THE HARMONY GUIDES

250 creative Knitting STITCHES

VOLUME 4

includes slip stitch mosaics, cross stitch
patterns and panels, cable panels

C&B

COLLINS & BROWN

First published for Lyric Books in 1990
as the Harmony Guide to Knitting Stitches, Volume III

Re-issued in 1998 by
Collins & Brown Limited
London House
Great Eastern Wharf
Parkgate Road
London SW11 4NQ

1 3 5 7 9 8 6 4 2

British Library Cataloguing-in-Publication Data:
A catalogue record for this book
is available from the British Library.

ISBN 1 85585 632 8

Printed and bound in Spain by Graficas Elkar

Contents

Equipment

Knitting Needles

Knitting needles are used in pairs to produce a flat knitted fabric. They are pointed at one end to form the stitches and have a knob at the other end to retain the stitches. They may be made of plastic, wood, bamboo, steel or alloy and range in size from 2mm to 17mm in diameter (see the conversion table below for the most commonly used). In the UK needles used to be sized by numbers - the higher the number, the smaller the needle. Metric sizing has now been adopted almost everywhere. Needles are also made in different lengths, - choose a length that will comfortably hold the stitches required for each project.

It is useful to have a range of sizes so that tension swatches can be knitted on various needles and compared.

Circular and double-pointed needles are used to produce a tubular fabric or flat rounds (such as circular shawls and table cloths). Many traditional fisherman's sweaters are knitted in the round and in some countries open fronted cardigans are first knitted in the round then cut at the front to create an opening which is then bound with a decorative edging to finish. Double-pointed needles are sold in sets of four or five. Circular needles consist of two needles joined by a flexible length of plastic. The plastic varies in length. Use the shorter lengths for knitting sleeves, neckband etc, and the longer lengths for larger pieces such as the body part of sweaters and skirts.

Cable needles are short double pointed needles used to hold the stitches of a cable to the back or front of the main body of the knitting.

Needle gauges are punched with holes corresponding to needle sizes and are marked with both the old numerical sizing and the metric sizing so you can easily check the size of any needle.

Stitch holders resemble large safety pins and are used to hold stitches while they are not being worked, for example, around a neckline when the neckband stitches will be picked up and worked after back and front have been joined. As an alternative, thread a wool sewing needle with a generous length of contrast-coloured yarn, thread it through the stitches to be held while they are still on the needle, then slip the stitches off the needle and knot both ends of the contrast yarn together.

Wool sewing needles are used to sew completed pieces of knitting together. They are large with a broad eye for easy threading and a blunt point that will slip between the knitted stitches without splitting and fraying the yarn. Do not use sharp pointed sewing needles to sew up knitting. A tapestry needle is also suitable.

A row counter is used to count the number of rows that have been knitted. It is a cylinder with a numbered dial that is pushed onto the needle and the dial is turned at the completion of each row.

A tape measure is essential for checking tension swatches and for measuring the length and width of completed knitting. For an accurate result, always smooth knitting out (without stretching) on a firm flat surface before measuring it.

A crochet hook is useful for picking up dropped stitches.

Knitting Yarn

Yarn is the term used for strands of spun fibre which are twisted together into a continuous thread of the required thickness. Yarn can be of animal origin (wool, angora, mohair, silk, alpaca), vegetable origin (cotton, linen) or man-made (nylon, acrylic, rayon). Knitting yarn may be made up from a combination of different fibres.

Each strand of yarn is known as a ply. A number of plys are twisted together to form the yarn. The texture and characteristics of the yarn may be varied by the combination of fibres and by the way in which the yarn is spun. Wool and other natural fibres are often combined with man-made fibres to make a yarn that is more economical and hard-wearing. Wool can also be treated to make it machine washable. The twist of the yarn can be varied too. A tightly twisted yarn is firm and smooth and knits up into a hard-wearing fabric. Loosely twisted yarn has a softer finish when knitted.

Buying Yarn

Yarn is most commonly sold ready wound into balls of specific weight measured in grams or ounces. Some yarn, particularly very thick yarn, is also sold in a coiled hank or skein and must be wound up into a ball before you begin knitting.

Yarn manufacturers (called spinners) wrap each ball with a paper band on which is printed a lot of necessary information. The ball band states the weight of the yarn and its composition. It will give instructions for washing and ironing and may state the ideal range of needle sizes to be used with the yarn. The ball band also carries the shade number and dye lot number. It is important that you use yarn of the same dye lot for a single project. Different dye lots vary subtly in shading which may not be apparent when you are holding two balls, but which will show as a variation in shade on the finished piece of knitting.

Always keep the ball band as a reference. The best way is to pin it to the tension swatch and keep them together with any left over yarn and spare buttons or other trimmings. That way you can always check the washing instructions and also have materials for repairs.

Charts

In many parts of the world knitters have become accustomed to working from charted instructions and find this method much easier. We feel that everyone should have this option and have therefore included both written and charted instructions for every pattern in this book

See page 8 for further details.

Knitting Needle Conversion Table

Canadian & Old UK Size	000	00	0	1	2	3	4	5	6	7	8	9	10	11	12	13	14
Metric Size (for UK)	10	9	8	7½	7	6½	6	5½	5	4½	4	3¾	3¼	3	2¾	2¼	2
US Size	15	13	11		10½		10	9	8	7	6	5	4	3	3	2	1	0

Crochet Hook Conversion Table

	Steel								Aluminium										
Old UK Size	6	5	4	3	2½	2	1	2/0	14	12	11	9	8	7	6	5	4	2	1/0	2/0	3/0
Metric Size	0.60	0.75	1.00	1.25	1.50	1.75	2.00	2.50	2.00	2.50	3.00	3.50	4.00	4.50	5.00	5.50	6.00	7.00	8.00	9.00	10.00
US Size	14	12	10	—	6	4	1	1/0	B	C	D	E	F	G	H	I	J	K	—	—	P

First Steps
Holding the Needles

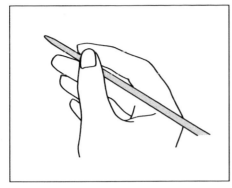

The **right needle** is held as if holding a pencil. For casting on and working the first few rows the knitted piece passes over the hand, between the thumb and the index finger. As work progresses let the thumb slide under the knitted piece, grasping the needle from below.

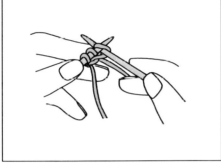

The **left needle** is held lightly, using the thumb and index finger to control the tip of the needle.

Holding the Yarn
Method 1

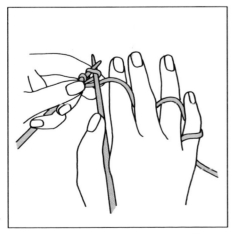

Holding yarn in right hand, pass under the little finger, then around same finger, over third finger, under centre finger and over index finger. The index finger is used to pass the yarn around the needle tip. The yarn circled around the little finger creates the necessary tension for knitting evenly.

Holding the Yarn
Method 2

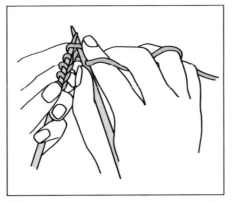

Holding yarn in right hand, pass under the little finger, over third finger, under centre finger and over index finger. The index finger is used to pass the yarn around the needle tip. The tension of the yarn is controlled by gripping it in the crook of the little finger.

Making a Slip Knot

A slip knot is the starting point for almost everything you do in knitting and is the basis of all casting on techniques.

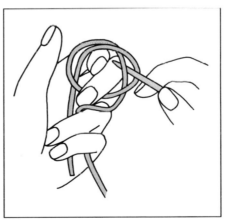

1. Wind the yarn around two fingers and over the two fingers again to the back of the first thread.

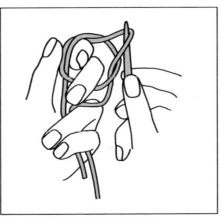

2. Using a knitting needle pull the back thread through the front one to form a loop.

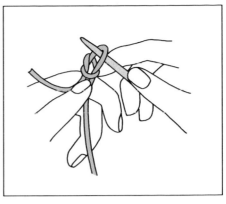

3. Pull end to tighten the loop.

Casting On

There are two common methods of casting on. The thumb method is used whenever a very elastic edge is required or when the rows immediately after the cast-on edge are to be worked in garter stitch or stocking stitch. The second method is the Cable or 'between stitches' method. This gives a very firm neat finish and is best for use before ribbing or any other firm type of stitch.

Thumb Method

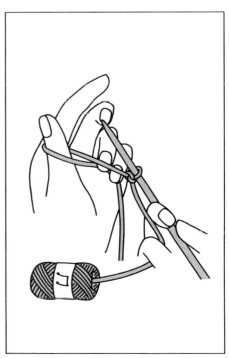

1. Make a slip knot about 1m (depending on the number of stitches required) from the end of the yarn. Hold the needle in the right hand with the ball end of the yarn over your first finger. *Wind the loose end of the yarn around the left thumb from front to back.

Basic Techniques

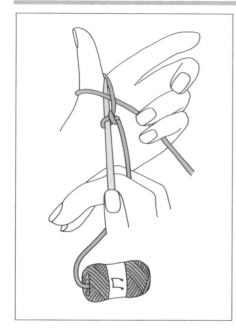

2. Insert the needle through the yarn on the thumb.

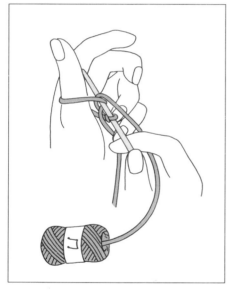

3. Take the ball end of yarn with your right forefinger over the point of the needle.

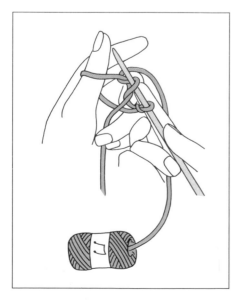

4. Pull a loop through to form the first stitch.

5. Remove your left thumb from the yarn and pull the loose end to secure the stitch. Repeat from * until the required number of stitches has been cast on.

Cable Method

This method requires the use of two needles.

1. Make a slip knot about 10 cm from the end of the yarn.

2. Insert right-hand needle through the slip knot and pass the yarn over the right needle.

3. Pull a loop through.

4. Place this loop on the left-hand needle.

5. Insert right-hand needle between the two stitches on the left-hand needle. Wind yarn round point of right-hand needle.

6. Draw a loop through, place this loop on left-hand needle.

Repeat steps 5 and 6 until the required number of stitches has been cast on.

The Basic Stitches
Knit Stitches

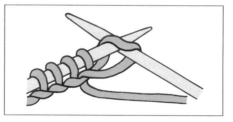

1. Hold the needle with the cast on stitches in the left hand. With the yarn at back of work, insert the right-hand needle from left to right through the front of the first stitch on left-hand needle.

2. Wind the yarn from left to right over the point of the right-hand needle.

3. Draw the yarn back through the stitch, thus forming a loop on the right-hand needle.

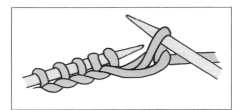

4.Slip the original stitch off the left-hand needle.

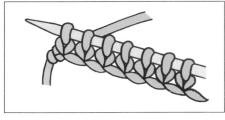

To knit a row, repeat steps 1 to 4 until all the stitches have been transferred from the left needle to the right needle. Turn the work and transfer the needle with the stitches on to the left hand to work the next row.

Purl Stitches

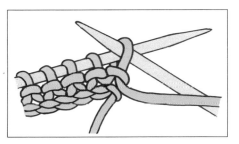

1. With the yarn at the front of the work insert the right-hand needle from right to left through the front of the first stitch on the left-hand needle.

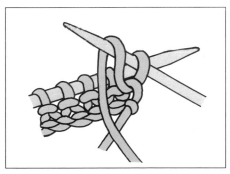

2. Wind the yarn from right to left over the point of the right-hand needle.

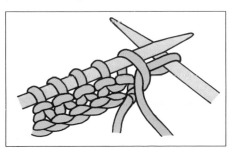

3. Draw a loop through onto the right-hand needle.

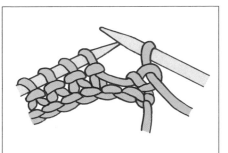

4. Slip the original stitch off the left-hand needle.

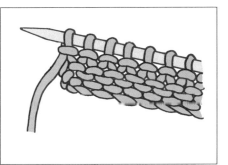

To purl a row, repeat steps 1 to 4 until all the stitches are transferred to the right-hand needle, then turn the work and transfer the needles to work the next row.

Casting Off

Always cast off in pattern. This means that in stocking stitch you cast off knitwise on a knit row and purlwise on a purl row. Casting off ribbing should always be done as if you were continuing to rib and most pattern stitches can also be followed during the course of the casting off.

Casting Off Knitwise

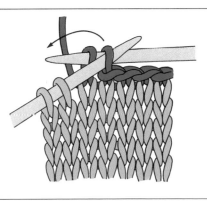

Knit the first two stitches. *Using the left-hand needle lift the first stitch over the second and drop it off the needle. Knit the next stitch and repeat from the * until all the stitches have been worked from the left-hand needle and one stitch only remains on the right-hand needle. Cut the yarn (leaving enough to sew in the end) and thread the cut end through the stitch on the needle. Draw the yarn up firmly to fasten off the last stitch.

Casting Off Purlwise

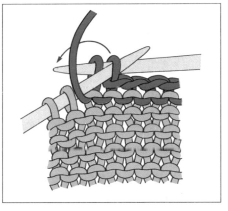

Purl the first two stitches, then *using the left-hand needle lift the first stitch over the second and drop it off the needle. Purl the next stitch and repeat from the * securing the last stitch as described above.

Tension or Gauge

Knitting tension refers to the number of stitches and rows in a given area. A frequently found tension indication given on garment instructions would be 22 sts and 30 rows = 10 cm [4 ins] square, measured over stocking stitch. It is necessary to produce fabric with the stated number of stitches and rows in order to obtain the correct measurements for the garment you intend to knit.

The needle size indicated in the pattern is the one which **most** knitters will use to achieve this tension, but it is the tension that is important, not the needle size.

The way to ensure that you do achieve a correct tension is to work a tension sample or swatch before starting the main part of the knitting. Care taken at this initial stage will avoid time wasted and disappointment that will result if the finished garment is unsatisfactory.

If you are going to use a stitch pattern from this book to design a garment of your own, a tension swatch or swatches must be knitted in order to calculate the number of stitches required. It is also worth experimenting with different tensions so that you find the best tension for the pattern and yarn. Some patterns look and feel better knitted loosely and others require a firmer tension to be at their best.

Charts

Most knitters have already used charts to knit fairisle or intarsia patterns. We have given **all** the patterns in this book both written and charted directions in the hope that you will discover how useful charts can be for other sorts of stitch patterns. A chart also gives a visual impression of how the finished pattern will appear, enabling instructions for long and complicated patterns to be given in a clear and concise way. This can also be very useful when learning a new stitch.

How to Read Charts

Charts are read exactly as the knitting is worked - from the bottom to the top. After the last row at the top has been worked repeat the sequence from row 1.

Each symbol represents an instruction. Symbols have been designed to resemble the actual appearance of the knitting. This is more difficult to do with multi-colour slip stitch patterns and these have to be knitted before the mosaic effects become obvious.

Before starting to knit look up all the symbols on your chosen chart so that you are familiar with the techniques involved. These are either shown with the pattern as a special abbreviation or on pages 9 and 10. A reminder of the more common abbreviations that are not shown as special abbreviations is given at the bottom of each page. (Refer to pages 9 and 10 for more detailed descriptions). **Make sure you understand the difference between working similar symbols on a right side row and a wrong side row.** Before working a particular pattern it is important to read the relevant information at the beginning of each chapter.

Each square represents a stitch and each horizontal line a row. Place a ruler above the line you are working and work the symbols one by one. If you are new to chart reading try comparing the charted instructions with the written ones.

The multi-coloured slip stitch patterns include suggested colours, indicated by a letter at the beginning of each row. These letters correspond to the colours shown on the Colour Chart on page 23.

For knitters who wish to follow the written directions it is still a good idea to look at the chart before starting, to see what the repeat looks like and how the pattern has been balanced.

Right Side and Wrong Side Rows

'Right side rows' are rows where the right side of the fabric is facing you when you work and 'wrong side rows' are rows where the wrong side of the work is facing you when you work. Row numbers are shown at the side of the charts **at the beginning of the row**. Right side rows are always read from right to left. Wrong side rows are always read from left to right.

Symbols on the charts are shown as they appear from the right side of the work. Therefore, a horizontal dash stands for a purl 'bump' on the right side regardless of whether it was achieved by purling on a right side row or knitting on a wrong side row. To make things clearer symbols on right side rows are slightly darker than wrong side rows.

Pattern Repeats and Multiples

The 'Multiple' or repeat of each pattern is given with each set of instructions, for example :- **'Multiple of 7 sts + 4'**. This means that you can cast on any number of stitches which is a multiple of 7, plus 4 stitches; for instance 14 + 4 sts, 21 + 4 sts, 28 + 4 sts etc.

In the written instructions the 7 stitches are shown in parentheses or brackets or follow an asterisk *, and these stitches are repeated across the row the required number of times. In charted instructions the pattern repeat is contained between heavier vertical lines. The extra stitches not included in the pattern repeat are there to 'balance' the row or make it symmetrical and are only worked once.

Some patterns require a foundation row and this row is worked once before commencing the pattern and does not form part of the repeat. On charts this row is marked by a letter **F** and is separated from the pattern repeat by a heavier horizontal line.

Panels

Panels are patterns worked over a given number of stitches without necessarily repeating them.

All the cable and twist panels in this book have been worked on a suggested background stitch. On the charts this is indicated by two stitches at either side of the panel. To work any of the panels you must cast on enough stitches to work the panel plus the required number of background stitches each side. It is extremely important when measuring a panel as part of a tension swatch to remember that there are stitches on either side which often lay underneath the edge of the panel. (See section on Cable and Cross Stitch Tension page 62).

Panels can be used on their own to liven up a plain garment. They can be inserted onto an overall background stitch which can be changed according to taste. For example, a panel given in this book on a background of reverse stocking stitch or garter stitch could be used on a sweater knitted in stocking stitch, double moss stitch or any other attractive background. In this case one or two stitches in reverse stocking stitch or garter stitch highlight the detail of the panel.

Panels can also be repeated to form an all-over pattern, or combined with other panels or pattern stitches to create a completely new effect.

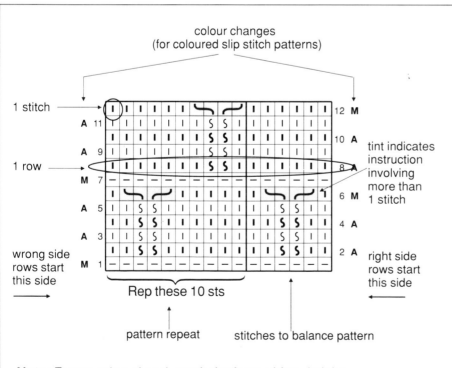

colour changes
(for coloured slip stitch patterns)

1 stitch

1 row

wrong side rows start this side

Rep these 10 sts

pattern repeat

stitches to balance pattern

tint indicates instruction involving more than 1 stitch

right side rows start this side

Note: For meaning of each symbol refer to abbreviations.

Abbreviations

Alt = alternate; **beg** = beginning; **cm** = centimetres; **dec** = decrease; **inc** = increase; **ins** = inches; **k** = knit; **KB1** = knit into back of stitch; **m** = metres; **mm** = millimetres; **p** = purl; **PB1** = purl into back of stitch; **psso** = pass slipped stitch over; **p2sso** = pass 2 slipped stitches over; **rep** = repeat; **sl** = slip; **st(s)** = stitch(es); **st st** = stocking stitch (1 row knit, 1 row purl); **tog** = together; **tbl** through back of loops; **yb** = yarn back; **yf** = yarn forward; **yfrn** = yarn forward and round needle; **yon** = yarn over needle; **yrn** = yarn round needle.

Basic Symbols

I	**K** knit on right side rows
−	**K** knit on wrong side rows
−	**P** purl on right side rows
I	**P** purl on wrong side rows
V	**KB1** knit into back of st on right side rows
<	**KB1** knit into back of st on wrong side rows
<	**PB1** purl into back of st on right side rows
V	**PB1** purl into back of st on wrong side rows
S	**sl 1** slip one st with yarn at back (wrong side) of work
S	**sl 1** slip one st with yarn at back (right side) of work
↯	**sl 1** slip one st with yarn at front (right side) of work
↯	**sl 1** slip one st with yarn at front (wrong side) of work

 yf, yfrn, yon, yrn (to make a st)

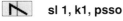 **k2tog**

sl 1, k1, psso

k3tog

k3tog tbl

sl 2tog knitwise, k1, p2sso

 **sl 1, k2tog, psso**

Note

Symbols are dark on right side rows and light on wrong side rows.

Common Abbreviations and Symbols

These techniques are used regularly throughout the book. If the pattern you are working contains an abbreviation or symbol that is not given as a special abbreviation it will be found here. At the foot of each page the abbreviation for any 'common' symbol used on that particular page is given.

Symbols for Right Side Rows

C2R (Cross 2 Right) = slip next st onto cable needle and hold at back of work, knit next st from left-hand needle, then knit st from cable needle.
Or without a cable needle:
C2R = knit into front of 2nd st on needle, then knit first st slipping both sts off needle at the same time (see page 44).

C2L (Cross 2 Left) = slip next st onto cable needle and hold at front of work, knit next st from left-hand needle, then knit st from cable needle.
Or without a cable needle:
C2L = knit into back of 2nd st on needle then knit first st slipping both sts off needle at the same time (see page 44).

T2B (Twist 2 Back) = slip next st onto cable needle and hold at back of work, knit next st from left-hand needle, then purl st from cable needle.
Or without a cable needle:
T2B = knit into front of 2nd st on needle then purl first st slipping both sts off needle at the same time (see page 44).

T2F (Twist 2 Front) = slip next st onto cable needle and hold at front of work, purl next st from left-hand needle, then knit st from cable needle.
Or without a cable needle:
T2F = purl into back of 2nd st on needle then knit first st slipping both sts off needle at the same time (see page 44).

Symbols for Wrong Side Rows

C2PR (Cross 2 Purl Right) = slip next st onto cable needle and hold at back (right side) of work, purl next st from left-hand needle, then purl st from cable needle.
Or without a cable needle:
C2PR = purl into front of 2nd st on needle, then purl first st slipping both sts off needle at the same time.

For North American Readers

English terms are used throughout this book. Please note equivalent American terms:
Tension - Gauge
Cast Off - Bind Off
Stocking Stitch - Stockinette Stitch
Yf, Yfrn, Yon and Yrn (to make a st) - Yarn Over

C2PL (Cross 2 Purl Left) = slip next st onto cable needle and hold at front (wrong side) of work, purl next st from left-hand needle, then purl st from cable needle.
Or without a cable needle:
C2PL = purl into back of 2nd st on needle, then purl first st slipping both sts off needle at the same time.

T2PR (Twist 2 Purl Right) = slip next st onto cable needle and hold at back (right side) of work, knit next st from left-hand needle, then purl st from cable needle.
Or without a cable needle:
T2PR = knit into front of 2nd st on needle, then purl first st slipping both sts off needle at the same time.

T2PL (Twist 2 Purl Left) = slip next st onto cable needle and hold at front (wrong side) of work, purl next st from left-hand needle, then knit st from cable needle.
Or without a cable needle:
T2PL = purl into back of 2nd st on needle, then knit first st slipping both sts off needle at the same time.

Symbols for Right Side Rows

C3R (Cable 3 Right) = slip next 2 sts onto cable needle and hold at back of work, knit next st from left-hand needle, then knit sts from cable needle.

C3L (Cable 3 Left) = slip next st onto cable needle and hold at front of work, knit next 2 sts from left-hand needle, then knit st from cable needle.

C3B (Cable 3 Back) = slip next st onto cable needle and hold at back of work, knit next 2 sts from left-hand needle, then knit st from cable needle.

C3F (Cable 3 Front) = slip next 2 sts onto cable needle and hold at front of work, knit next st from left-hand needle, then knit sts from cable needle.

T3B (Twist 3 Back) = slip next st onto cable needle and hold at back of work, knit next 2 sts from left-hand needle, then purl st from cable needle.

T3F (Twist 3 Front) = slip next 2 sts onto cable needle and hold at front of work, purl next st from left-hand needle, then knit sts from cable needle.

C4B (Cable 4 Back) = slip next 2 sts onto cable needle and hold at back of work, knit next 2 sts from left-hand needle, then knit sts from cable needle.

C4F (Cable 4 Front) = slip next 2 sts onto cable needle and hold at front of work, knit next 2 sts from left-hand needle, then knit sts from cable needle.

Abbreviations and Symbols

C4R (Cable 4 Right) = slip next st onto cable needle and hold at back of work, knit next 3 sts from left-hand needle, then knit st from cable needle.

C4L (Cable 4 Left) = slip next 3 sts onto cable needle and hold at front of work, knit next st from left-hand needle, then knit sts from cable needle.

T4B (Twist 4 Back) = slip next 2 sts onto cable needle and hold at back of work, knit next 2 sts from left-hand needle, then purl sts from cable needle.

T4F (Twist 4 Front) = slip next 2 sts onto cable needle and hold at front of work, purl next 2 sts from left-hand needle, then knit sts from cable needle.

T4R (Twist 4 Right) = slip next st onto cable needle and hold at back of work, knit next 3 sts from left-hand needle, then purl st from cable needle.

T4L (Twist 4 Left) = slip next 3 sts onto cable needle and hold at front of work, purl next st from left-hand needle, then knit sts from cable needle.

T5B (Twist 5 Back) = slip next 3 sts onto cable needle and hold at back of work, knit next 2 sts from left-hand needle, then purl sts from cable needle.

T5F (Twist 5 Front) = slip next 2 sts onto cable needle and hold at front of work, purl next 3 sts from left-hand needle, then knit sts from cable needle.

 **T5L (Twist 5 Left)** = slip next 2 sts onto cable needle and hold at front of work, k2, p1 from left-hand needle, then knit sts from cable needle.

C6B (Cable 6 Back) = slip next 3 sts onto cable needle and hold at back of work, knit next 3 sts from left-hand needle, then knit sts from cable needle.

C6F (Cable 6 Front) = slip next 3 sts onto cable needle and hold at front of work, knit next 3 sts from left-hand needle, then knit sts from cable needle.

C6R (Cross 6 Right) = slip next 4 sts onto cable needle and hold at back of work, knit next 2 sts from left-hand needle, then knit sts from cable needle.

C6L (Cross 6 Left) = slip next 2 sts onto cable needle and hold at front of work, knit next 4 sts from left-hand needle, then knit sts from cable needle.

T6B (Twist 6 Back) = slip next 3 sts onto cable needle and hold

at back of work, knit next 3 sts from left-hand needle, then purl sts from cable needle.

 **T6F (Twist 6 Front)** = slip next 3 sts onto cable needle and hold at front of work, purl next 3 sts from left-hand needle, then knit sts from cable needle.

C8B (Cable 8 Back) = slip next 4 sts onto cable needle and hold at back of work, knit next 4 sts from left-hand needle, then knit sts from cable needle.

C8F (Cable 8 Front) = slip next 4 sts onto cable needle and hold at front of work, knit next 4 sts from left-hand needle, then knit sts from cable needle.

C10B (Cable 10 Back) = slip next 5 sts onto cable needle and hold at back of work, knit next 5 sts from left-hand needle, then knit sts from cable needle.

C10F (Cable 10 Front) = slip next 5 sts onto cable needle and hold at front of work, knit next 5 sts from left-hand needle, then knit sts from cable needle.

 **C12B (Cable 12 Back)** = slip next 6 sts onto cable needle and hold at back of work, knit next 6 sts from left-hand needle, then knit sts from cable needle.

 **C12F (Cable 12 Front)** = slip next 6 sts onto cable needle and hold at front of work, knit next 6 sts from left-hand needle, then knit sts from cable needle.

Knit and Purl Textures

Inexperienced knitters will be able to knit most of the patterns in this section without difficulty. It is also a good idea for knitters unfamiliar with charts to knit a simple knit and purl pattern from the written instructions and then try knitting the same pattern following the charted instructions. (See pages 6 and 7 for the basic knit and purl stitches).

A rich variety of patterns can be made from basic knit and purl stitches. By combining knit and purl stitches in different ways the resulting fabric may curl in or out or lie flat. The fabric can be made elastic in different directions, horizontally as in rib or vertically with garter stitch stripes.

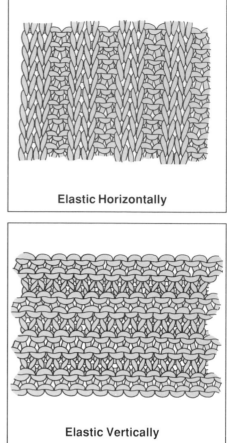

Elastic Horizontally

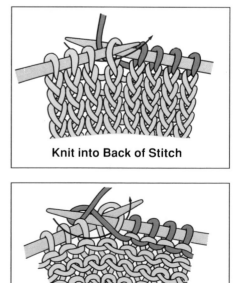

Elastic Vertically

By combining areas of garter stitch, stocking stitch and reverse stocking stitch, interesting texture patterns can be built up.

Knit and Purl into Back of Stitch

Follow the instructions for Basic Knit or Basic Purl Stitch on pages 6 and 7 **but** insert the needle through the back of loop, thus twisting the stitch. This makes the stitch much firmer and also makes it stand out more.

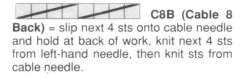

Knit into Back of Stitch

Purl into Back of Stitch

I.1

Multiple of 14 sts + 1.

1st row (right side): K7, p1, *k13, p1; rep from * to last 7 sts, k7.

2nd and every alt row: Purl.

3rd row: K6, p3, *k11, p3; rep from * to last 6 sts, k6.

5th row: K5, p5, *k9, p5; rep from * to last 5 sts, k5.

7th row: K4, p7, *k7, p7; rep from * to last 4 sts, k4.

9th row: K3, p9, *k5, p9; rep from * to last 3 sts, k3.

11th row: K2, p11, *k3, p11; rep from * to last 2 sts, k2.

13th row: K1, *p13, k1; rep from * to end.

15th row: P1, *k13, p1; rep from * to end.

17th row: P2, k11, *p3, k11; rep from * to last 2 sts, p2.

19th row: P3, k9, *p5, k9; rep from * to last 3 sts, p3.

21st row: P4, k7, *p7, k7; rep from * to last 4 sts, p4.

23rd row: P5, k5, *p9, k5; rep from * to last 5 sts, p5.

25th row: P6, k3, *p11, k3; rep from * to last 6 sts, p6.

27th row: P7, k1, *p13, k1; rep from * to last 7 sts, p7.

28th row: Purl.

Rep these 28 rows.

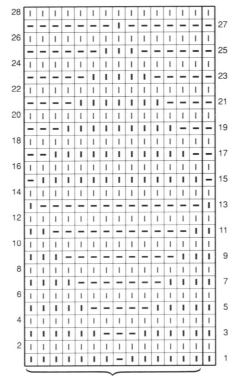

Rep these 14 sts

I.2

Multiple of 6 sts + 3.

Work 4 rows in st st, starting knit (right side).

5th row: K1, *p1, k1; rep from * to end.
6th row: P1, *k1, p1; rep from * to end.
Rep the last 2 rows once more.

9th row: K1, p1, k1, *p3, k1, p1, k1; rep from * to end.

10th row: P1, k1, p1, *k3, p1, k1, p1; rep from * to end.
Rep the last 2 rows once more.
Rep these 12 rows.

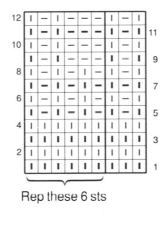

Rep these 6 sts

I.3

Multiple of 10 sts + 6.

1st row (right side): P1, *k4, p1; rep from * to end.

2nd row: K1, *p4, k1; rep from * to end.

Rep the last 2 rows once more, then 1st row again.

6th row: K6, *p4, k6; rep from * to end.

7th row: As 1st row.

Rep the last 2 rows twice more.

12th row: As 2nd row.

13th row: As 1st row.

Rep the last 2 rows once more.

16th row: K1, p4, *k6, p4; rep from * to last st, k1.

17th row: As 1st row.

Rep the last 2 rows once more, then 16th row again.

Rep these 20 rows.

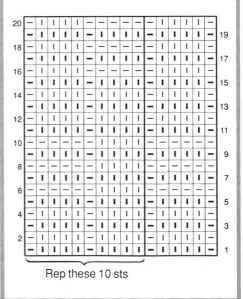

Rep these 10 sts

I. Knit and Purl Textures

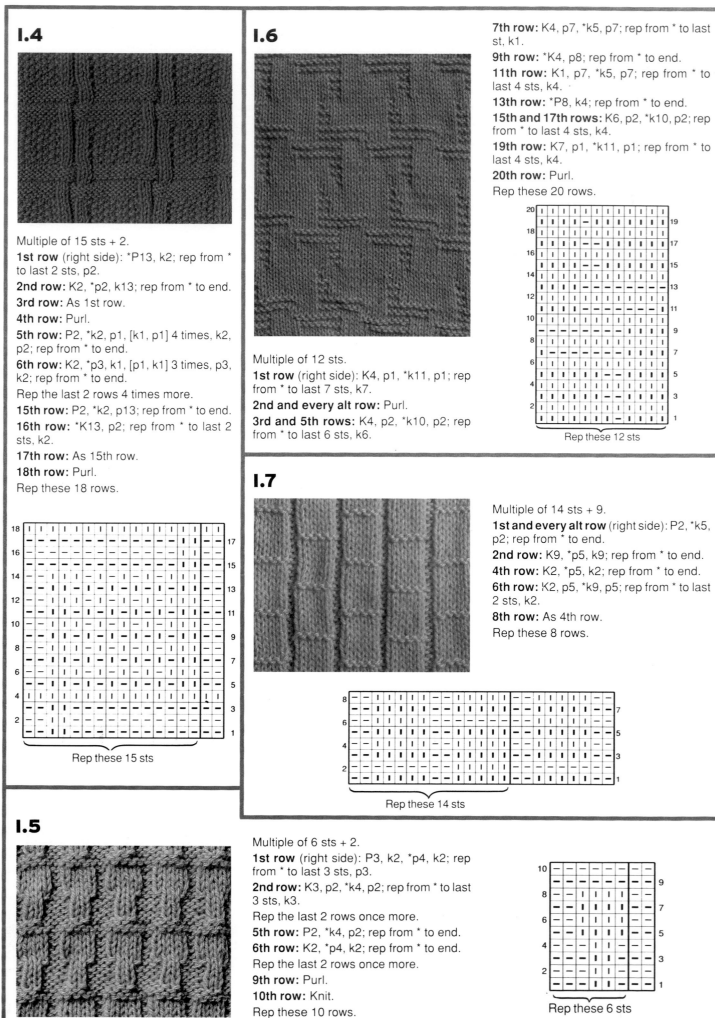

I.4

Multiple of 15 sts + 2.

1st row (right side): *P13, k2; rep from * to last 2 sts, p2.

2nd row: K2, *p2, k13; rep from * to end.

3rd row: As 1st row.

4th row: Purl.

5th row: P2, *k2, p1, [k1, p1] 4 times, k2, p2; rep from * to end.

6th row: K2, *p3, k1, [p1, k1] 3 times, p3, k2; rep from * to end.

Rep the last 2 rows 4 times more.

15th row: P2, *k2, p13; rep from * to end.

16th row: *K13, p2; rep from * to last 2 sts, k2.

17th row: As 15th row.

18th row: Purl.

Rep these 18 rows.

I.5

Multiple of 6 sts + 2.

1st row (right side): P3, k2, *p4, k2; rep from * to last 3 sts, p3.

2nd row: K3, p2, *k4, p2; rep from * to last 3 sts, k3.

Rep the last 2 rows once more.

5th row: P2, *k4, p2; rep from * to end.

6th row: K2, *p4, k2; rep from * to end.

Rep the last 2 rows once more.

9th row: Purl.

10th row: Knit.

Rep these 10 rows.

I.6

Multiple of 12 sts.

1st row (right side): K4, p1, *k11, p1; rep from * to last 7 sts, k7.

2nd and every alt row: Purl.

3rd and 5th rows: K4, p2, *k10, p2; rep from * to last 6 sts, k6.

7th row: K4, p7, *k5, p7; rep from * to last st, k1.

9th row: *K4, p8; rep from * to end.

11th row: K1, p7, *k5, p7; rep from * to last 4 sts, k4.

13th row: *P8, k4; rep from * to end.

15th and 17th rows: K6, p2, *k10, p2; rep from * to last 4 sts, k4.

19th row: K7, p1, *k11, p1; rep from * to last 4 sts, k4.

20th row: Purl.

Rep these 20 rows.

Rep these 12 sts

I.7

Multiple of 14 sts + 9.

1st and every alt row (right side): P2, *k5, p2; rep from * to end.

2nd row: K9, *p5, k9; rep from * to end.

4th row: K2, *p5, k2; rep from * to end.

6th row: K2, p5, *k9, p5; rep from * to last 2 sts, k2.

8th row: As 4th row.

Rep these 8 rows.

Rep these 14 sts

Rep these 15 sts

Rep these 6 sts

I.8

Multiple of 8 sts.

1st row (right side): *K1, p1, k1, p5; rep from * to end.

2nd row: *K5, p1, k1, p1; rep from * to end.

3rd row: *K1, p1, k5, p1; rep from * to end.

4th and 5th rows: *K1, p5, k1, p1; rep from * to end.

6th row: As 3rd row.

7th row: As 2nd row.

8th row: *K1, p1, k1, p5; rep from * to end.

9th row: P4, k1, p1, k1, *p5, k1, p1, k1; rep from * to last st, p1.

10th row: [K1, p1] twice, *k5, p1, k1, p1; rep from * to last 4 sts, k4.

11th row: K3, p1, k1, p1, *k5, p1, k1, p1; rep from * to last 2 sts, k2.

12th and 13th rows: P2, k1, p1, k1, *p5, k1, p1, k1; rep from * to last 3 sts, p3.

14th row: As 11th row.

15th row: As 10th row.

16th row: As 9th row.

Rep these 16 rows.

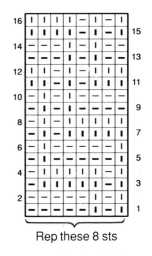

Rep these 8 sts

I.9

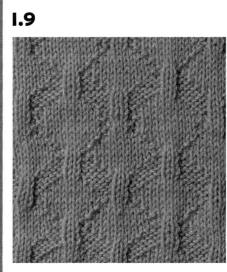

Multiple of 14 sts + 2.

1st row (right side): K2, *p1, k10, p1, k2; rep from * to end.

2nd row: P3, k1, p8, k1, *p4, k1, p8, k1; rep from * to last 3 sts, p3.

3rd row: K4, p1, *k6, p1; rep from * to last 4 sts, k4.

4th row: P5, k1, p4, k1, *p8, k1, p4, k1; rep from * to last 5 sts, p5.

5th row: K6, p1, k2, p1, *k10, p1, k2, p1; rep from * to last 6 sts, k6.

6th row: P5, k2, p2, k2, *p8, k2, p2, k2; rep from * to last 5 sts, p5.

7th row: K4, p3, k2, p3, *k6, p3, k2, p3; rep from * to last 4 sts, k4.

8th row: P3, k4, p2, k4, *p4, k4, p2, k4; rep from * to last 3 sts, p3.

9th row: K2, *p5, k2; rep from * to end.

10th row: P2, *k4, p4, k4, p2; rep from * to end.

11th row: K2, *p3, k6, p3, k2; rep from * to end.

12th row: P2, *k2, p8, k2, p2; rep from * to end.

Rep these 12 rows.

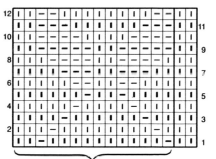

Rep these 14 sts

I.10

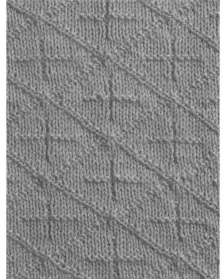

Multiple of 20 sts + 1.

1st row (right side): P1, *k7, p2, k1, p2, k7, p1; rep from * to end.

2nd row: K1, *p6, k2, p3, k2, p6, k1; rep from * to end.

3rd row: P1, *k5, [p2, k5] twice, p1; rep from * to end.

4th row: K1, *p4, k2, p7, k2, p4, k1; rep from * to end.

5th row: K4, p2, k4, p1, k4, p2, *k7, p2, k4, p1, k4, p2; rep from * to last 4 sts, k4.

6th row: P3, k2, p5, k1, p5, *[k2, p5] twice, k1, p5; rep from * to last 5 sts, k2, p3.

7th row: K2, p2, k6, p1, k6, p2, *k3, p2, k6, p1, k6, p2; rep from * to last 2 sts, k2.

8th row: P1, *k2, p7, k1, p7, k2, p1; rep from * to end.

9th row: P2, k4, p9, k4, *p3, k4, p9, k4; rep from * to last 2 sts, p2.

10th row: As 8th row.

11th row: As 7th row.

12th row: As 6th row.

13th row: As 5th row.

14th row: As 4th row.

15th row: As 3rd row.

16th row: As 2nd row.

17th row: As 1st row.

18th row: K5, p4, k3, p4, *k9, p4, k3, p4; rep from * to last 5 sts, k5.

Rep these 18 rows.

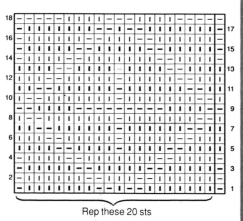

Rep these 20 sts

I. Knit and Purl Textures

I.11

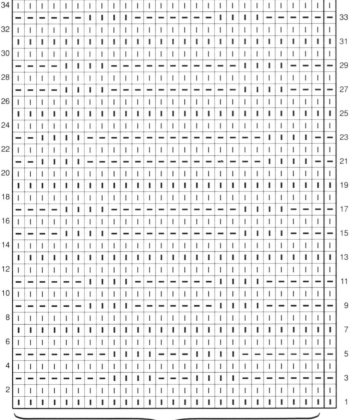

Multiple of 26 sts + 1.

1st row (right side): Knit.

2nd and every alt row: Purl.

3rd and 5th rows: P8, k4, p3, k4, *p15, k4, p3, k4; rep from * to last 8 sts, p8.

7th row: Knit.

9th and 11th rows: P6, k4, p7, k4, *p11, k4, p7, k4; rep from * to last 6 sts, p6.

13th row: Knit.

15th and 17th rows: P4, k4, p11, k4, *p7, k4, p11, k4; rep from * to last 4 sts, p4.

19th row: Knit.

21st and 23rd rows: P2, k4, p15, k4, *p3, k4, p15, k4; rep from * to last 2 sts, p2.

25th row: Knit.

27th and 29th rows: As 15th row.

31st row: Knit.

33rd and 35th rows: As 9th row.

36th row: Purl.

Rep these 36 rows.

Rep these 26 sts

I.13

Multiple of 10 sts + 3.

1st row (right side): P1, k1, p1, *k7, p1, k1, p1; rep from * to end.

2nd row: K1, p1, k1, *p7, k1, p1, k1; rep from * to end.

Rep the last 2 rows once more.

5th row: P1, k1, *p9, k1; rep from * to last st, p1.

6th row: As 2nd row.

Rep the last 2 rows once more.

9th and 10th rows: As 1st and 2nd rows.

Rep the last 2 rows once more.

Rep these 12 rows.

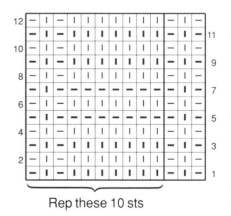

Rep these 10 sts

I.12

Multiple of 6 sts + 1.

1st row (right side): K1, *p5, k1; rep from * to end.

2nd row: P1, *k5, p1; rep from * to end.

Rep the last 2 rows twice more.

7th row: P1, *k5, p1; rep from * to end.

8th row: K1, *p5, k1; rep from * to end.

Rep the last 2 rows twice more.

Rep these 12 rows.

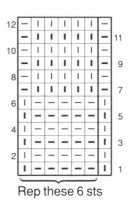

Rep these 6 sts

I.14

Multiple of 24 sts + 2.

1st row (right side): P2, *k2, p18, k2, p2; rep from * to end.

2nd row: K2, *p2, k18, p2, k2; rep from * to end.

3rd row: P2, *k18, p2, k2, p2; rep from * to end.

4th row: K2, *p2, k2, p18; rep from * to end.

5th row: P2, *k2, p14, [k2, p2] twice; rep from * to end.

6th row: *[K2, p2] twice, k14, p2; rep from * to last 2 sts, k2.

7th row: P2, k2, p2, k10, p2, *[k2, p2] 3 times, k10, p2; rep from * to last 8 sts, [k2, p2] twice.

8th row: K2, [p2, k2] twice, p10, k2, *[p2, k2] 3 times, p10, k2; rep from * to last 4 sts, p2, k2.

9th row: [P2, k2] twice, p6, k2, *[p2, k2] 4 times, p6, k2; rep from * to last 10 sts, p2, [k2, p2] twice.

10th row: [K2, p2] 3 times, k6, *p2, [k2, p2] 4 times, k6; rep from * to last 8 sts, [p2, k2] twice.

11th row: P2, *k2, p2; rep from * to end.

12th row: K2, *p2, k2; rep from * to end.

13th row: [P2, k2] 3 times, p6, k2, *[p2, k2] 4 times, p6, k2; rep from * to last 6 sts, p2, k2, p2.

14th row: [K2, p2] twice, k6, *p2, [k2, p2] 4 times, k6; rep from * to last 12 sts, [p2, k2] 3 times.

15th row: P2, [k2, p2] twice, k10, p2, *[k2, p2] 3 times, k10, p2; rep from * to last 4 sts, k2, p2.

16th row: K2, p2, k2, p10, k2, *[p2, k2] 3 times, p10, k2; rep from * to last 8 sts, [p2, k2] twice.

17th row: *[P2, k2] twice, p14, k2; rep from * to last 2 sts, p2.

18th row: K2, p2, k14, p2, *[k2, p2] twice, k14, p2; rep from * to last 6 sts, k2, p2, k2.

19th row: P2, *k2, p2, k18, p2; rep from * to end.

20th row: K2, *p18, k2, p2, k2; rep from * to end.

Rep these 20 rows.

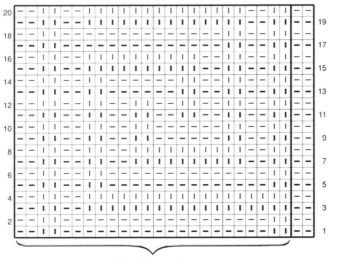

Rep these 24 sts

I.15

Multiple of 6 sts + 3.

1st and every alt row (right side): Knit.

2nd row: Knit.

4th and 6th rows: P3, *k3, p3; rep from * to end.

8th and 10th rows: Knit.

12th and 14th rows: K3, *p3, k3; rep from * to end.

16th row: Knit.

Rep these 16 rows.

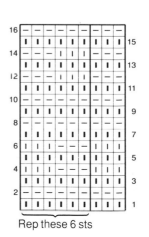

Rep these 6 sts

I.16

Multiple of 8 sts.

1st row (right side): P1, k6, *p2, k6; rep from * to last st, p1.

2nd row: K1, p5, *k3, p5; rep from * to last 2 sts, k2.

3rd row: P3, k4, *p4, k4; rep from * to last st, p1.

4th row: K1, p3, k2, p1, *k2, p3, k2, p1; rep from * to last st, k1.

5th row: P1, k2, *p2, k2; rep from * to last st, p1.

6th row: K1, p1, k2, p3, *k2, p1, k2, p3; rep from * to last st, k1.

7th row: P1, k4, *p4, k4; rep from * to last 3 sts, p3.

8th row: K2, p5, *k3, p5; rep from * to last st, k1.

9th row: As 1st row.

10th row: K1, p6, *k2, p6; rep from * to last st, k1.

Rep these 10 rows.

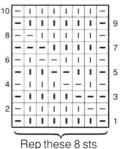

Rep these 8 sts

I. Knit and Purl Textures

I.17

Multiple of 20 sts + 10.

1st row (right side): P2, *k2, p2; rep from * to end.

2nd row: K2, *p2, k2; rep from * to end.

3rd row: [K2, p2] twice, *k4, p2, k2, p2; rep from * to last 2 sts, k2.

4th row: [P2, k2] twice, *p4, k2, p2, k2; rep from * to last 2 sts, p2.

Rep the last 4 rows once more, then 1st and 2nd rows again.

11th row: As 2nd row.

12th row: P2, *k2, p2; rep from * to end.

13th row: [K2, p2] 3 times, [k4, p2] twice, *[k2, p2] twice, [k4, p2] twice; rep from * to last 6 sts, k2, p2, k2.

14th row: [P2, k2] twice, *[p4, k2] twice, [p2, k2] twice; rep from * to last 2 sts, p2.

Rep the last 4 rows once more, then 11th and 12th rows again.

Rep these 20 rows.

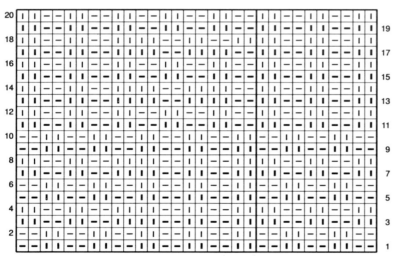

Rep these 20 sts

I.19

Multiple of 12 sts + 1.

1st and every alt row (right side): Knit.

2nd row: P5, k3, *p9, k3; rep from * to last 5 sts, p5.

4th row: P4, k5, *p7, k5; rep from * to last 4 sts, p4.

6th row: P3, k3, p1, k3, *p5, k3, p1, k3; rep from * to last 3 sts, p3.

8th row: P2, k3, *p3, k3; rep from * to last 2 sts, p2.

10th row: P1, *k3, p5, k3, p1; rep from * to end.

12th row: Purl.

Rep these 12 rows.

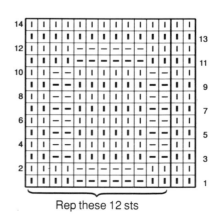

Rep these 12 sts

I.18

Multiple of 12 sts + 2.

1st row (right side): K4, p6, *k6, p6; rep from * to last 4 sts, k4.

2nd row: P4, k6, *p6, k6; rep from * to last 4 sts, p4.

3rd row: K2, *p2, k6, p2, k2; rep from * to end.

4th row: P2, *k2, p6, k2, p2; rep from * to end.

Rep the last 2 rows 3 times more.

11th and 12th rows: As 1st and 2nd rows.

13th row: Knit.

14th row: Purl.

Rep these 14 rows.

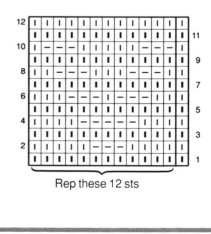

Rep these 12 sts

I.20

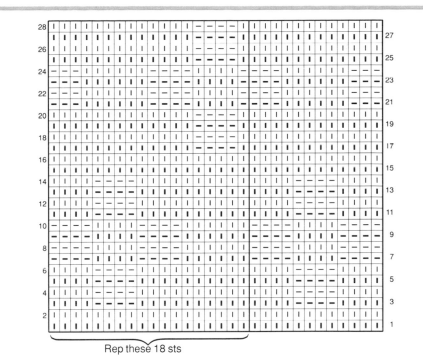

Rep these 18 sts

Multiple of 18 sts + 12.

1st row (right side): Knit.

2nd row: Purl.

3rd row: K4, p4, *k14, p4; rep from * to last 4 sts, k4.

4th row: P4, k4, *p14, k4; rep from * to last 4 sts, p4.

Rep the last 2 rows once more.

7th row: P4, k4, p4, *k6, p4, k4, p4; rep from * to end.

8th row: K4, p4, k4, *p6, k4, p4, k4; rep from * to end.

Rep the last 2 rows once more.

11th and 12th rows: As 3rd and 4th rows.

Rep the last 2 rows once more.

15th row: Knit.

16th row: Purl.

17th row: K13, p4, *k14, p4; rep from * to last 13 sts, k13.

18th row: P13, k4, *p14, k4; rep from * to last 13 sts, p13.

Rep the last 2 rows once more.

21st row: P3, k6, *p4, k4, p4, k6; rep from * to last 3 sts, p3.

22nd row: K3, p6, *k4, p4, k4, p6; rep from * to last 3 sts, k3.

Rep the last 2 rows once more.

25th and 26th rows: As 17th and 18th rows.

Rep the last 2 rows once more.

Rep these 28 rows.

I.21

Multiple of 20 sts + 1.

1st row (right side): K6, p9, *k11, p9; rep from * to last 6 sts, k6.

2nd row: P5, k11, *p9, k11; rep from * to last 5 sts, p5.

3rd row: K4, p13, *k7, p13; rep from * to last 4 sts, k4.

4th row: P3, k4, p7, k4, *p5, k4, p7, k4; rep from * to last 3 sts, p3.

5th row: K3, p3, k9, p3, *k5, p3, k9, p3; rep from * to last 3 sts, k3.

6th row: P3, k2, p11, k2, *p5, k2, p11, k2; rep from * to last 3 sts, p3.

7th row: K3, p1, k13, p1, *k5, p1, k13, p1; rep from * to last 3 sts, k3.

8th row: As 3rd row.

9th row: As 2nd row.

10th row: K6, p9, *k11, p9; rep from * to last 6 sts, k6.

11th row: K3, p4, k7, p4, *k5, p4, k7, p4; rep from * to last 3 sts, k3.

12th row: P4, k3, *p7, k3; rep from * to last 4 sts, p4.

13th row: K5, p2, k7, p2, *k9, p2, k7, p2; rep from * to last 5 sts, k5.

14th row: P6, k1, p7, k1, *p11, k1, p7, k1; rep from * to last 6 sts, p6.

Rep these 14 rows.

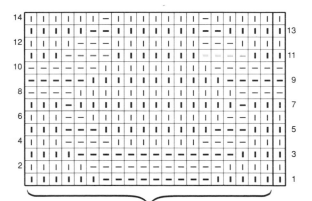

Rep these 20 sts

I. Knit and Purl Textures

I.22

Multiple of 16 sts + 1.

1st row (right side): [K1, p1] twice, [k4, p1] twice, *[k1, p1] 3 times, [k4, p1] twice; rep from * to last 3 sts, k1, p1, k1.

2nd row: K1, p1, k1, p4, k3, p4, *k1, [p1, k1] twice, p4, k3, p4; rep from * to last 3 sts, k1, p1, k1.

3rd row: K1, *p1, k4, p5, k4, p1, k1; rep from * to end.

4th row: K1, *p4, k7, p4, k1; rep from * to end.

5th row: K4, p4, k1, p4, *k7, p4, k1, p4; rep from * to last 4 sts, k4.

6th row: P4, k3, p1, k1, p1, k3, *p7, k3, p1, k1, p1, k3; rep from * to last 4 sts, p4.

7th row: K4, p2, k1, [p1, k1] twice, p2, *k7, p2, k1, [p1, k1] twice, p2; rep from * to last 4 sts, k4.

8th row: P4, k1, [p1, k1] 4 times, *p7, k1, [p1, k1] 4 times; rep from * to last 4 sts, p4.

9th row: P1, k4, p1, [K1, p1] 3 times, *[k4, p1] twice, [k1, p1] 3 times; rep from * to last 5 sts, k4, p1.

10th row: K2, p4, k1, [p1, k1] twice, p4, *k3, p4, k1, [p1, k1] twice, p4; rep from * to last 2 sts, k2.

11th row: P3, k4, p1, k1, p1, k4, *p5, k4, p1, k1, p1, k4; rep from * to last 3 sts, p3.

12th row: K4, p4, k1, p4, *k7, p4, k1, p4; rep from * to last 4 sts, k4.

13th row: K1, *p4, k7, p4, k1; rep from * to end.

14th row: K1, *p1, k3, p7, k3, p1, k1; rep from * to end.

15th row: K1, p1, k1, p2, k7, p2, *k1, [p1, k1] twice, p2, k7, p2; rep from * to last 3 sts, k1, p1, k1.

16th row: K1, [p1, k1] twice, p7, k1, *[p1, k1] 4 times, p7, k1; rep from * to last 4 sts, [p1, k1] twice.

Rep these 16 rows.

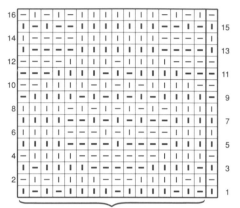

Rep these 16 sts

I.23

Multiple of 15 sts.

1st row (right side): P1, k4, p5, k4, *p2, k4, p5, k4; rep from * to last st, p1.

2nd row: K2, p4, k3, p4, *k4, p4, k3, p4; rep from * to last 2 sts, k2.

3rd row: P3, k4, p1, k4, *p6, k4, p1, k4; rep from * to last 3 sts, p3.

4th row: K4, p7, *k8, p7; rep from * to last 4 sts, k4.

5th row: P5, k5, *p10, k5; rep from * to last 5 sts, p5.

6th row: P1, k5, p3, k5, *p2, k5, p3, k5; rep from * to last st, p1.

7th row: K2, p5, k1, p5, *k4, p5, k1, p5; rep from * to last 2 sts, k2.

8th row: P3, k9, *p6, k9; rep from * to last 3 sts, p3.

9th row: As 7th row.

10th row: As 6th row.

11th row: As 5th row.

12th row: As 4th row.

13th row: As 3rd row.

14th row: As 2nd row.

Rep these 14 rows.

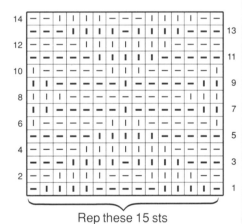

Rep these 15 sts

I.23A

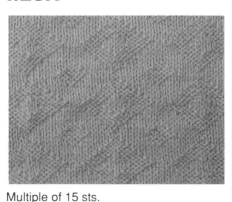

Multiple of 15 sts.
Worked as **I.23** using reverse side as right side.

I.24

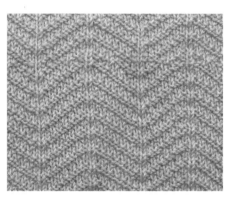

Multiple of 16 sts + 1.

1st row (right side): [K2, p2] twice, k1, p2, k2, p2, *k3, p2, k2, p2, k1, p2, k2, p2; rep from * to last 2 sts, k2.

2nd row: P1, *k2, p2, k2, p3, k2, p2, k2, p1; rep from * to end.

3rd row: K1, *p1, k2, p2, k5, p2, k2, p1, k1; rep from * to end.

4th row: P3, k2, p2, k1, p1, k1, p2, k2, *p5, k2, p2, k1, p1, k1, p2, k2; rep from * to last 3 sts, p3.

Rep these 4 rows.

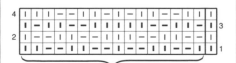

Rep these 16 sts

18

I.25

Rep these 15 sts

Multiple of 15 sts + 2.

1st row (right side): P6, k2, p1, k2, *p10, k2, p1, k2; rep from * to last 6 sts, p6.

2nd row: K6, p2, k1, p2, *k10, p2, k1, p2; rep from * to last 6 sts, k6.

Rep the last 2 rows once more.

5th row: P5, k2, p3, k2, *p8, k2, p3, k2; rep from * to last 5 sts, p5.

6th row: K5, p2, k3, p2, *k8, p2, k3, p2; rep from * to last 5 sts, k5.

Rep the last 2 rows once more.

9th row: P4, k2, p2, k1, p2, k2, *p6, k2, p2, k1, p2, k2; rep from * to last 4 sts, p4.

10th row: K4, p2, k2, p1, k2, p2, *k6, p2, k2, p1, k2, p2; rep from * to last 4 sts, k4.

Rep the last 2 rows once more.

13th row: P3, k2, p2, k1, p1, k1, p2, k2, *p4, k2, p2, k1, p1, k1, p2, k2; rep from * to last 3 sts, p3.

14th row: K3, p2, k2, p1, k1, p1, k2, p2, *k4, p2, k2, p1, k1, p1, k2, p2; rep from * to last 3 sts, k3.

Rep the last 2 rows once more.

17th row: P2, *k2, p2, k1, [p1, k1] twice, p2, k2, p2; rep from * to end.

18th row: K2, *p2, k2, p1, [k1, p1] twice, k2, p2, k2; rep from * to end.

Rep the last 2 rows once more.

21st and 22nd rows: As 13th and 14th rows.

Rep these 2 rows once more.

25th and 26th rows: As 9th and 10th rows.

Rep these 2 rows once more.

29th and 30th rows: As 5th and 6th rows.

Rep these 2 rows once more.

Rep these 32 rows.

Multiple of 6 sts + 2.

1st row (right side): P2, *k4, p2; rep from * to end.

2nd row: K2, *p4, k2; rep from * to end.

Rep the last 2 rows 3 times more.

9th row: K1, *p2, k4; rep from * to last st, p1.

10th row: *P4, k2; rep from * to last 2 sts, p2.

11th row: K3, p2, *k4, p2; rep from * to last 3 sts, k3.

12th row: P2, *k2, p4; rep from * to end.

13th row: P1, *k4, p2; rep from * to last st, k1.

14th, 15th and 16th rows: As 8th, 9th and 10th rows.

17th row: As 11th row.

18th row: P3, k2, *p4, k2; rep from * to last 3 sts, p3.

Rep the last 2 rows 3 times more.

25th row: *K4, p2, rep from * to last 2 sts, k2.

26th row: P1, *k2, p4; rep from * to last st, k1.

27th row: As 1st row.

28th row: K1, *p4, k2; rep from * to last st, p1.

29th row: K2, *p2, k4; rep from * to end.

30th row: P3, k2, *p4, k2; rep from * to last 3 sts, p3.

31st row: *K4, p2; rep from * to last 2 sts, k2.

32nd row: As 26th row.

Rep these 32 rows.

I.26

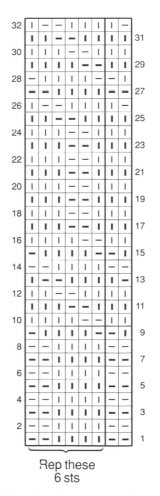

Rep these 6 sts

I. Knit and Purl Textures

I.27

Multiple of 12 sts + 7.

1st row (right side): K3, p1, k3, *p2, k1, p2, k3, p1, k3; rep from * to end.

2nd row: P3, k1, p3, *k2, p1, k2, p3, k1, p3; rep from * to end.

3rd row: K2, p1, k1, p1, k2, *p2, k1, p2, k2, p1, k1, p1, k2; rep from * to end.

4th row: P2, k1, p1, k1, p2, *k2, p1, k2, p2, k1, p1, k1, p2; rep from * to end.

5th row: K1, [p1, k1] 3 times, *[p2, k1] twice, [p1, k1] 3 times; rep from * to end.

6th row: P1, [k1, p1] 3 times, *[k2, p1] twice, [k1, p1] 3 times; rep from * to end.

7th and 8th rows: As 3rd and 4th rows.

9th and 10th rows: As 1st and 2nd rows.

11th row: [K1, p2] twice, *k3, p1, k3, p2, k1, p2; rep from * to last st, k1.

12th row: [P1, k2] twice, *p3, k1, p3, k2, p1, k2; rep from * to last st, p1.

13th row: [K1, p2] twice, *k2, p1, k1, p1, k2, p2, k1, p2; rep from * to last st, k1.

14th row: [P1, k2] twice, *p2, k1, p1, k1, p2, k2, p1, k2; rep from * to last st, p1.

15th row: [K1, p2] twice, k1, *[p1, k1] 3 times, [p2, k1] twice; rep from * to end.

16th row: [P1, k2] twice, p1, *[k1, p1] 3 times, [k2, p1] twice; rep from * to end.

17th and 18th rows: As 13th and 14th rows.

19th and 20th rows: As 11th and 12th rows.

Rep these 20 rows.

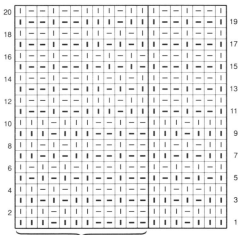

Rep these 12 sts

I.28

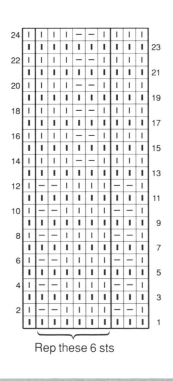

Rep these 6 sts

I.29

Multiple of 10 sts.

1st row (right side): P7, k2, *p8, k2; rep from * to last st, p1.

2nd row: *P1, k1, p2, k6; rep from * to end.

3rd row: *P5, k2, p1, k2; rep from * to end.

4th row: *P3, k1, p2, k4; rep from * to end.

5th row: *P3, k2, p1, k4; rep from * to end.

6th row: *P5, k1, p2, k2; rep from * to end.

7th row: *P1, k2, p1, k6; rep from * to end.

8th row: As 6th row.

9th row: As 5th row.

10th row: As 4th row.

11th row: As 3rd row.

12th row: As 2nd row.

13th row: As 1st row.

14th row: *P2, k8; rep from * to end.

Rep these 14 rows.

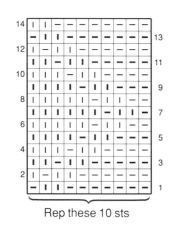

Rep these 10 sts

Multiple of 6 sts + 4.

1st row (right side): Knit.

2nd row: P1, k2, *p4, k2; rep from * to last st, p1.

Rep the last 2 rows 5 times more.

13th row: Knit.

14th row: P4, *k2, p4; rep from * to end.

Rep the last 2 rows 5 times more.

Rep these 24 rows.

I.30

Multiple of 24 sts + 3.

1st row (right side): P1, KB1, *p5, KB1, [p1, KB1] 6 times, p5, KB1; rep from * to last st, p1.

2nd row: K1, p1, *k5, p1, [k1, p1] 6 times, k5, p1; rep from * to last st, k1.

3rd row: As 1st row.

4th row: K1, p1, *k7, p1, [k1, p1] 4 times, k7, p1; rep from * to last st, k1.

5th row: P1, KB1, *p7, KB1, [p1, KB1] 4 times, p7, KB1; rep from * to last st, p1.

6th row: K1, p1, k9, p1, [k1, p1] twice, *[k9, p1] twice, [k1, p1] twice; rep from * to last 11 sts, k9, p1, k1.

7th row: P1, KB1, p9, KB1, [p1, KB1] twice, *[p9, KB1] twice, [p1, KB1] twice; rep from * to last 11 sts, p9, KB1, p1.

8th row: K1, p1, *k11, p1; rep from * to last st, k1.

9th row: P1, KB1, *p11, KB1; rep from * to last st, p1.

10th row: *[K1, p1] twice, [k9, p1] twice; rep from * to last 3 sts, k1, p1, k1.

11th row: *[P1, KB1] twice, [p9, KB1] twice; rep from * to last 3 sts, p1, KB1, p1.

12th row: [K1, p1] 3 times, [k7, p1] twice, *[k1, p1] 4 times, [k7, p1] twice; rep from * to last 5 sts, k1, [p1, k1] twice.

13th row: [P1, KB1] 3 times, [p7, KB1] twice, *[p1, KB1] 4 times, [p7, KB1] twice; rep from * to last 5 sts, p1, [KB1, p1] twice.

14th row: [K1, p1] 4 times, [k5, p1] twice, *[k1, p1] 6 times, [k5, p1] twice; rep from * to last 7 sts, k1, [p1, k1] 3 times.

15th row: [P1, KB1] 4 times, [p5, KB1] twice, *[p1, KB1] 6 times, [p5, KB1] twice; rep from * to last 7 sts, p1, [KB1, p1] 3 times.

Rep the last 2 rows twice more.

20th and 21st rows: As 12th and 13th rows.

22nd and 23rd rows: As 10th and 11th rows.

24th and 25th rows: As 8th and 9th rows.

26th and 27th rows: As 6th and 7th rows.

28th and 29th rows: As 4th and 5th rows.

30th row: As 2nd row.

31st and 32nd rows: As 1st and 2nd rows.

Rep these 32 rows.

I.31

Multiple of 10 sts + 7.

1st row (right side): P3, KB1, *p4, KB1; rep from * to last 3 sts, p3.

2nd row: K3, PB1, *k4, PB1; rep from * to last 3 sts, k3.

3rd row: P2, [KB1] 3 times, *p3, KB1, p3, [KB1] 3 times; rep from * to last 2 sts, p2.

4th row: K2, [PB1] 3 times, *k3, PB1, k3, [PB1] 3 times; rep from * to last 2 sts, k2.

Rep the last 2 rows once more.

7th and 8th rows: As 1st and 2nd rows.

Rep the last 2 rows once more.

11th row: P3, KB1, p3, *[KB1] 3 times, p3, KB1, p3; rep from * to end.

12th row: K3, PB1, k3, *[PB1] 3 times, k3, PB1, k3; rep from * to end.

Rep the last 2 rows once more.

15th and 16th rows: As 1st and 2nd rows.

Rep these 16 rows.

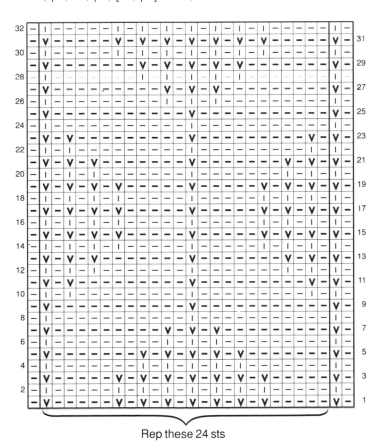

Rep these 24 sts

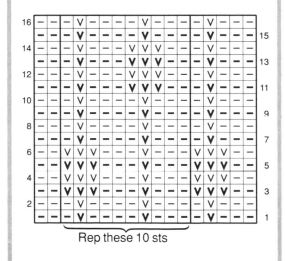

Rep these 10 sts

V = KB1, V = PB1.

I. Knit and Purl Textures

I.32

Multiple of 10 sts + 5.

1st row (right side): K5, *KB1, [p1, KB1] twice, k5; rep from * to end.

2nd row: K5, *PB1, [k1, PB1] twice, k5; rep from * to end.

Rep the last 2 rows twice more.

7th row: KB1, [p1, KB1] twice, *k5, KB1, [p1, KB1] twice; rep from * to end.

8th row: PB1, [k1, PB1] twice, *k5, PB1, [k1, PB1] twice; rep from * to end.

Rep the last 2 rows twice more.

Rep these 12 rows.

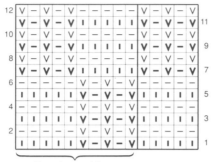

Rep these 10 sts

I.34

Multiple of 6 sts + 3.

Note: Slip sts purlwise with yarn at back of work (wrong side) = S on diagram.

Foundation row: K1, p1, *k2, p1; rep from * to last st, k1.

1st row (right side): K1, sl 1, *k2, sl 1; rep from * to last st, k1.

2nd row: K1, p1, *k2, p1; rep from * to last st, k1.

Rep the last 2 rows once more.

5th row: K1, sl 1, *k5, sl 1; rep from * to last st, k1.

6th row: K1, p1, *k5, p1; rep from * to last st, k1.

Rep the last 2 rows once more.

9th and 10th rows: As 1st and 2nd rows.

Rep the last 2 rows once more.

13th row: K4, sl 1, *k5, sl 1; rep from * to last 4 sts, k4.

14th row: K4, p1, *k5, p1; rep from * to last 4 sts, k4.

Rep the last 2 rows once more.

Rep the last 16 rows.

I.33

Multiple of 14 sts + 5.

Note: Slip sts purlwise with yarn at wrong side of work, (S or S on diagram, see page 9).

1st row (right side): Purl.

2nd row: Knit.

3rd row: Purl.

4th row: P8, sl 3, *p11, sl 3; rep from * to last 8 sts, p8.

5th row: K8, sl 3, *k11, sl 3; rep from * to last 8 sts, k8.

Rep the last 2 rows once more, then 4th row again.

9th, 10th and 11th rows: As 1st, 2nd and 3rd rows.

12th row: P1, sl 3, *p11, sl 3; rep from * to last st, p1.

13th row: K1, sl 3, *k11, sl 3; rep from * to last st, k1.

Rep the last 2 rows once more, then 12th row again.

Rep these 16 rows.

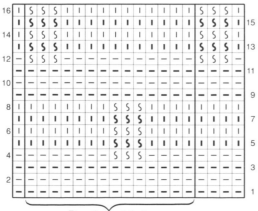

Rep these 14 sts

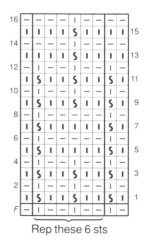

Rep these 6 sts

A slip stitch is one that is passed from the left to the right needle without being knitted. There are two ways of slipping stitches.

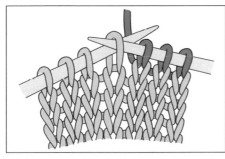

Purlwise where the right-hand needle is inserted as if to purl. This method is used when the slip stitch is to be worked on the following row, e.g. slip stitch and lace patterns.

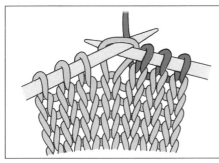

Knitwise where the right-hand needle is inserted as if to knit. In this case the slip stitch becomes twisted. Occasionally twisted slip stitches can become a feature of the stitch pattern. Unless otherwise stated always slip stitches purlwise.

Pattern Effects

A multitude of patterns can be created using combinations of effects produced by slipping stitches.

The yarn can be carried across the front or back of the work whilst the stitch is being slipped. It will form a 'bar' across the slipped stitch.

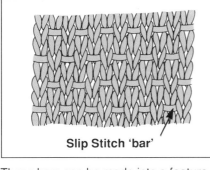

Slip Stitch 'bar'

These bars can be made into a feature of a stitch pattern (e.g. III.3 and III.6) or hidden from view by always carrying the yarn on the wrong side of the work as in mosaic patterns (e.g. II.1 and II.2) or honeycomb patterns (e.g. II.19 and II.6).

Mosaic Patterns

Mosaic patterns give the impression that two or more colours have been used in the same row. In reality only one colour is used at a time in a stripe sequence. This means that the effect is similar to fairisle but without the difficulty of handling more than one colour in a row. Multi-coloured effects are achieved by slipping stitches of one colour over rows of stitches worked in another colour.

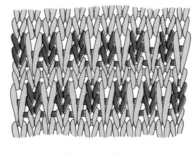

Mosaic Effect

Honeycomb Patterns

By slipping stitches at intervals over several rows the fabric contracts into hexagonal shapes. This honeycomb effect can be emphasised by using contrast colours.

Honeycomb Effect

Colour Chart

Multi-coloured slip stitch patterns include suggested colours which have been indicated by a letter shown on the colour chart below. These letters are given either at the beginning of the row in written instructions or next to the row number on charts.

The colours shown are approximate equivalents to yarn colours used in the samples.

Keeping Yarn on Wrong Side

When following a slip stitch pattern from this book, unless otherwise stated, carry the yarn across the wrong side of the work (i.e. the back of the work on right side rows and the front of the work on wrong side rows). If necessary the yarn is brought forward or taken back before working the next stitch, without making a stitch.

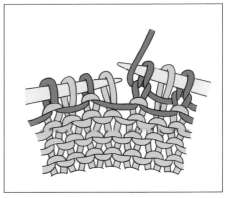

1. Bring the yarn from back to front of work under needles.

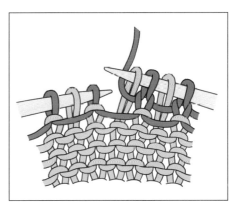

2. Take yarn from front to back of work under needles.

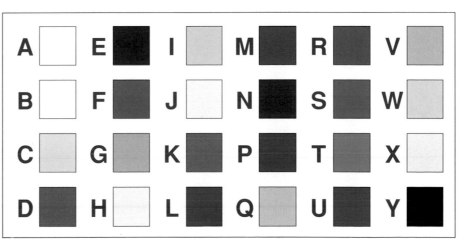

II. Slip Stitch Mosaics

II.1

13th and 14th rows: As 1st and 2nd rows.

15th and 16th rows: Using G k1, sl 1, *k11, sl 1; rep from * to last st, k1.

17th and 18th rows: Using Y k2, sl 1, k9, *sl 1, k1, sl 1, k9; rep from * to last 3 sts, sl 1, k2.

19th and 20th rows: Using G [k1, sl 1] twice, k7, *[sl 1, k1] twice, sl 1, k7; rep from * to last 4 sts, [sl 1, k1] twice.

21st and 22nd rows: As 17th and 18th rows.

23rd and 24th rows: As 15th and 16th rows.

Rep these 24 rows.

Multiple of 12 sts + 3.

1st row (right side): Using Y knit.

2nd row: Using Y knit.

3rd and 4th rows: Using G k7, sl 1, *k11, sl 1; rep from * to last 7 sts, k7.

5th and 6th rows: Using Y k6, sl 1, k1, sl 1, *k9, sl 1, k1, sl 1; rep from * to last 6 sts, k6.

7th and 8th rows: Using G k5, [sl 1, k1] twice, sl 1, *k7, [sl 1, k1] twice, sl 1; rep from * to last 5 sts, k5.

9th and 10th rows: As 5th and 6th rows.

11th and 12th rows: As 3rd and 4th rows.

II.3

Multiple of 8 sts + 2.

Foundation row: Using B purl.

1st row (right side): Using K k3, sl 1, k2, sl 1, *k4, sl 1, k2, sl 1; rep from * to last 3 sts, k3.

2nd row: Using K p3, sl 1, p2, sl 1, *p4, sl 1, p2, sl 1; rep from * to last 3 sts, p3.

3rd row: Using B k1, sl 1, k2, *sl 2, k2; rep from * to last 2 sts, sl 1, k1.

4th row: Using B p1, sl 1, p2, *sl 2, p2; rep from * to last 2 sts, sl 1, p1.

5th and 6th rows: As 1st and 2nd rows.

7th row: Using B k2, *sl 1, k4, sl 1, k2; rep from * to end.

8th row: Using B p2, *sl 1, p4, sl 1, p2; rep from * to end.

9th and 10th rows: As 3rd and 4th rows **but** using K instead of B.

11th and 12th rows: As 7th and 8th rows.

Rep the last 12 rows.

II.2

Multiple of 8 sts + 2.

Foundation row (wrong side): Using B knit.

1st and 2nd rows: Using P k3, sl 1, k2, sl 1, *k4, sl 1, k2, sl 1; rep from * to last 3 sts, k3.

3rd and 4th rows: Using B k1, sl 1, k2, *sl 2, k2; rep from * to last 2 sts, sl 1, k1.

5th and 6th rows: As 1st and 2nd rows.

7th and 8th rows: Using B k2, *sl 1, k4, sl 1, k2; rep from * to end.

9th and 10th rows: As 3rd and 4th rows **but** using P instead of B.

11th and 12th rows: As 7th and 8th rows.

Rep the last 12 rows.

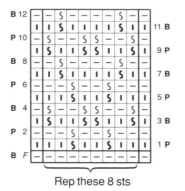

Rep these 8 sts

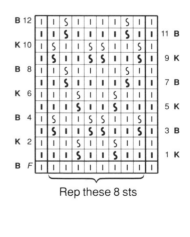

Rep these 8 sts

Rep these 12 sts

Colour key on page 23

II.4

Mutliple of 16 sts + 3.

Foundation row: Using P purl.

1st row (right side): Using G k2, *sl 1, [k1, sl 1] twice, k11; rep from * to last st, k1.

2nd row: Using G p12, sl 1, [p1, sl 1] twice, *p11, sl 1, [p1, sl 1] twice; rep from * to last 2 sts, p2.

3rd row: Using P k1, sl 1, *k7, sl 1, [k1, sl 1] 4 times; rep from * to last st, k1.

4th row: Using P p1, *sl 1, [k1, sl 1] 4 times, p7; rep from * to last 2 sts, sl 1, p1.

5th row: Using G k4, sl 1, [k1, sl 1] twice, *k11, sl 1, [k1, sl 1] twice; rep from * to last 10 sts, k10.

6th row: Using G p10, sl 1, [p1, sl 1] twice, *p11, sl 1, [p1, sl 1] twice; rep from * to last 4 sts, p4.

7th row: Using P [k1, sl 1] twice, k7, *sl 1, [k1, sl 1] 4 times, k7; rep from * to last 8 sts, [sl 1, k1] 4 times.

8th row: Using P p1, sl 1, [k1, sl 1] 3 times, p7, *sl 1, [k1, sl 1] 4 times, p7; rep from * to last 4 sts, sl 1, k1, sl 1, p1.

9th row: Using G k6, sl 1, [k1, sl 1] twice, *k11, sl 1, [k1, sl 1] twice; rep from * to last 8 sts, k8.

10th row: Using G p8, sl 1, [p1, sl 1] twice, *p11, sl 1, [p1, sl 1] twice; rep from * to last 6 sts, p6.

11th row: Using P [k1, sl 1] 3 times, k7, *sl 1, [k1, sl 1] 4 times, k7; rep from * to last 6 sts, [sl 1, k1] 3 times.

12th row: Using P p1, sl 1, [k1, sl 1] twice, p7, *sl 1, [k1, sl 1] 4 times, p7; rep from * to last 6 sts, sl 1, [k1, sl 1] twice, p1.

13th row: Using G k8, sl 1, [k1, sl 1] twice, *k11, sl 1, [k1, sl 1] twice; rep from * to last 6 sts, k6.

14th row: Using G p6, sl 1, [p1, sl 1] twice, *p11, sl 1, [p1, sl 1] twice; rep from * to last 8 sts, p8.

15th row: Using P [k1, sl 1] 4 times, k7, *sl 1, [k1, sl 1] 4 times, k7; rep from * to

last 4 sts, [sl 1, k1] twice.

16th row: Using P p1, sl 1, k1, sl 1, p7, *sl 1, [k1, sl 1] 4 times, p7; rep from * to last 8 sts, sl 1, [k1, sl 1] 3 times, p1.

17th row: Using G k10, sl 1, [k1, sl 1] twice, *k11, sl 1, [k1, sl 1] twice; rep from * to last 4 sts, k4.

18th row: Using G p4, sl 1, [p1, sl 1] twice, *p11, sl 1, [p1, sl 1] twice; rep from * to last 10 sts, p10.

19th row: Using P [k1, sl 1] 5 times, k7, *sl 1, [k1, sl 1] 4 times, k7; rep from * to last 2 sts, sl 1, k1.

20th row: Using P p1, sl 1, *p7, sl 1, [k1, sl 1] 4 times; rep from * to last st, p1.

21st row: Using G k12, sl 1, [k1, sl 1] twice, *k11, sl 1, [k1, sl 1] twice; rep from * to last 2 sts, k2.

22nd row: Using G p2, *sl 1, [p1, sl 1] twice, p11; rep from * to last st, p1.

23rd and 24th rows: As 19th and 20th rows.

25th and 26th rows: As 17th and 18th rows.

27th and 28th rows: As 15th and 16th rows.

29th and 30th rows: As 13th and 14th rows.

31st and 32nd rows: As 11th and 12th rows.

33rd and 34th rows: As 9th and 10th rows.

35th and 36th rows: As 7th and 8th rows.

37th and 38th rows: As 5th and 6th rows.

39th and 40th rows: As 3rd and 4th rows.

Rep the last 40 rows.

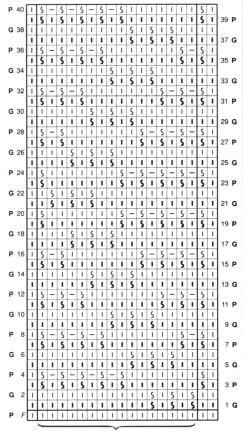

Rep these 16 sts

II.5

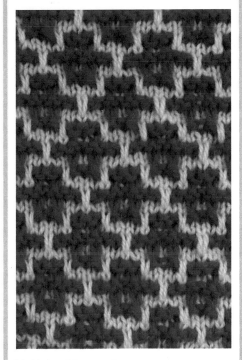

Multiple of 8 sts + 3.

Foundation row (wrong side): Using J purl.

1st and 2nd rows: Using M k3, *sl 1, k3; rep from * to end.

3rd row: Using J k4, sl 1, k1, sl 1, *k5, sl 1, k1, sl 1; rep from * to last 4 sts, k4.

4th row: Using J p4, sl 1, p1, sl 1, *p5, sl 1, p1, sl 1: rep from * to last 4 sts, p4.

5th and 6th rows: Using M k1, sl 1, *k7, sl 1; rep from * to last st, k1.

7th and 8th rows: As 3rd and 4th rows.

9th and 10th rows: As 1st and 2nd rows.

11th row: Using J k2, sl 1, k5, *sl 1, k1, sl 1, k5; rep from * to last 3 sts, sl 1, k2.

12th row: Using J p2, sl 1, p5, *sl 1, p1, sl 1, p5; rep from * to last 3 sts, sl 1, p2.

13th and 14th rows: Using M k5, sl 1, *k7, sl 1; rep from * to last 5 sts, k5.

15th and 16th rows: As 11th and 12th rows.

Rep the last 16 rows.

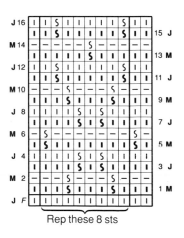

Rep these 8 sts

II. Slip Stitch Mosaics

II.6

Multiple of 8 sts + 6.
Foundation row: Using H purl.
1st row (right side): Using V knit.
2nd row: Using V k6, *sl 2, k6; rep from * to end.
Rep the last row twice more.
5th row: Using K k6, *sl 2, k6; rep from * to end.
6th row: Using K p6, *sl 2, p6; rep from * to end.
Rep the last 2 rows once more.
9th row: Using V knit.
10th row: Using V k2, sl 2, *k6, sl 2; rep from * to last 2 sts, k2.
Rep the last row twice more.
13th row: Using H k2, sl 2, *k6, sl 2; rep from * to last 2 sts, k2.
14th row: Using H p2, sl 2, *p6, sl 2; rep from * to last 2 sts, p2.
Rep the last 2 rows once more.
Rep the last 16 rows.

II.6 chart

H 16	I	I	S	S	I	I	I	I	I	I	S	S	I	I	
H 14	I	I	S	S	I	I	I	I	I	I	S	S	I	I	15 H
V 12	I	I	S	S	I	I	I	I	I	I	S	S	I	I	13 H
V 10	–	–	S	S	–	–	–	–	–	–	S	S	–	–	11 V
K 8	–	–	S	S	–	–	–	–	–	–	S	S	–	–	
K 6	I	I	I	I	I	I	S	S	I	I	I	I	I	I	9 V
V 4	I	I	I	I	I	I	S	S	I	I	I	I	I	I	7 K
V 2	I	I	I	I	I	I	S	S	I	I	I	I	I	I	5 K
	–	–	–	–	–	–	S	S	–	–	–	–	–	–	3 V
	I	I	I	I	I	I	S	S	I	I	I	I	I	I	
	–	–	–	–	–	–	S	S	–	–	–	–	–	–	1 V
H F	I	I	I	I	I	I	I	I	I	I	I	I	I	I	

Rep these 8 sts

II.6A

As **II.6** but working Foundation row, 13th, 14th, 15th and 16th rows in K.

Multiple of 8 sts + 7.
1st row (right side): Using H knit.
2nd row: Using H knit.
3rd row: Using Q k1, sl 1, k3, *sl 1, [k1, sl 1] twice, k3; rep from * to last 2 sts, sl 1, k1.
4th row: Using Q k1, sl 1, p3, *sl 1, [k1, sl 1] twice, p3; rep from * to last 2 sts, sl 1, k1.
5th and 6th rows: Using H k2, sl 3, *k5, sl 3; rep from * to last 2 sts, k2.
7th and 8th rows: As 3rd and 4th rows.
9th and 10th rows: Using H knit.
11th row: Using Q [k1, sl 1] 3 times, *k3, sl 1, [k1, sl 1] twice; rep from * to last st, k1.
12th row: Using Q [k1, sl 1] 3 times, *p3, sl 1, [k1, sl 1] twice; rep from * to last st, k1.
13th and 14th rows: Using H k6, *sl 3, k5; rep from * to last st, k1.
15th and 16th rows: As 11th and 12th rows.
Rep these 16 rows.

II.7

II.8

Multiple of 10 sts + 5.
Using V work 4 rows in st st, starting knit (1st row is right side).
5th and 6th rows: Using K knit.
Using V work 4 rows in st st, starting knit.
11th and 12th rows: Using K k1, sl 3, *k3, sl 1, k3, sl 3; rep from * to last st, k1.
13th row: Using V knit.
14th row: Using V purl.
Rep the last 4 rows once more, then 11th and 12th rows again.
Rep these 20 rows.

II.8 chart

K 20	–	S	S	S	–	–	–	S	–	–	–	S	S	S	–	19 K
V 18	I	S	S	S	I	I	I	S	I	I	I	S	S	S	I	17 V
K 16	I	I	I	I	I	I	I	I	I	I	I	I	I	I	I	15 K
V 14	–	S	S	S	–	–	–	S	–	–	–	S	S	S	–	13 V
K 12	I	S	S	S	I	I	I	S	I	I	I	S	S	S	I	11 K
V 10	–	S	S	S	–	–	–	S	–	–	–	S	S	S	–	9 V
V 8	I	I	I	I	I	I	I	I	I	I	I	I	I	I	I	7 V
K 6	I	I	I	I	I	I	I	I	I	I	I	I	I	I	I	5 K
V 4	–	–	–	–	–	–	–	–	–	–	–	–	–	–	–	3 V
V 2	I	I	I	I	I	I	I	I	I	I	I	I	I	I	I	1 V

Rep these 10 sts

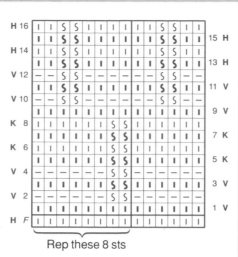

II.7 chart

Q 16	–	S	–	S	–	S	I	I	I	S	–	S	–	S	–	
	I	S	I	S	I	S	I	I	I	S	I	S	I	S	I	15 Q
H 14	I	I	I	I	I	I	S	S	S	I	I	I	I	I	I	13 H
Q 12	–	S	–	S	–	S	I	I	I	S	–	S	–	S	–	
	I	S	I	S	I	S	I	I	I	S	I	S	I	S	I	11 Q
H 10	I	I	I	I	I	I	I	I	I	I	I	I	I	I	I	9 H
Q 8	–	S	I	I	I	S	–	S	–	S	I	I	I	S	–	
	I	S	I	I	I	S	I	S	I	S	I	I	I	S	I	7 Q
H 6	–	S	S	S	–	–	–	–	–	S	S	S	–	–	–	
	I	S	S	S	I	I	I	I	I	S	S	S	I	I	I	5 H
Q 4	I	S	I	S	–	S	–	S	I	S	I	S	–	S	–	
	I	S	I	S	I	S	I	S	I	S	I	S	I	S	I	3 Q
H 2	I	I	I	I	I	I	I	I	I	I	I	I	I	I	I	
	I	I	I	I	I	I	I	I	I	I	I	I	I	I	I	1 H

Rep these 8 sts

Colour key on page 23

II.9

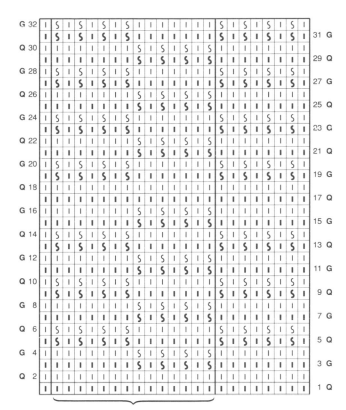

Rep these 14 sts

Multiple of 14 sts + 9.

1st row (right side): Using Q knit.

2nd row: Using Q purl.

3rd row: Using G k8, *sl 1, [k1, sl 1] 3 times, k7; rep from * to last st, k1.

4th row: Using G p8, *sl 1, [p1, sl 1] 3 times, p7; rep from * to last st, p1.

5th row: Using Q [k1, sl 1] 4 times, *k7, sl 1, [k1, sl 1] 3 times; rep from * to last st, k1.

6th row: Using Q [p1, sl 1] 4 times, *p7, sl 1, [p1, sl 1] 3 times; rep from * to last st, p1.

Rep the last 4 rows twice more, then 3rd and 4th rows again.

17th and 18th rows: As 1st and 2nd rows.

19th and 20th rows: As 5th and 6th rows **but** using G instead of Q.

21st and 22nd rows: As 3rd and 4th rows **but** using Q instead of G.

Rep the last 4 rows twice more, then 19th and 20th rows again.

Rep these 32 rows.

II.10

Multiple of 8 sts + 1.

1st row (right side): Using Q knit.

2nd row: Using Q knit.

3rd and 4th rows: Using K k1, *sl 1, k1; rep from * to end.

5th and 6th rows: As 1st and 2nd rows.

7th and 8th rows: Using K k1, *sl 1, k5, sl 1, k1; rep from * to end.

9th and 10th rows: Using Q k2, sl 1, *k3, sl 1; rep from * to last 2 sts, k2.

11th and 12th rows: As 3rd and 4th rows.

13th and 14th rows: As 9th and 10th rows.

15th and 16th rows: As 7th and 8th rows.

Rep these 16 rows.

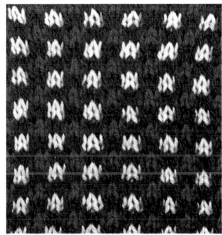

Rep these 8 sts

II.11

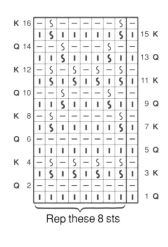

Multiple of 4 sts + 2.

1st row (right side): Using N knit.

2nd row: Using R p1, *sl 2, p2; rep from * to last st, p1.

3rd row: Using R k3, sl 2, *k2, sl 2; rep from * to last st, k1.

4th row: Using N purl.

5th row: Using B k1, *sl 2, k2; rep from * to last st, k1.

6th row: Using B p3, sl 2, *p2, sl 2; rep from * to last st, p1.

Rep these 6 rows.

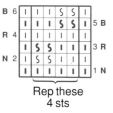

Rep these 4 sts

II. Slip Stitch Mosaics

II.12

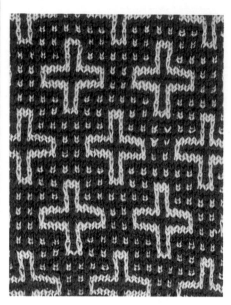

Multiple of 16 sts + 5.

Foundation row: Using S purl.

1st row (right side): Using B k4, *[sl 1, k1] twice, sl 1, k3; rep from * to last st, k1.

2nd row: Using B p4, *[sl 1, p1] twice, sl 1, p3; rep from * to last st, p1.

3rd row: Using S k9, sl 1, k1, sl 1, *k13, sl 1, k1, sl 1; rep from * to last 9 sts, k9.

4th row: Using S p9, sl 1, p1, sl 1, *p13, sl 1, p1, sl 1; rep from * to last 9 sts, p9.

5th row: Using B k2, sl 1, *k1, sl 1; rep from * to last 2 sts, k2.

6th row: Using B p2, sl 1, *p1, sl 1; rep from * to last 2 sts, p2.

7th and 8th rows: As 3rd and 4th rows.

9th row: Using B k2, sl 1, k1, [sl 1, k5] twice, *[sl 1, k1] twice, [sl 1, k5] twice; rep from * to last 5 sts, sl 1, k1, sl 1, k2.

10th row: Using B p2, sl 1, p1, [sl 1, p5] twice, *[sl 1, p1] twice, [sl 1, p5] twice; rep from * to last 5 sts, sl 1, p1, sl 1, p2.

11th row: Using S k5, *sl 1, k9, sl 1, k5; rep from * to end.

12th row: Using S p5, *sl 1, p9, sl 1, p5; rep from * to end.

13th and 14th rows: As 9th and 10th rows.

15th, 16th, 17th and 18th rows: As 3rd, 4th, 5th and 6th rows.

19th and 20th rows: As 3rd and 4th rows.

21st and 22nd rows: As 1st and 2nd rows.

23rd row: Using S [k1, sl 1] twice, *k13, sl 1, k1, sl 1; rep from * to last st, k1.

24th row: Using S [p1, sl 1] twice, *p13, sl 1, p1, sl 1; rep from * to last st, p1.

25th and 26th rows: As 5th and 6th rows.

27th and 28th rows: As 23rd and 24th rows.

29th row: Using B k2, sl 1, *k5, [sl 1, k1] twice, sl 1, k5, sl 1; rep from * to last 2 sts, k2.

30th row: Using B p2, sl 1, *p5, [sl 1, p1] twice, sl 1, p5, sl 1; rep from * to last 2 sts, p2.

31st row: Using S k7, sl 1, k5, sl 1, *k9, sl 1, k5, sl 1; rep from * to last 7 sts, k7.

32nd row: Using S p7, sl 1, p5, sl 1, *p9, sl 1, p5, sl 1; rep from * to last 7 sts, p7.

33rd and 34th rows: As 29th and 30th rows.

35th and 36th rows: As 23rd and 24th rows.

37th and 38th rows: As 5th and 6th rows.

39th and 40th rows: As 23rd and 24th rows.

Rep the last 40 rows.

II.13

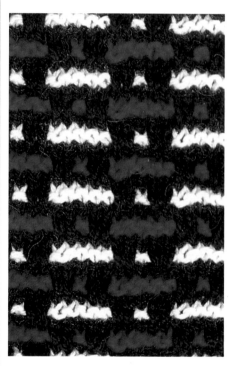

Multiple of 10 sts + 7.

1st row (right side): Using Y knit.

2nd row: Using Y purl.

3rd and 4th rows: Using A k6, *sl 2, k1 sl 2, k5; rep from * to last st, k1.

5th and 6th rows: As 1st and 2nd rows.

7th and 8th rows: Using L [k1, sl 2] twice, *k5, sl 2, k1, sl 2; rep from * to last st, k1.

Rep these 8 rows.

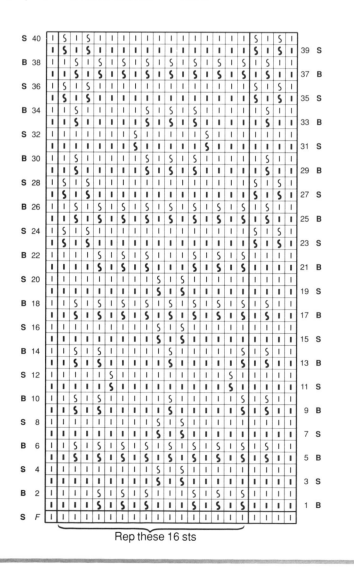

Rep these 16 sts

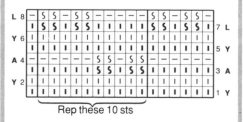

Rep these 10 sts

Colour key on page 23

II.14

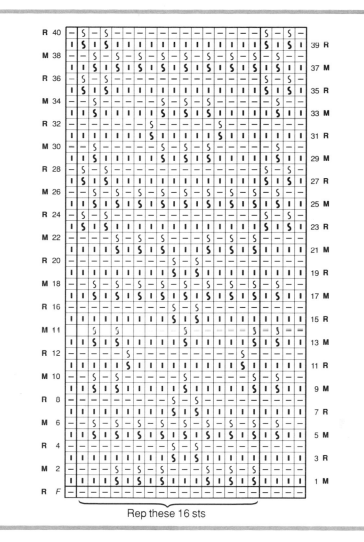

Multiple of 16 sts + 5.

Foundation row (wrong side): Using R knit.

1st and 2nd rows: Using M k4, *sl 1, [k1, sl 1] twice, k3; rep from * to last st, k1.

3rd and 4th rows: Using R k9, sl 1, k1, sl 1, *k13, sl 1, k1, sl 1; rep from * to last 9 sts, k9.

5th and 6th rows: Using M k2, sl 1, *k1, sl 1; rep from * to last 2 sts, k2.

7th and 8th rows: As 3rd and 4th rows.

9th and 10th rows: Using M k2, sl 1, k1, [sl 1, k5] twice, *sl 1, [k1, sl 1] twice, k5, sl 1, k5; rep from * to last 5 sts, sl 1, k1, sl 1, k2.

11th and 12th rows: Using R k5, *sl 1, k9, sl 1, k5; rep from * to end.

13th and 14th rows: As 9th and 10th rows.

15th, 16th, 17th and 18th rows: As 3rd, 4th, 5th and 6th rows.

19th and 20th rows: As 3rd and 4th rows.

21st and 22nd rows: As 1st and 2nd rows.

23rd and 24th rows: Using R [k1, sl 1] twice, *k13, sl 1, k1, sl 1; rep from * to last st, k1.

25th and 26th rows: As 5th and 6th rows.

27th and 28th rows: As 23rd and 24th rows.

29th and 30th rows: Using M k2, sl 1, *k5, sl 1, [k1, sl 1] twice, k5, sl 1; rep from * to last 2 sts, k2.

31st and 32nd rows: Using R k7, sl 1, k5, sl 1, *k9, sl 1, k5, sl 1; rep from * to last 7 sts, k7.

33rd and 34th rows: As 29th and 30th rows.

35th and 36th rows: As 23rd and 24th rows.

37th and 38th rows: As 5th and 6th rows.

39th and 40th rows: As 23rd and 24th rows.

Rep the last 40 rows.

Rep these 16 sts

II.15

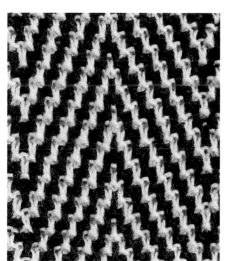

Multiple of 24 sts + 3.

Foundation row (wrong side): Using A purl.

1st and 2nd rows: Using Y k1, sl 1, *k2, sl 1; rep from * to last st, k1.

3rd and 4th rows: Using A [k2, sl 1] 4 times, k3, sl 1, [k2, sl 1] 3 times, *k1, sl 1, [k2, sl 1] 3 times, k3, sl 1, [k2, sl 1] 3 times; rep from * to last 2 sts, k2.

5th and 6th rows: Using Y k3, *[sl 1, k2] 3 times, sl 1, k1, sl 1, [k2, sl 1] 3 times, k3; rep from * to end.

7th and 8th rows: As 1st and 2nd rows **but** using A instead of Y.

9th and 10th rows: As 3rd and 4th rows **but** using Y instead of A.

11th and 12th rows: As 5th and 6th rows **but** using A instead of Y.

Rep the last 12 rows.

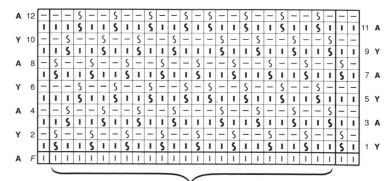

Rep these 24 sts

II.16

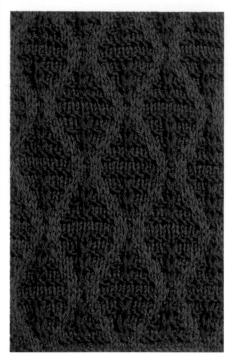

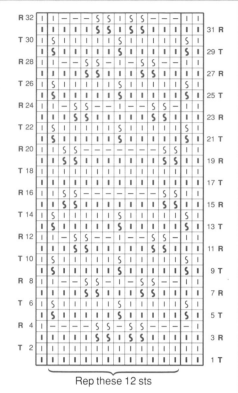

Rep these 12 sts

Mutliple of 12 sts + 3.

1st row (right side): Using T knit.

2nd row: Using T purl.

3rd row: Using R k5, sl 2, k1, sl 2, *k7, sl 2, k1, sl 2; rep from * to last 5 sts, k5.

4th row: Using R p1, k4, sl 2, k1, sl 2, *k7, sl 2, k1, sl 2; rep from * to last 5 sts, k4, p1.

5th row: Using T k1, sl 1, *k5, sl 1; rep from * to last st, k1.

6th row: Using T p1, sl 1, *p5, sl 1; rep from * to last st, p1.

7th row: Using R k4, sl 2, k3, sl 2, *k5, sl 2, k3, sl 2; rep from * to last 4 sts, k4.

8th row: Using R p2, *k2, sl 2, k1, p1, k1, sl 2, k2, p1; rep from * to last st, p1.

9th and 10th rows: As 5th and 6th rows.

11th row: Using R k3, *sl 2, k5, sl 2, k3; rep from * to end.

12th row: Using R p2, *k1, sl 2, k2, p1, k2, sl 2, k1, p1; rep from * to last st, p1.

13th and 14th rows: As 5th and 6th rows.

15th row: Using R k2, sl 2, k7, sl 2, *k1, sl 2, k7, sl 2; rep from * to last 2 sts, k2.

16th row: Using R p2, *sl 2, k7, sl 2, p1; rep from * to last st, p1.

17th and 18th rows: As 1st and 2nd rows.

19th and 20th rows: As 15th and 16th rows.

21st and 22nd rows: As 5th and 6th rows.

23rd and 24th rows: As 11th and 12th rows.

25th, 26th, 27th and 28th rows: As 5th, 6th, 7th and 8th rows.

29th and 30th rows: As 5th and 6th rows.

31st row: As 3rd row.

32nd row: Using R p2, *k3, sl 2, p1, sl 2, k3, p1; rep from * to last st, p1.

Rep these 32 rows.

II.17

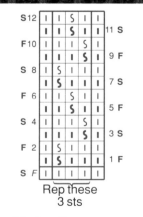

Rep these 3 sts

Multiple of 3 sts + 2.

Foundation row: Using S purl.

1st row (right side): Using F k3, sl 1, *k2, sl 1; rep from * to last st, k1.

2nd row: Using F p1, *sl 1, p2; rep from * to last st, p1.

3rd row: Using S k1, *sl 1, k2; rep from * to last st, k1.

4th row: Using S p3, sl 1, *p2, sl 1; rep from * to last st, p1.

5th row: Using F k2, *sl 1, k2; rep from * to end.

II.18

Multiple of 4 sts + 3.

1st row (right side): Using R knit.

2nd row: Using R purl.

3rd and 4th rows: Using T k1, sl 1, *k3, sl 1; rep from * to last st, k1.

5th and 6th rows: As 1st and 2nd rows.

7th and 8th rows: Using G k3, *sl 1, k3; rep from * to end.

Rep the last 2 rows once more.

11th and 12th rows: As 1st and 2nd rows.

13th and 14th rows: As 3rd and 4th rows.

15th and 16th rows: As 1st and 2nd rows.

17th and 18th rows: As 7th and 8th rows **but** using K instead of G.

Rep the last 2 rows once more.

Rep these 20 rows.

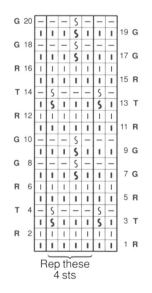

Rep these 4 sts

6th row: Using F p2, *sl 1, p2; rep from * to end.

7th and 8th rows: As 1st and 2nd rows **but** using S instead of F.

9th and 10th rows: As 3rd and 4th rows **but** using F instead of S.

11th and 12th rows: As 5th and 6th rows **but** using S instead of F.

Rep the last 12 rows.

Colour key on page 23

II.19

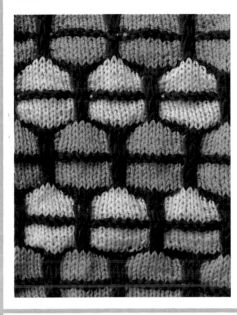

II.20

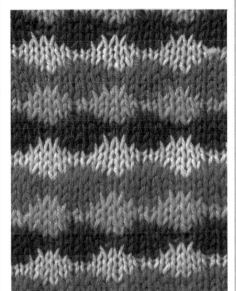

Multiple of 10 sts + 4.

1st row (right side): Using R knit.

2nd row: Using R purl.

3rd row: Using V k1, sl 2, *k8, sl 2; rep from * to last st, k1.

4th row: Using V p1, sl 2, *p8, sl 2; rep from * to last st, p1.

Rep the last 2 rows twice more.

9th row: As 1st row.

10th row: Using R p3, *k8, p2; rep from * to last st, p1.

Rep 3rd and 4th rows 3 times more, then 1st and 2nd rows again.

19th row: Using A k6, sl 2, *k8, sl 2; rep from * to last 6 sts, k6.

20th row: Using A p6, sl 2, *p8, sl 2; rep from * to last 6 sts, p6.

Rep the last 2 rows twice more.

25th row: As 1st row.

26th row: Using R p1, k5, p2, *k8, p2; rep from * to last 6 sts, k5, p1.

Rep 19th and 20th rows 3 times more.

Rep these 32 rows.

A 32	I	I	I	I	I	S	S	I	I	I	I	I						
	I	I	I	I	I	S	S	I	I	I	I	I			31	A	
A 30	I	I	I	I	I	S	S	I	I	I	I	I					
	I	I	I	I	I	S	S	I	I	I	I	I			29	A	
A 28	I	I	I	I	I	S	S	I	I	I	I	I					
	I	I	I	I	I	S	S	I	I	I	I	I			27	A	
R 26	I	–	–	–	–	–	I	I	–	–	–	–	I				
	I	I	I	I	I	I	I	I	I	I	I	I			25	R	
A 24	I	I	I	I	I	S	S	I	I	I	I	I					
	I	I	I	I	I	S	S	I	I	I	I	I			23	A	
A 22	I	I	I	I	I	S	S	I	I	I	I	I					
	I	I	I	I	I	S	S	I	I	I	I	I			21	A	
A 20	I	I	I	I	I	S	S	I	I	I	I	I					
	I	I	I	I	I	S	S	I	I	I	I	I			19	A	
R 18	I	I	I	I	I	I	I	I	I	I	I	I					
	I	I	I	I	I	I	I	I	I	I	I	I			17	R	
V 16	I	S	S	I	I	I	I	I	I	I	S	S	I				
	I	S	S	I	I	I	I	I	I	I	S	S	I		15	V	
V 14	I	S	S	I	I	I	I	I	I	I	S	S	I				
	I	S	S	I	I	I	I	I	I	I	S	S	I		13	V	
V 12	I	S	S	I	I	I	I	I	I	I	S	S	I				
	I	S	S	I	I	I	I	I	I	I	S	S	I		11	V	
R 10	I	I	I	–	–	–	–	–	–	–	I	I	I				
	I	I	I	I	I	I	I	I	I	I	I	I	I		9	R	
V 8	I	S	S	I	I	I	I	I	I	I	S	S	I				
	I	S	S	I	I	I	I	I	I	I	S	S	I		7	V	
V 6	I	S	S	I	I	I	I	I	I	I	S	S	I				
	I	S	S	I	I	I	I	I	I	I	S	S	I		5	V	
V 4	I	S	S	I	I	I	I	I	I	I	S	S	I				
	I	S	S	I	I	I	I	I	I	I	S	S	I		3	V	
R 2	I	I	I	I	I	I	I	I	I	I	I	I	I				
	I	I	I	I	I	I	I	I	I	I	I	I	I		1	R	

Rep these 10 sts

Multiple of 6 sts + 2.

1st row (right side): Using B knit.

2nd row: Using B purl.

3rd row: Using F k2, *sl 4, k2; rep from * to end.

4th row: Using F p3, sl 2, *p4, sl 2; rep from * to last 3 sts, p3.

5th and 6th rows: As 1st and 2nd rows **but** using F instead of B.

7th row: Using H k1, sl 2, k2, *sl 4, k2; rep from * to last 3 sts, sl 2, k1.

8th row: Using H p1, sl 1, p4, *sl 2, p4; rep from * to last 2 sts, sl 1, p1.

9th and 10th rows: As 1st and 2nd rows **but** using H instead of B.

11th and 12th rows: As 3rd and 4th rows **but** using G instead of F.

13th and 14th rows: As 1st and 2nd rows **but** using G instead of B.

15th and 16th rows: As 7th and 8th rows **but** using B instead of H.

Rep these 16 rows.

B 16	I	S	I	I	I	I	S	I		
	I	S	S	I	I	S	S	I	15	B
G 14	I	I	I	I	I	I	I	I		
	I	I	I	I	I	I	I	I	13	G
G 12	I	I	I	S	S	I	I	I		
	I	I	S	S	S	S	I	I	11	G
H 10	I	I	I	I	I	I	I	I		
	I	I	I	I	I	I	I	I	9	H
H 8	I	S	I	I	I	I	S	I		
	I	S	S	I	I	S	S	I	7	H
F 6	I	I	I	I	I	I	I	I		
	I	I	I	I	I	I	I	I	5	F
F 4	I	I	I	S	S	I	I	I		
	I	I	S	S	S	S	I	I	3	F
B 2	I	I	I	I	I	I	I	I		
	I	I	I	I	I	I	I	I	1	B

Rep these 6 sts

II.21

Multiple of 4 sts + 3.

Foundation row: Using T purl.

1st row (right side): Using N k2, *[sl 1, k1] twice; rep from * to last st, k1.

2nd row: Using N p2, *[sl 1, p1] twice; rep from * to last st, p1.

3rd row: Using T k3, *sl 1, k3; rep from * to end.

4th row: Using T p3, *sl 1, p3; rep from * to end.

5th row: Using N k1, sl 1, *k3, sl 1; rep from * to last st, k1.

6th row: Using N p1, sl 1, *k3, sl 1; rep from * to last st, p1.

7th and 8th rows: As 3rd and 4th rows.

9th and 10th rows: As 1st and 2nd rows.

11th row: As 5th row **but** using T instead of N.

12th row: Using I p1, sl 1, *p3, sl 1; rep from * to last st, p1.

13th row: As 3rd row **but** using N instead of T.

14th row: Using N p1, k2, sl 1, *k3, sl 1; rep from * to last 3 sts, k2, p1.

15th and 16th row: As 11th and 12th rows.

Rep the last 16 rows.

T 16	I	S	I	I	I	S	I		
	I	S	I	I	I	S	I	15	T
N 14	I	–	–	S	–	–	I		
	I	I	I	S	I	I	I	13	N
T 12	I	S	I	I	I	S	I		
	I	S	I	I	I	S	I	11	T
N 10	I	I	S	I	S	I	I		
	I	I	S	I	S	I	I	9	N
T 8	I	I	I	S	I	I	I		
	I	I	I	S	I	I	I	7	T
N 6	I	S	–	–	–	S	I		
	I	S	I	I	I	S	I	5	N
T 4	I	I	I	S	I	I	I		
	I	I	I	S	I	I	I	3	T
N 2	I	I	S	I	S	I	I		
	I	I	S	I	S	I	I	1	N
T F	I	I	I	I	I	I	I		

Rep these 4 sts

II. Slip Stitch Mosaics

II.22

Multiple of 26 sts + 2.

Foundation row: Using X purl.

1st row (right side): Using Y *k13, [sl 1, k1] 6 times, sl 1; rep from * to last 2 sts, k2.

2nd row: Using Y p2, *[sl 1, p1] 6 times, sl 1, p13; rep from * to end.

3rd row: Using X k12, [sl 1, k1] 6 times, sl 1, *k13, [sl 1, k1] 6 times, sl 1; rep from * to last 3 sts, k3.

4th row: Using X p3, [sl 1, p1] 6 times, sl 1, *p13, [sl 1, p1] 6 times, sl 1; rep from * to last 12 sts, p12.

5th row: Using Y k11, [sl 1, k1] 5 times, sl 1, *k15, [sl 1, k1] 5 times, sl 1; rep from * to last 6 sts, k6.

6th row: Using Y p6, [sl 1, p1] 5 times, sl 1, *p15, [sl 1, p1] 5 times, sl 1; rep from * to last 11 sts, p11.

7th row: Using X k8, [sl 1, k1] 6 times, sl 1, *k13, [sl 1, k1] 6 times, sl 1; rep from * to last 7 sts, k7.

8th row: Using X p7, [sl 1, p1] 6 times, sl 1, *p13, [sl 1, p1] 6 times, sl 1; rep from * to last 8 sts, p8.

9th row: Using Y k7, [sl 1, k1] 5 times, sl 1, *k15, [sl 1, k1] 5 times, sl 1; rep from * to last 10 sts, k10.

10th row: Using Y p10, [sl 1, p1] 5 times, sl 1, *p15, [sl 1, p1] 5 times, sl 1; rep from * to last 7 sts, p7.

11th row: Using X k4, [sl 1, k1] 6 times, sl 1, *k13, [sl 1, k1] 6 times, sl 1; rep from * to last 11 sts, k11.

12th row: Using X p11, [sl 1, p1] 6 times, sl 1, *p13, [sl 1, p1] 6 times, sl 1; rep from * to last 4 sts, p4.

13th row: Using Y [k1, sl 1] 7 times, *k13, [sl 1, k1] 6 times, sl 1; rep from * to last 14 sts, k14.

14th row: Using Y p14, *[sl 1, p1] 6 times, sl 1, p13; rep from * to last 14 sts, [sl 1, k1] 7 times.

15th row: Using X k14, *[sl 1, k1] 6 times, sl 1, k13; rep from * to last 14 sts, [sl 1, k1] 7 times.

16th row: Using X [p1, sl 1] 7 times, *p13, [sl 1, p1] 6 times, sl 1; rep from * to last 14 sts, p14.

17th row: Using Y [k1, sl 1] twice, k11, *[sl 1, k1] 7 times, sl 1, k11; rep from * to last 13 sts, sl 1, [k1, sl 1] 5 times, k2.

18th row: Using Y p2, [sl 1, p1] 5 times, sl 1, p11, *[sl 1, p1] 7 times, sl 1, p11; rep from * to last 4 sts, [sl 1, p1] twice.

19th row: Using X k2, sl 1, k1, sl 1, k13, *[sl 1, k1] 6 times, sl 1, k13; rep from * to last 10 sts, [sl 1, k1] 5 times.

20th row: Using X [p1, sl 1] 5 times, p13, *[sl 1, p1] 6 times, sl 1, p13; rep from * to last 5 sts, sl 1, p1, sl 1, p2.

21st row: Using Y [k1, sl 1] 4 times, k11, *[sl 1, k1] 7 times, sl 1, k11; rep from * to last 9 sts, sl 1, [k1, sl 1] 3 times, k2.

22nd row: Using Y p2, [sl 1, p1] 3 times, sl 1, p11, *[sl 1, p1] 7 times, sl 1, p11; rep from * to last 8 sts, [sl 1, p1] 4 times.

23rd row: Using X k2, [sl 1, k1] 3 times, sl 1, k13, *[sl 1, k1] 6 times, sl 1, k13; rep from * to last 6 sts, [sl 1, k1] 3 times.

24th row: Using X [p1, sl 1] 3 times, p13, *[sl 1, p1] 6 times, sl 1, p13; rep from * to last 9 sts, sl 1, [p1, sl 1] 3 times, p2.

25th row: Using Y [k1, sl 1] 6 times, k11, *[sl 1, k1] 7 times, sl 1, k11; rep from * to last 5 sts, sl 1, k1, sl 1, k2.

26th row: Using Y p2, sl 1, p1, sl 1, p11, *[sl 1, p1] 7 times, sl 1, p11; rep from * to last 12 sts, [sl 1, p1] 6 times.

27th row: Using X k2, [sl 1, k1] 5 times, sl 1, k11, *[sl 1, k1] 7 times, sl 1, k11; rep from * to last 4 sts, [sl 1, k1] twice.

28th row: Using X [p1, sl 1] twice, p11, *[sl 1, p1] 7 times, sl 1, p11; rep from * to last 13 sts, sl 1, [p1, sl 1] 5 times, p2.

Rep the last 28 rows.

II.23

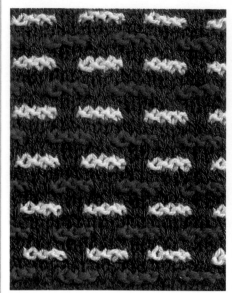

Multiple of 6 sts + 4.

1st row (right side): Using N knit.

2nd row: Using N purl.

3rd and 4th rows: Using M k4, *sl 2, k4; rep from * to end.

5th row: Using N knit.

6th row: Using N purl.

7th and 8th rows: Using B k1, sl 2, *k4, sl 2; rep from * to last st, k1.

Rep these 8 rows.

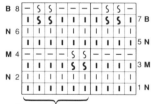

Rep these 6 sts

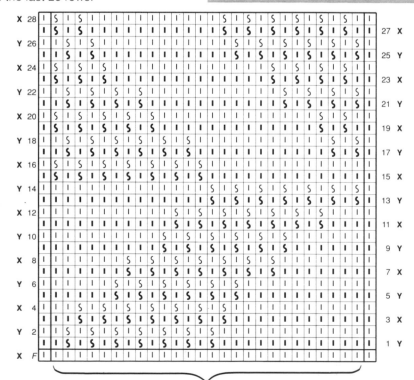

Rep these 26 sts

Colour key on page 23

II.24

Multiple of 12 sts + 3.

Foundation row: Using M purl.

1st row (right side): Using G k1, sl 1, *k11, sl 1; rep from * to last st, k1.

2nd row: Using G p1, sl 1, *p11, sl 1; rep from * to last st, p1.

3rd row: Using M k4, [sl 1, k1] 3 times, sl 1, *k5, [sl 1, k1] 3 times, sl 1; rep from * to last 4 sts, k4.

4th row: Using M p4, [sl 1, k1] 3 times, sl 1, *p5, [sl 1, k1] 3 times, sl 1; rep from * to last 4 sts, p4.

5th row: Using G k3, *sl 1, k7, sl 1, k3; rep from * to end.

6th row: Using G p3, *sl 1, p7, sl 1, p3; rep from * to end.

7th row: Using M k2, sl 1, k3, *sl 1, k1, sl 1, k3; rep from * to last 3 sts, sl 1, k2.

8th row: Using M p1, k1, sl 1, p3, *sl 1, k1, sl 1, p3; rep from * to last 3 sts, sl 1, k1, p1.

9th row: Using G k5, sl 1, k3, sl 1, *k7, sl 1, k3, sl 1; rep from * to last 5 sts, k5.

10th row: Using G p5, sl 1, p3, sl 1, *p7, sl 1, p3, sl 1; rep from * to last 5 sts, p5.

11th row: Using M k2, sl 1, k1, sl 1, k5, *[sl 1, k1] 3 times, sl 1, k5; rep from * to last 5 sts, sl 1, k1, sl 1, k2.

12th row: Using M p1, [k1, sl 1] twice, p5, *[sl 1, k1] 3 times, sl 1, p5; rep from * to last 5 sts, [sl 1, k1] twice, p1.

13th row: Using G k7, sl 1, *k11, sl 1; rep from * to last 7 sts, k7.

14th row: Using G p7, sl 1, *p11, sl 1; rep from * to last 7 sts, p7.

15th and 16th rows: As 11th and 12th rows.

17th and 18th rows: As 9th and 10th rows.

19th and 20th rows: As 7th and 8th rows.

21st and 22nd rows: As 5th and 6th rows.

23rd and 24th rows: As 3rd and 4th rows.
Rep the last 24 rows.

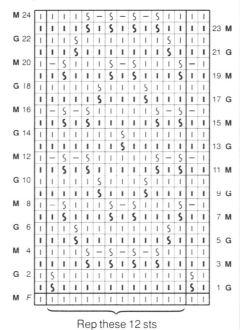

Rep these 12 sts

II.25

Multiple of 16 sts + 3.

Foundation row (wrong side): Using N knit.

1st and 2nd rows: Using B [k1, sl 1] 3 times, k7, *sl 1, [k1, sl 1] 4 times, k7; rep from * to last 6 sts, [sl 1, k1] 3 times.

3rd and 4th rows: Using N k6, sl 1, [k1, sl 1] 3 times, *k9, sl 1, [k1, sl 1] 3 times; rep from * to last 6 sts, k6.

5th and 6th rows: Using B [k1, sl 1] twice, k5, sl 1, k5, *sl 1, [k1, sl 1] twice, k5, sl 1, k5; rep from * to last 4 sts, [sl 1, k1] twice.

7th and 8th rows: Using N k4, sl 1, k1, sl 1, *k5, sl 1, k1, sl 1; rep from * to last 4 sts, k4.

9th and 10th rows: Using B k1, sl 1, *k5, sl 1, [k1, sl 1] twice, k5, sl 1; rep from * to last st, k1.

11th and 12th rows: Using N k2, sl 1, k1, sl 1, k9, *sl 1, [k1, sl 1] 3 times, k9; rep from * to last 5 sts, sl 1, k1, sl 1, k2.

II.26

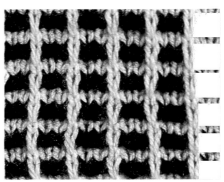

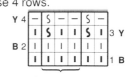

Multiple of 3 sts + 3.

1st row (right side): Using B knit.

2nd row: Using B purl.

3rd and 4th rows: Using Y k1, sl 1, *k2, sl 1; rep from * to last st, k1.

Rep these 4 rows.

Y 4	−	S	−	−	S	−	
	I	S	I	I	S	I	3 Y
B 2	I	I	I	I	I	I	
	I	I	I	I	I	I	1 B

Rep these
3 sts

13th and 14th rows: Using B k5, sl 1, [k1, sl 1] 4 times, *k7, sl 1, [k1, sl 1] 4 times; rep from * to last 5 sts, k5.

15th and 16th rows: Using N k2, sl 1, k13, *sl 1, k1, sl 1, k13; rep from * to last 3 sts, sl 1, k2.

17th and 18th rows: As 13th and 14th rows.

19th and 20th rows: As 11th and 12th rows.

21st and 22nd rows: As 9th and 10th rows.

23rd and 24th rows: As 7th and 8th rows.

25th and 26th rows: As 5th and 6th rows.

27th and 28th rows: As 3rd and 4th rows.
Rep the last 28 rows.

Rep these 16 sts

II. Slip Stitch Mosaics

II.27

Multiple of 22 sts + 13.

1st row (right side): Using B knit.

2nd row: Using B purl.

3rd row: Using P k12, *[sl 1, k1] 5 times, sl 1, k11; rep from * to last st, k1.

4th row: Using P p12, *[sl 1, k1] 5 times, sl 1, p11; rep from * to last st, k1.

Rep the last 4 rows twice more.

13th and 14th rows: As 1st and 2nd rows.

15th row: Using P [k1, sl 1] 6 times, *k11, [sl 1, k1] 5 times, sl 1; rep from * to last st, k1.

16th row: Using P p1, [sl 1, k1] 5 times, sl 1, *p11, [sl 1, k1] 5 times, sl 1; rep from * to last st, p1.

Rep the last 4 rows twice more.

Rep these 24 rows.

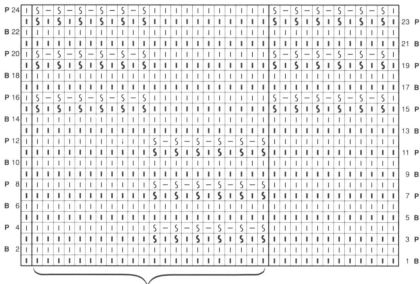

Rep these 22 sts

II.29

Multiple of 10 sts + 8.

1st row (right side): Using T knit.

2nd row: Using T purl.

Rep the last 2 rows once more.

5th and 6th rows: Using R k8, *sl 2, k8; rep from * to end.

7th row: Using R p8, *sl 2, p8; rep from * to end.

8th row: As 6th row.

Rep these 8 rows.

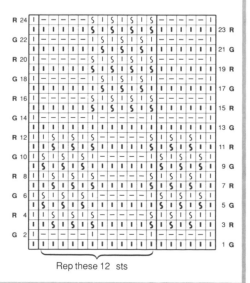

Rep these 10 sts

II.28

Multiple of 12 sts + 7.

1st row (right side): Using G knit.

2nd row: Using G p1, *k5, p1; rep from * to end.

3rd row: Using R k2, sl 1, [k1, sl 1] twice, k5, *sl 1, [k1, sl 1] 3 times, k5; rep from * to last 7 sts, sl 1, [k1, sl 1] twice, k2.

4th row: Using R p2, sl 1, [p1, sl 1] twice, k5, *sl 1, [p1, sl 1] 3 times, k5; rep from * to last 7 sts, sl 1, [p1, sl 1] twice, p2.

5th row: Using G [k1, sl 1] 3 times, *k7, sl 1, [k1, sl 1] twice; rep from * to last st, k1.

6th row: Using G [p1, sl 1] 3 times, p1, *k5, p1, [sl 1, p1] 3 times; rep from * to end.

Rep the last 4 rows once more.

11th row: As 3rd row.

12th row: As 4th row.

13th row: As 1st row.

14th row: As 2nd row.

15th row: Using R k6, sl 1, [k1, sl 1] 3 times, *k5, sl 1, [k1, sl 1] 3 times; rep from * to last 6 sts, k6.

16th row: Using R p1, k5, *sl 1, [p1, sl 1] 3 times, k5; rep from * to last st, p1.

17th row: Using G k7, *sl 1, [k1, sl 1]

twice, k7; rep from * to end.

18th row: Using G p1, k5, p1, *[sl 1, p1] 3 times, k5, p1; rep from * to end.

Rep the last 4 rows once more.

23rd row: As 15th row.

24th row: As 16th row.

Rep these 24 rows.

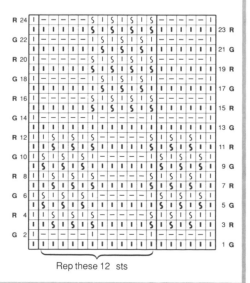

Rep these 12 sts

Colour key on page 23

II.30

Multiple of 8 sts + 5.

1st row (right side): Using F knit.

2nd row: Using F knit.

3rd and 4th rows: Using R [k1, sl 1] twice, *k5, sl 1, k1, sl 1; rep from * to last st, k1.

5th and 6th rows: Using F k4, *sl 1, k3; rep from * to last st, k1.

Rep the last 4 rows twice more.

15th and 16th rows: As 3rd and 4th rows.

17th and 18th rows: As 1st and 2nd rows.

19th and 20th rows: As 3rd and 4th rows.

21st and 22nd rows: Using F k4, *sl 1, [k1, sl 1] twice, k3; rep from * to last st, k1.

23rd and 24th rows: As 3rd and 4th rows.

Rep the last 4 rows twice more.

Rep these 32 rows.

II.31

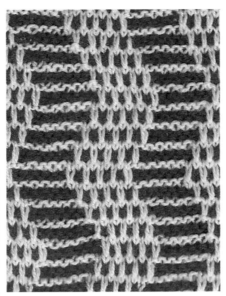

Multiple of 15 sts + 11.

1st row (right side): Using A knit.

2nd row: Using A k1, p9, k6, *p9, k6; rep from * to last 10 sts, p10.

3rd row: Using P [k1, sl 1] 5 times, *k6, [sl 1, k1] 4 times, sl 1; rep from * to last st, k1.

4th row: Using P k1, *[sl 1, p1] 4 times, sl 1, k6; rep from * to last 10 sts, [sl 1, p1] 5 times.

5th and 6th rows: As 1st and 2nd rows.

7th row: Using P k2, [sl 1, k1] 3 times, sl 1, *k6, [sl 1, k1] 4 times, sl 1; rep from * to last 2 sts, k2.

8th row: Using P k2, *[sl 1, p1] 4 times, sl 1, k6; rep from * to last 9 sts, [sl 1, k1] 3 times, sl 1, p2.

9th row: Using A knit.

10th row: Using A k2, p9, *k6, p9; rep from * to end.

11th row: Using P [k1, sl 1] 4 times, *k6, [sl 1, k1] 4 times, sl 1; rep from * to last 3 sts, k3.

12th row: Using P k3, *[sl 1, k1] 4 times, sl 1, k6; rep from * to last 8 sts, [sl 1, k1] 4 times.

13th row: Using A knit.

14th row: Using A k3, *p9, k6; rep from * to last 8 sts, p8.

15th row: Using P k2, [sl 1, k1] twice, sl 1, *k6, [sl 1, k1] 4 times, sl 1; rep from * to last 4 sts, k4.

16th row: Using P k4, *[sl 1, p1] 4 times, sl 1, k6; rep from * to last 7 sts, [sl 1, p1] twice, sl 1, p2.

17th row: Using A knit.

18th row: Using A k4, *p9, k6; rep from * to last 7 sts, p7.

19th row: Using P [k1, sl 1] 3 times, *k6, [sl 1, k1] 4 times, sl 1; rep from * to last 5 sts, k5.

20th row: Using P k5, *[sl 1, p1] 4 times, sl 1, k6; rep from * to last 6 sts, [sl 1, p1] 3 times.

21st row: Using A knit.

22nd row: Using A k5, *p9, k6; rep from * to last 6 sts, p6.

23rd and 24th rows: As 15th and 16th rows.

25th and 26th rows: As 1st and 18th rows.

27th and 28th rows: As 11th and 12th rows.

29th and 30th rows: As 1st and 14th rows.

31st and 32nd rows: As 7th and 8th rows.

Rep these 32 rows.

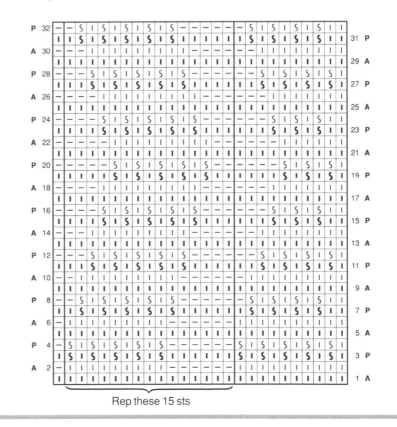

II. Slip Stitch Mosaics

II.32

Multiple of 6 sts + 2.

Foundation row: Using B purl.

1st row (right side): Using K k1, *sl 2, k4; rep from * to last st, k1.

2nd row: Using K p1, k2, p2, sl 2, *k2, p2, sl 2; rep from * to last st, p1.

3rd row: Using Q k3, sl 2, *k4, sl 2; rep from * to last 3 sts, k3.

4th row: Using Q p3, sl 2, k2, *p2, sl 2, k2; rep from * to last st, p1.

5th row: Using H k5, sl 2, *k4, sl 2; rep from * to last st, k1.

6th row: Using H p1, *sl 2, k2, p2; rep from * to last st, p1.

7th and 8th rows: As 1st and 2nd rows **but** using B instead of K.

9th and 10th rows: As 3rd and 4th rows **but** using K instead of Q.

11th and 12th rows: As 5th and 6th rows **but** using Q instead of H.

13th and 14th rows: As 1st and 2nd rows **but** using H instead of K.

15th and 16th rows: As 3rd and 4th rows **but** using B instead of Q.

17th and 18th rows: As 5th and 6th rows **but** using K instead of H.

19th and 20th rows: As 1st and 2nd rows **but** using Q instead of K.

21st and 22nd rows: As 3rd and 4th rows **but** using H instead of Q.

23rd and 24th rows: As 5th and 6th rows **but** using B instead of H.

Rep the last 24 rows.

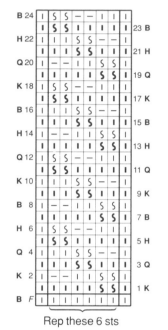

Rep these 6 sts

II.33

Multiple of 8 sts + 7.

1st row (right side): Using K knit.

2nd row: Using K knit.

3rd row: Using X k5, *[sl 1, k1] twice, sl 1, k3; rep from * to last 2 sts, k2.

4th row: Using X p5, *[sl 1, k1] twice, sl 1, p3; rep from * to last 2 sts, p2.

5th and 6th rows: Using K k2, sl 3, *k5, sl 3; rep from * to last 2 sts, k2.

Rep the last 4 rows once more, then 3rd and 4th rows again.

13th and 14th rows: As 1st and 2nd rows.

15th row: Using X [k1, sl 1] 3 times, *k3, [sl 1, k1] twice, sl 1; rep from * to last st, k1.

16th row: Using X p1, [sl 1, k1] twice, sl 1, *p3, [sl 1, k1] twice, sl 1; rep from * to last st, p1.

17th and 18th rows: Using K k6, *sl 3, k5; rep from * to last st, k1.

Rep the last 4 rows once more, then 15th and 16th rows again.

Rep these 24 rows.

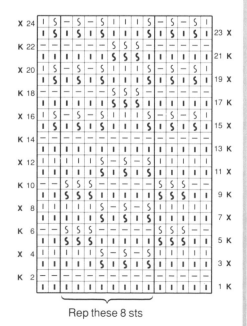

Rep these 8 sts

II.34

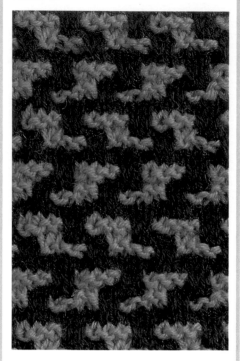

Multiple of 6 sts + 2.

1st row (right side): Using N knit.

2nd row: Using N purl.

3rd and 4th rows: Using G k3, sl 2, *k4, sl 2; rep from * to last 3 sts, k3.

5th row: Using N k1, *sl 2, k4; rep from * to last st, k1.

6th row: Using N p5, sl 2, *p4, sl 2; rep from * to last st, p1.

7th row: Using G k5, sl 2, *k4, sl 2; rep from * to last st, k1.

8th row: Using G k1, *sl 2, k4; rep from * to last st, k1.

9th and 10th rows: As 1st and 2nd rows.

11th row: Using G k2, *sl 2, k4; rep from * to end.

12th row: Using G *k4, sl 2; rep from * to last 2 sts, k2.

13th row: Using N *k4, sl 2; rep from * to last 2 sts, k2.

14th row: Using N p2, *sl 2, p4; rep from * to end.

15th and 16th rows: Using G k1, sl 1, k4, *sl 2, k4; rep from * to last 2 sts, sl 1, k1.

Rep these 16 rows.

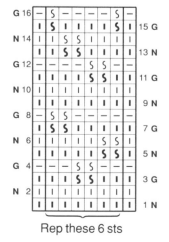

Rep these 6 sts

Colour key on page 23

II.35

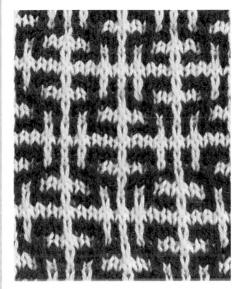

Multiple of 12 sts + 3.

1st row (right side): Using B knit.

2nd row: Using B purl.

3rd row: Using N k1, sl 1, *k3, [sl 1, k1] twice, sl 1, k3, sl 1; rep from * to last st, k1.

4th row: Using N p1, sl 1, *p3, [sl 1, p1] twice, sl 1, p3, sl 1; rep from * to last st, p1.

5th row: Using B k4, [sl 1, k1] 3 times, sl 1, *k5, [sl 1, k1] 3 times, sl 1; rep from * to last 4 sts, k4.

6th row: Using B p4, [sl 1, p1] 3 times, sl 1, *p5, [sl 1, p1] 3 times, sl 1; rep from * to last 4 sts, p4.

7th row: Using N k1, sl 1, *k5, sl 1; rep from * to last st, k1.

8th row: Using N p1, sl 1, *p5, sl 1; rep from * to last st, p1.

9th row: Using B k2, sl 1, k1, sl 1, k5, *[sl 1, k1] 3 times, sl 1, k5; rep from * to last 5 sts, sl 1, k1, sl 1, k2.

10th row: Using B p2, sl 1, p1, sl 1, p5, *[sl 1, p1] 3 times, sl 1, p5; rep from * to last 5 sts, sl 1, p1, sl 1, p2.

11th row: Using N [k1, sl 1] twice, k3, sl 1, k3, *[sl 1, k1] twice, [sl 1, k3] twice; rep from * to last 4 sts, [sl 1, k1] twice.

12th row: Using N [p1, sl 1] twice, p3, sl 1, p3, *[sl 1, p1] twice, [sl 1, p3] twice; rep from * to last 4 sts, [sl 1, p1] twice.

13th and 14th rows: As 1st and 2nd rows.

15th and 16th rows: As 11th and 12th rows.

17th and 18th rows: As 9th and 10th rows.

19th and 20th rows: As 7th and 8th rows.

21st and 22nd rows: As 5th and 6th rows.

23rd and 24th rows: As 3rd and 4th rows.

Rep these 24 rows.

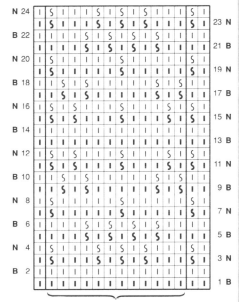

Rep these 12 sts

II.36

Multiple of 6 sts + 2.

1st row (right side): Using N knit.

2nd row: Using N purl.

3rd row: Using F k6, sl 1, *k5, sl 1; rep from * to last st, k1.

4th row: Using F p1, *sl 1, p5; rep from * to last st, p1.

5th row: Using N *k1, sl 1, k3, sl 1; rep from * to last 2 sts, k2.

6th row: Using N p2, sl 1, p3, sl 1, *p1, sl 1, p3, sl 1; rep from * to last st, p1.

7th row: Using F k4, sl 1, k1, sl 1, *k3, sl 1, k1, sl 1; rep from * to last st, k1.

8th row: Using F p1, *sl 1, p1, sl 1, p3; rep from * to last st, p1.

9th row: Using N *k3, sl 1, k1, sl 1; rep from * to last 2 sts, k2.

10th row: Using N p2, *sl 1, p1, sl 1, p3; rep from * to end.

11th row: Using F k4, sl 1, *k5, sl 1; rep from * to last 3 sts, k3.

12th row: Using F p3, sl 1, *p5, sl 1; rep from * to last 4 sts, p4.

Rep these 12 rows.

Rep these 6 sts

II.37

Multiple of 8 sts + 5.

1st row (wrong side): Using Y purl.

2nd and 3rd rows: Using M k1, sl 3, *k5, sl 3; rep from * to last st, k1.

4th row: Using Y k6, sl 1, *k7, sl 1; rep from * to last 6 sts, k6.

5th row: Using Y p6, sl 1, *p7, sl 1; rep from * to last 6 sts, p6.

6th, 7th and 8th rows: As 2nd, 3rd and 4th rows.

9th row: Using Y purl.

10th row: Using M k5, *sl 3, k5; rep from * to end.

11th row: Using M, p1, k4, sl 3, *k5, sl 3; rep from * to last 5 sts, k4, p1.

12th row: Using Y k2, sl 1, *k7, sl 1; rep from * to last 2 sts, k2.

13th row: Using Y p2, sl 1, *p7, sl 1; rep from * to last 2 sts, p2.

14th, 15th and 16th rows: As 10th, 11th and 12th rows.

Rep these 16 rows.

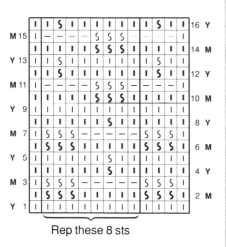

Rep these 8 sts

II. Slip Stitch Mosaics

II.38

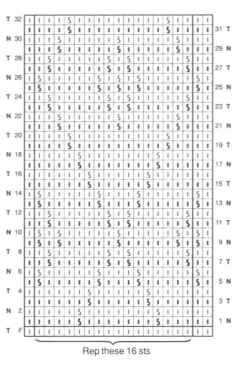

Rep these 16 sts

Multiple of 16 sts + 3.

Foundation row: Using T purl.

1st row (right side): Using N k5, sl 1, *k7, sl 1; rep from * to last 5 sts, k5.

2nd row: Using N p5, sl 1, *p7, sl 1; rep from * to last 5 sts, p5.

3rd row: Using T k6, sl 1, k5, sl 1, *k9, sl 1, k5, sl 1; rep from * to last 6 sts, k6.

4th row: Using T p6, sl 1, p5, sl 1, *p9, sl 1, p5, sl 1; rep from * to last 6 sts, p6.

5th row: Using N k1, sl 1, *k5, sl 1, k3, sl 1, k5, sl 1; rep from * to last st, k1.

6th row: Using N p1, sl 1, *p5, sl 1, p3, sl 1, p5, sl 1; rep from * to last st, p1.

7th row: Using T k2, sl 1, k5, *sl 1, k1, sl 1, k5; rep from * to last 3 sts, sl 1, k2.

8th row: Using T p2, sl 1, p5, *sl 1, p1, sl 1, p5; rep from * to last 3 sts, sl 1, p2.

9th row: Using N [k1, sl 1] twice, k5, sl 1, k5, *[sl 1, k1] twice, [sl 1, k5] twice; rep from * to last 4 sts, [sl 1, k1] twice.

10th row: Using N [p1, sl 1] twice, p5, sl 1, p5, *[sl 1, p1] twice, [sl 1, p5] twice; rep from * to last 4 sts, [sl 1, p1] twice.

11th and 12th rows: As 7th and 8th rows.

13th and 14th rows: As 5th and 6th rows.

15th and 16th rows: As 3rd and 4th rows.

17th and 18th rows: As 1st and 2nd rows.

19th row: Using T k4, sl 1, k9, sl 1, *k5, sl 1, k9, sl 1; rep from * to last 4 sts, k4.

20th row: Using T p4, sl 1, p9, sl 1, *p5, sl 1, p9, sl 1; rep from * to last 4 sts, p4.

21st row: Using N k3, *[sl 1, k5] twice, sl 1, k3; rep from * to end.

22nd row: Using N p3, *[sl 1, p5] twice, sl 1, p3; rep from * to end.

23rd and 24th rows: As 7th and 8th rows.

25th row: Using N k1, sl 1, *k5, [sl 1, k1] twice, sl 1, k5, sl 1; rep from * to last st, k1.

26th row: Using N p1, sl 1, *p5, [sl 1, p1] twice, sl 1, p5, sl 1; rep from * to last st, p1.

27th and 28th rows: As 7th and 8th rows.

29th and 30th rows: As 21st and 22nd rows.

31st and 32nd rows: As 19th and 20th rows.

Rep the last 32 rows.

II.39

Multiple of 21 sts + 11.

Foundation row: Using Y purl.

1st row (right side): Using B [k1, sl 1] 5 times, *k12, sl 1, [k1, sl 1] 4 times; rep from * to last st, k1.

2nd row: Using B [p1, sl 1] 5 times, *p12, sl 1, [p1, sl 1] 4 times; rep from * to last st, p1.

3rd row: Using Y k2, sl 1, [k1, sl 1] 3 times, *k14, sl 1, [k1, sl 1] 3 times; rep from * to last 2 sts, k2.

4th row: Using Y p2, sl 1, [p1, sl 1] 3 times, *p14, sl 1, [p1, sl 1] 3 times; rep from * to last 2 sts, p2.

Rep the last 4 rows.

Rep these 21 sts

II.40

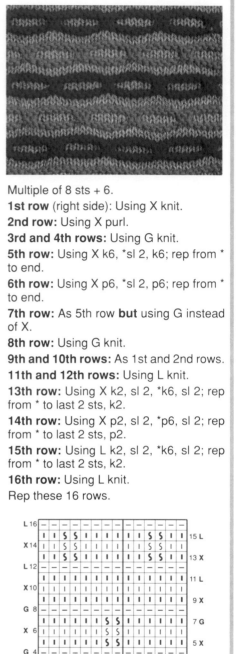

Multiple of 8 sts + 6.

1st row (right side): Using X knit.

2nd row: Using X purl.

3rd and 4th rows: Using G knit.

5th row: Using X k6, *sl 2, k6; rep from * to end.

6th row: Using X p6, *sl 2, p6; rep from * to end.

7th row: As 5th row **but** using G instead of X.

8th row: Using G knit.

9th and 10th rows: As 1st and 2nd rows.

11th and 12th rows: Using L knit.

13th row: Using X k2, sl 2, *k6, sl 2; rep from * to last 2 sts, k2.

14th row: Using X p2, sl 2, *p6, sl 2; rep from * to last 2 sts, p2.

15th row: Using L k2, sl 2, *k6, sl 2; rep from * to last 2 sts, k2.

16th row: Using L knit.

Rep these 16 rows.

Rep these 8 sts

II.40A

As **II.40** but working 11th, 12th, 15th and 16th rows in G.

II.41

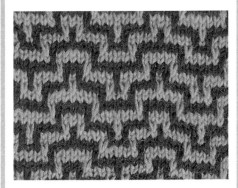

Multiple of 14 sts + 3.

1st row (right side): Using N knit.

2nd row: Using N purl.

3rd row: Using X k1, sl 1, *k6, sl 1; rep from * to last st, k1.

4th row: Using X p1, sl 1, *p6, sl 1; rep from * to last st, p1.

5th row: Using N k2, sl 1, k4, *sl 1, k1, sl 1, k4; rep from * to last 3 sts, sl 1, k2.

6th row: Using N p2, sl 1, p4, *sl 1, p1, sl 1, p4; rep from * to last 3 sts, sl 1, p2.

7th row: Using X [k1, sl 1] twice, k2, *sl 1, [k1, sl 1] twice, k2; rep from * to last 4 sts, [sl 1, k1] twice.

8th row: Using X [p1, sl 1] twice, p2, *sl 1, [p1, sl 1] twice, p2; rep from * to last 4 sts, [sl 1, p1] twice.

9th row: Using N k2, sl 1, k4, *sl 1, k1, sl 1, k4; rep from * to last 3 sts, sl 1, k2.

10th row: Using N p2, sl 1, p4, *sl 1, p1, sl 1, p4; rep from * to last 3 sts, sl 1, p2.

11th row: Using X [k1, sl 1] twice, k4, sl 1, k4, *sl 1, [k1, sl 1] twice, k4, sl 1, k4; rep from * to last 4 sts, [sl 1, k1] twice.

12th row: Using X [p1, sl 1] twice, p4, sl 1, p4, *sl 1, [p1, sl 1] twice, p4, sl 1, p4; rep from * to last 4 sts, [sl 1, p1] twice.

13th row: Using N k2, sl 1, k11, *sl 1, k1, sl 1, k11; rep from * to last 3 sts, sl 1, k2.

14th row: Using N p2, sl 1, p11, *sl 1, p1, sl 1, p11; rep from * to last 3 sts, sl 1, p2.

15th row: Using X k1, sl 1, *k13, sl 1; rep from * to last st, k1.

16th row: Using X p1, sl 1, *p13, sl 1; rep from * to last st, p1.

17th and 18th rows: As 1st and 2nd rows.

19th and 20th rows: As 15th and 16th rows.

21st and 22nd rows: As 13th and 14th rows.

23rd and 24th rows: As 11th and 12th rows.

25th and 26th rows: As 9th and 10th rows.

27th and 28th rows: As 7th and 8th rows.

29th and 30th rows: As 5th and 6th rows.

31st and 32nd rows: As 3rd and 4th rows.

Rep these 32 rows.

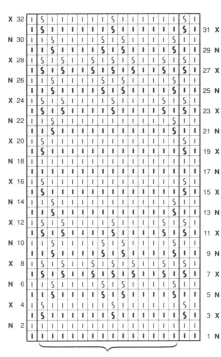

Rep these 14 sts

II.42

Multiple of 7 sts + 4.

1st row (right side): Using M knit.

2nd row: Using M purl.

3rd row: Using A k1, sl 2, *k5, sl 2; rep from * to last st, k1.

4th row: Using A p1, sl 2, *p5, sl 2; rep from * to last st, p1.

5th row: Using M k3, *sl 2, k1, sl 2, k2; rep from * to last st, k1.

6th row: Using M p3, *sl 2, k1, sl 2, p2; rep from * to last st, p1.

7th and 8th rows: As 3rd and 4th rows.

Rep these 8 rows.

Rep these 7 sts

II.43

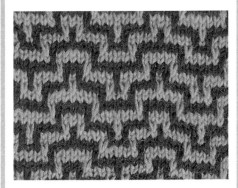

Multiple of 12 sts + 5.

Foundation row: Using N purl.

1st row (right side): Using G k4, *sl 1, k7, sl 1, k3; rep from * to last st, k1.

2nd row: Using G p4, *sl 1, p7, sl 1, p3; rep from * to last st, p1.

3rd row: Using N k5, *sl 1, k5; rep from * to end.

4th row: Using N p5, *sl 1, p5; rep from * to end.

5th row: Using G k6, sl 1, k3, sl 1, *k7, sl 1, k3, sl 1; rep from * to last 6 sts, k6.

6th row: Using G p6, sl 1, p3, sl 1, *p7, sl 1, p3, sl 1; rep from * to last 6 sts, p6.

7th row: Using N k2, sl 1, k4, sl 1, k1, sl 1, *[k4, sl 1] twice, k1, sl 1; rep from * to last 7 sts, k4, sl 1, k2.

8th row: Using N p2, sl 1, *p4, sl 1, p1, sl 1, p4, sl 1; rep from * to last 2 sts, p2.

9th row: Using G [k1, sl 1] twice, *[k4, sl 1] twice, k1, sl 1; rep from * to last st, k1.

10th row: Using G [p1, sl 1] twice, *[p4, sl 1] twice, p1, sl 1; rep from * to last st, p1.

11th and 12th rows: As 1st and 2nd rows **but** using N instead of G.

13th and 14th rows: As 3rd and 4th rows **but** using G instead of N.

15th and 16th rows: As 5th and 6th rows **but** using N instead of G.

17th and 18th rows: As 7th and 8th rows **but** using G instead of N.

19th and 20th rows: As 9th and 10th rows **but** using N instead of G.

Rep the last 20 rows.

Rep these 12 sts

II. Slip Stitch Mosaics

II.44

Multiple of 3 sts + 2.

Foundation row: Using N knit.

1st row (right side): Using G k3, sl 1, *k2, sl 1; rep from * to last st, k1.

2nd row: Using G k1, *sl 1, k2; rep from * to last st, k1.

3rd and 4th rows: Using N k2, *sl 1, k2; rep from * to end.

5th row: As 2nd row.

6th row: As 1st row.

7th and 8th rows: As 1st and 2nd rows **but** using N instead of G.

9th and 10th rows: As 3rd and 4th rows **but** using G instead of N.

11th and 12th rows: As 5th and 6th rows **but** using N instead of G.

Rep the last 12 rows.

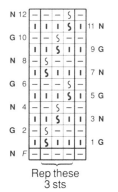

II.45

Multiple of 6 sts + 5.

Foundation row (wrong side): Using V purl.

1st and 2nd rows: Using H k1, sl 3, *k3, sl 3; rep from * to last st, k1.

3rd and 4th rows: Using I k4, *sl 3, k3; rep from * to last st, k1.

5th and 6th rows: As 1st and 2nd rows **but** using V instead of H.

7th and 8th rows: As 3rd and 4th rows **but** using H instead of I.

9th and 10th rows: As 1st and 2nd rows **but** using I instead of H.

11th and 12th rows: As 3rd and 4th rows **but** using V instead of I.

Rep the last 12 rows.

II.46

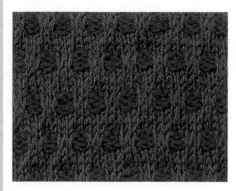

Multiple of 4 sts + 4.

Using S work 4 rows in st st, starting knit (right side).

5th row: Using R k1, sl 2, *k2, sl 2; rep from * to last st, k1.

6th row: Using R p1, sl 2, *k2, sl 2; rep from * to last st, p1.

7th row: Using R k1, sl 2, *p2, sl 2; rep from * to last st, k1.

8th row: As 6th row.

Using S work 4 rows in st st, starting knit.

13th row: Using R k3, *sl 2, k2; rep from * to last st, k1.

14th row: Using R p1, k2, *sl 2, k2; rep from * to last st, p1.

15th row: Using R k1, p2, *sl 2, p2; rep from * to last st, k1.

16th row: As 14th row.

Rep these 16 rows.

II.47

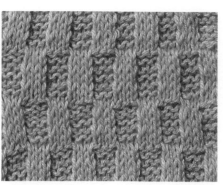

Multiple of 6 sts + 5.

1st row (right side): Using J knit.

2nd row: Using J p1, k3, *p3, k3; rep from * to last st, p1.

3rd row: Using V k4, sl 3, *k3, sl 3; rep from * to last 4 sts, k4.

4th row: Using V p1, k3, *sl 3, k3; rep from * to last st, p1.

Rep the last 4 rows twice more.

13th row: Using J knit.

14th row: Using J p4, k3, *p3, k3; rep from * to last 4 sts, p4.

15th row: Using V k1, sl 3, *k3, sl 3; rep from * to last st, k1.

16th row: Using V p1, sl 3, *k3, sl 3; rep from * to last st, p1.

Rep the last 4 rows twice more.

Rep these 24 rows.

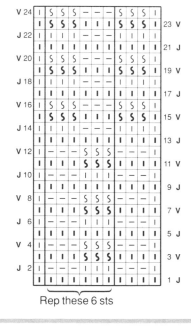

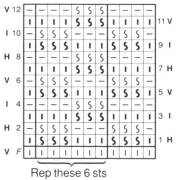

Colour key on page 23

III.1

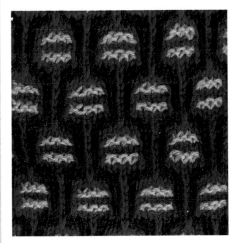

Multiple of 8 sts + 3.

Special Abbreviation

ᗐ **PW2** = p1 wrapping yarn twice around needle.

Foundation row: Using M purl.

1st row (right side): Using N k1, sl 1, *k3, sl 1; rep from * to last st, k1.

2nd row: Using N p1, sl 1, *p2, PW2, sl 1, PW2, p2, sl 1; rep from * to last st, p1.

3rd row: Using M k4, sl 1, k1, sl 1, *k5, sl 1, k1, sl 1; rep from * to last 4 sts, k4.

4th row: Using M p4, sl 1, p1, sl 1, *p5, sl 1, p1, sl 1; rep from * to last 4 sts, p4.

5th row: Using H k3, *sl 5, k3; rep from * to end.

6th row: Using H p1, k2, sl 5, *k3, sl 5; rep from * to last 3 sts, k2, p1.

Rep the last 4 rows once more, then 3rd and 4th rows again.

13th row: As 1st row.

14th row: Using N p1, sl 1, *PW2, p2, sl 1, p2, PW2, sl 1; rep from * to last st, p1.

15th row: Using M k2, sl 1, k5, *sl 1, k1, sl 1, k5; rep from * to last 3 sts, sl 1, k2.

16th row: Using M p2, sl 1, p5, *sl 1, p1, sl 1, p5; rep from * to last 3 sts, sl 1, p2.

17th row: Using H k1, sl 3, k3, *sl 5, k3; rep from * to last 4 sts, sl 3, k1.

18th row: Using H p1, sl 3, k3, *sl 5, k3; rep from * to last 4 sts, sl 3, p1.

Rep the last 4 rows once more, then 15th and 16th rows again.

Rep the last 24 rows.

(chart: Rep these 8 sts)

III.2

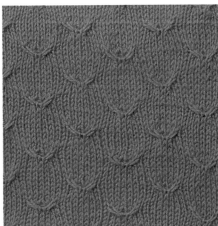

Multiple of 14 sts + 8.

1st row (right side): Knit.

2nd row: Purl.

3rd row: K3, sl 2, *k12, sl 2; rep from * to last 3 sts, k3.

4th row: P3, sl 2, *p12, sl 2; rep from * to last 3 sts, p3.

5th row: K1, C3R, C3L, *k8, C3R, C3L; rep from * to last st, k1.

Work 3 rows in st st, starting purl.

9th row: K10, sl 2, *k12, sl 2; rep from * to last 10 sts, k10.

10th row: P10, sl 2, *p12, sl 2; rep from * to last 10 sts, p10.

11th row: K8, *C3R, C3L, k8; rep from * to end.

12th row: Purl.

Rep these 12 rows.

(chart: Rep these 14 sts)

III.3

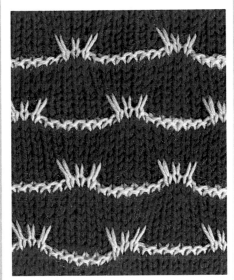

Multiple of 10 sts + 7.

1st row (right side): Using P knit.

2nd row: Using P purl.

3rd row: Using B knit.

4th row: Using B k2, p3, *k7, p3; rep from * to last 2 sts, k2.

5th row: Using P k2, sl 3, *k7, sl 3; rep from * to last 2 sts, k2.

6th row: Using P p2, sl 3, *p7, sl 3; rep from * to last 2 sts, p2.

Rep the last 2 rows once more.

9th row: Using P k1, C2R, k1, C2L, *k5, C2R, k1, C2L; rep from * to last st, k1.

Using P work 3 rows in st st, starting purl.

13th row: Using B knit.

14th row: Using B k7, *p3, k7; rep from * to end.

15th row: Using P k7, *sl 3, k7; rep from * to end.

16th row: Using P p7, *sl 3, p7; rep from * to end.

Rep the last 2 rows once more.

19th row: Using P k6, *C2R, k1, C2L, k5; rep from * to last st, k1.

20th row: Using P purl.

Rep these 20 rows.

(chart: Rep these 10 sts)

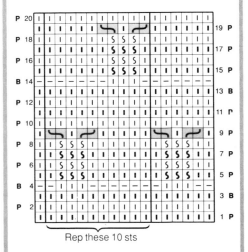

⬚⬚ = C3R, ⬚⬚ = C3L, ⬚ = C2R, ⬚ = C2L.

III.4

Multiple of 6 sts + 2.

1st row (wrong side): Using H k1, p1, k4, *p2, k4; rep from * to last 2 sts, p1, k1.

2nd row: Using V k1, sl 1, k4, *sl 2, k4; rep from * to last 2 sts, sl 1, k1.

3rd row: Using V p1, sl 1, p4, *sl 2, p4; rep from * to last 2 sts, sl 1, p1.

4th row: Using H k1, *C3L, C3R; rep from * to last st, k1.

5th row: Using H k3, p2, *k4, p2; rep from * to last 3 sts, k3.

6th row: Using V k3, sl 2, *k4, sl 2; rep from * to last 3 sts, k3.

7th row: Using V p3, sl 2, *p4, sl 2; rep from * to last 3 sts, p3.

8th row: Using H k1, *C3R, C3L; rep from * to last st, k1.

Rep these 8 rows.

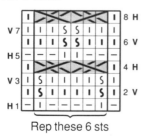

Rep these 6 sts

III.5

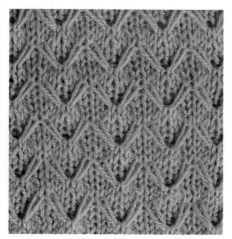

Multiple of 6 sts + 2.

Special Abbreviation

PW2 = p1 wrapping yarn twice round needle.

1st row (wrong side): P1, PW2, p4, *[PW2] twice, p4; rep from * to last 2 sts, PW2, p1.

2nd row: K1, sl 1, k4, *sl 2, k4; rep from * to last 2 sts, sl 1, k1.

3rd row: P1, sl 1, p4, *sl 2, p4; rep from * to last 2 sts, sl 1, p1.

Rep the last 2 rows once more.

6th row: K1, *C3L, C3R; rep from * to last st, k1.

Rep these 6 rows.

III.6

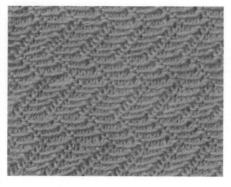

Multiple of 5 sts + 2.

Note: Slip sts purlwise with yarn at front of work (right side), = ⭍ on diagram.

1st and every alt row (wrong side): Purl.

2nd row: P1, *sl 3, p2; rep from * to last st, p1.

4th row: P2, *sl 3, p2; rep from * to end.

6th row: P3, sl 3, *p2, sl 3; rep from * to last st, p1.

8th row: P1, sl 1, p2, *sl 3, p2; rep from * to last 3 sts, sl 2, p1.

10th row: P1, sl 2, p2, *sl 3, p2; rep from * to last 2 sts, sl 1, p1.

12th row: As 8th row.

14th row: As 6th row.

16th row: As 4th row.

Rep these 16 rows.

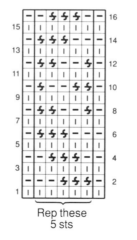

Rep these
5 sts

III.7

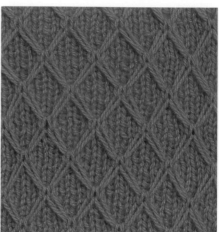

Multiple of 6 sts + 2.

Special Abbreviation

PW2 = p1 wrapping yarn twice round needle.

1st row (wrong side): P1, PW2, p4, *[PW2] twice, p4; rep from * to last 2 sts, PW2, p1.

2nd row: K1, sl 1, k4, *sl 2, k4; rep from * to last 2 sts, sl 1, k1.

3rd row: P1, sl 1, p4, *sl 2, p4; rep from * to last 2 sts, sl 1, p1.

Rep the last 2 rows once more.

6th row: K1, *C3L, C3R; rep from * to last st, k1.

7th row: P3, [PW2] twice, *p4, [PW2] twice; rep from * to last 3 sts, p3.

8th row: K3, sl 2, *k4, sl 2; rep from * to last 3 sts, k3.

9th row: P3, sl 2, *p4, sl 2; rep from * to last 3 sts, p3.

Rep the last 2 rows once more.

12th row: K1, *C3R, C3L; rep from * to last st, k1.

Rep these 12 rows.

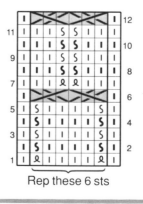

Rep these 6 sts

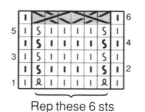

Rep these 6 sts

Colour key on page 23   ⬥⬥ = C3R,   ⬥⬥ = C3L.

III.8

Multiple of 6 sts + 3.

Note: Slip stitches with yarn at front of work, (wrong side), = ⅂ on diagram.

Special Abbreviation

⋒ **PU1 (Pick up 1)** = insert point of right-hand needle upwards under the loose strand of the slip stitches 3 rows below and knit it together with the next stitch.

Foundation row: Using I knit.

1st row (wrong side): Using I p2, *yb, sl 5, yf, p1; rep from * to last st, p1.

2nd row: Using B knit.

3rd row: Using B purl.

4th row: Using I k1, sl 3, PU1, *sl 5, PU1; rep from * to last 4 sts, sl 3, k1.

5th row: Using I p1, yb, sl 3, yf, p1, *yb, sl 5, yf, p1; rep from * to last 4 sts, yb, sl 3, yf, p1.

6th row: Using B knit.

7th row: Using B purl.

8th row: Using I k1, PU1, *sl 5, PU1; rep from * to last st, k1.

Rep the last 8 rows.

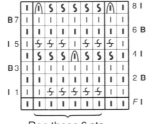

Rep these 6 sts

III.9

Multiple of 6 sts + 2.

Note: Slip sts purlwise with yarn at front of work (right side), = ⅃ on diagram.

1st and every alt row (wrong side): Purl.

2nd, 4th, 6th and 8th rows: K1, sl 2, k2, *sl 4, k2; rep from * to last 3 sts, sl 2, k1.

10th, 12th, 14th and 16th rows: K2, *sl 4, k2; rep from * to end.

Rep these 16 rows.

III.10

Multiple of 7 sts + 1.

Special Abbreviation

⋈ **C4 (Cross 4)** = slip next st onto cable needle and hold at front of work, knit into front of 3rd st on left-hand needle, knit 1st and 2nd sts then knit stitch from cable needle.

1st row (right side): Knit.

2nd row: P3, k2, *p5, k2; rep from * to last 3 sts, p3.

Rep the last 2 rows once more, then 1st row again.

6th row: [K2, sl 1] twice, *k3, sl 1, k2, sl 1; rep from * to last 2 sts, k2.

7th row: P2, sl 1, k2, sl 1, *p3, sl 1, k2, sl 1; rep from * to last 2 sts, p2.

8th row: As 6th row.

9th row: K2, C4, *k3, C4; rep from * to last 2 sts, k2.

10th row: As 2nd row.

Rep these 10 rows.

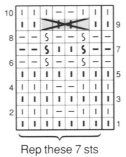

Rep these 7 sts

III.11

Multiple of 9 sts + 1.

Special Abbreviations

◣ **S1R (Slip 1 Right)** = slip next st onto cable needle and hold at back of work, slip next st purlwise from left-hand needle then knit st from cable needle.

◢ **S1L (Slip 1 Left)** = slip next st onto cable needle and hold at front of work, knit next st from left-hand needle, then slip st purlwise from cable needle.

Foundation row: Using B purl.

1st row (right side): Using W k3, S1R, S1L, *k5, S1R, S1L; rep from * to last 3 sts, k3.

2nd row: Using W p3, sl 1, p2, sl 1, *p5, sl 1, p2, sl 1; rep from * to last 3 sts, p3.

3rd and 4th rows: As 1st and 2nd rows **but** using B instead of W.

Rep the last 4 rows.

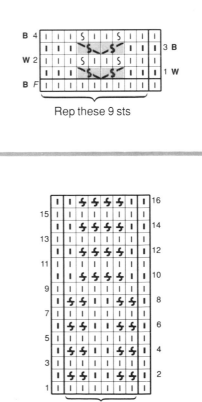

Rep these 9 sts

Rep these 6 sts

Cross Stitch Patterns

These are very small cables involving only 2 stitches. This can be done either with or without a cable needle. Instructions for cable needle methods are given on page 9. It is well worth experimenting with both methods to discover which method suits you best.

Crossing Stitches Without a Cable Needle

The following instructions can be substituted for cable method abbreviations (see page 9).

C2R (Cross 2 Right)

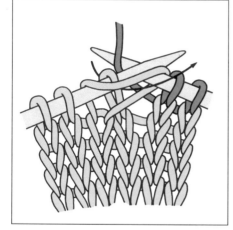

1. Miss the first stitch on the left-hand needle and knit the second stitch, working through the front of the loop only.

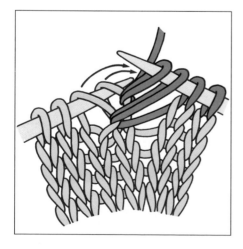

2. Do not slip the worked stitch off the needle, but twist the needle back and knit the missed stitch through the front of the loop. Then slip both stitches off the needle together.

C2L (Cross 2 Left)

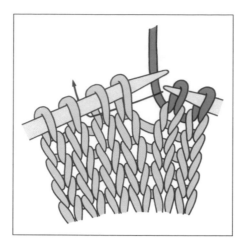

Work as given for C2R, but knit the second stitch on the left-hand needle through the **back** of the loop working behind the first stitch.

T2B (Twist 2 Back)

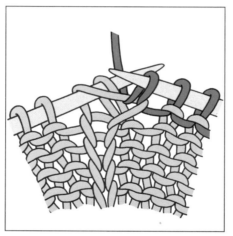

1. Miss the first stitch, then knit the second stitch through the front of the loop.

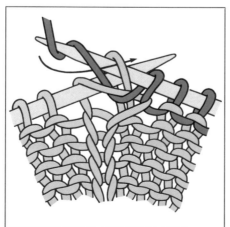

2. Without slipping the worked stitch off the needle, purl the missed stitch through the front of the loop, then slip both stitches off the needle at the same time.

T2F (Twist 2 Front)

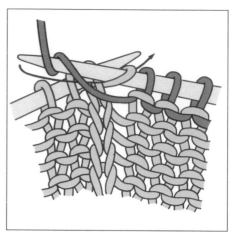

1. Miss the first stitch and purl the following stitch through the **back** of the loop working behind the first stitch.

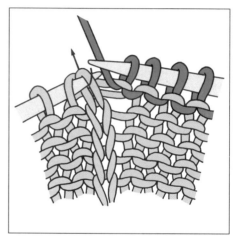

2. Without slipping the purled stitch off the needle, bring the needle to the front of the work and knit the missed stitch then slip both stitches off the needle at the same time.

For crossing stitches without a cable needle on wrong side rows see written instructions on page 9.

Cross Stitch Tension

Fabrics produced from patterns with lots of cross stitches in them tend to be quite rigid. This can be alleviated by working on slightly larger needles than you would usually use for the chosen yarn. (See Cable and Cross Stitch Tension on page 62).

IV.1

Multiple of 16 sts + 1.

1st and every alt row (wrong side): Purl.
2nd row: K1, *C2L, [C2R] twice, k3, [C2L] twice, C2R, k1; rep from * to end.
4th row: K2, C2L, [C2R] twice, k1, [C2L] twice, C2R, *k3, C2L, [C2R] twice, k1, [C2L] twice, C2R; rep from * to last 2 sts, k2.
6th row: K1, *[C2L] twice, C2R, k3, C2L, [C2R] twice, k1; rep from * to end.
8th row: K2, [C2L] twice, C2R, k1, C2L, [C2R] twice, *k3, [C2L] twice, C2R, k1, C2L, [C2R] twice; rep from * to last 2 sts, k2.
10th row: K1, *[C2L] 3 times, k3, [C2R] 3

times, k1; rep from * to end.
12th row: K2, [C2L] 3 times, k1, [C2R] 3 times, *k3, [C2L] 3 times, k1, [C2R] 3 times; rep from * to last 2 sts, k2.
14th row: As 10th row.
16th row: As 8th row.
18th row: As 6th row.
20th row: As 4th row.
22nd row: As 2nd row.
24th row: K2, [C2R] 3 times, k1, [C2L] 3 times, *k3, [C2R] 3 times, k1, [C2L] 3 times; rep from * to last 2 sts, k2.
26th row: K1, *[C2R] 3 times, k3, [C2L] 3 times, k1; rep from * to end.
28th row: As 24th row.
Rep these 28 rows.

Rep these 16 sts

IV.2

Multiple of 8 sts + 2.

1st row (wrong side): K1, p1, k2, *p2, k2; rep from * to last 2 sts, p1, k1.

2nd row: P1, k1, p1, T2B, T2F, p1, *k2, p1, T2B, T2F, p1; rep from * to last 2 sts, k1, p1.
3rd row: [K1, p1] twice, k2, p1, k1, *p2, k1, p1, k2, p1, k1; rep from * to last 2 sts, p1, k1.
4th row: P1, k1, T2B, p2, T2F, *k2, T2B, p2, T2F; rep from * to last 2 sts, k1, p1.
5th row: K1, p2, k4, *p4, k4; rep from * to last 3 sts, p2, k1.
6th row: Knit.
7th row: As 1st row.
8th row: P1, *T2F, p1, k2, p1, T2B; rep from * to last st, p1.
9th row: K2, *p1, k1, p2, k1, p1, k2; rep from * to end.
10th row: P2, *T2F, k2, T2B, p2; rep from * to end.
11th row: K3, p4, *k4, p4; rep from * to last 3 sts, k3.
12th row: Knit.
Rep these 12 rows.

IV.3

Multiple of 7 sts + 1.

1st row (right side): P3, k2, *p5, k2; rep from * to last 3 sts, p3.
2nd row: K3, p2, *k5, p2; rep from * to last 3 sts, k3.
3rd row: P2, C2R, C2L, *p3, C2R, C2L; rep from * to last 2 sts, p2.
4th row: K2, p4, *k3, p4; rep from * to last 2 sts, k2.
5th row: P1, *C2R, k2, C2L, p1; rep from * to end.
6th row: K1, *p6, k1; rep from * to end.
7th row: P1, *k6, p1; rep from * to end.
8th row: As 6th row.
9th row: P1, *T2F, k2, T2B, p1; rep from * to end.
10th row: As 4th row.
11th row: P2, T2F, T2B, *p3, T2F, T2B; rep from * to last 2 sts, p2.
12th row: As 2nd row.
Rep these 12 rows.

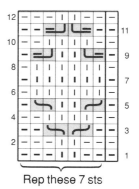

Rep these 7 sts

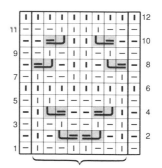

Rep these 8 sts

 = C2R, = C2L, = T2B, = T2F.

IV. Cross Stitch Patterns

IV.4

Multiple of 12 sts + 4.

1st row (wrong side): K7, p2, *k10, p2; rep from * to last 7 sts, k7.

2nd row: K7, C2R, *k10, C2R; rep from * to last 7 sts, k7.

3rd row: As 1st row.

4th row: K6, C2R, C2L, *k8, C2R, C2L; rep from * to last 6 sts, k6.

5th row: K6, p1, k2, p1, *k8, p1, k2, p1; rep from * to last 6 sts, k6.

6th row: K5, C2R, k2, C2L, *k6, C2R, k2, C2L; rep from * to last 5 sts, k5.

7th row: K5, p1, k4, p1, *k6, p1, k4, p1; rep from * to last 5 sts, k5.

8th row: K4, *C2R, k4, C2L, k4; rep from * to end.

9th row: K4, *p1, k6, p1, k4; rep from * to end.

10th row: K3, *C2R, k6, C2L, k2; rep from

* to last st, k1.

11th row: K3, p1, k8, p1, *k2, p1, k8, p1; rep from * to last 3 sts, k3.

12th row: K2, *C2R, k8, C2L; rep from * to last 2 sts, k2.

13th row: K1, p2, *k10, p2; rep from * to last st, k1.

14th row: K1, C2L, *k10, C2L; rep from * to last st, k1.

15th row: As 13th row.

16th row: K2, *C2L, k8, C2R; rep from * to last 2 sts, k2.

17th row: As 11th row.

18th row: K3, *C2L, k6, C2R, k2; rep from * to last st, k1.

19th row: As 9th row.

20th row: K4, *C2L, k4, C2R, k4; rep from * to end.

21st row: As 7th row.

22nd row: K5, C2L, k2, C2R, *k6, C2L, k2, C2R; rep from * to last 5 sts, k5.

23rd row: As 5th row.

24th row: K6, C2L, C2R, *k8, C2L, C2R; rep from * to last 6 sts, k6.

Rep these 24 rows.

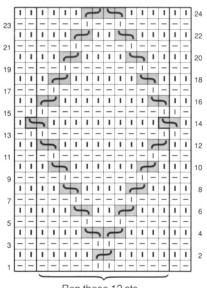

Rep these 12 sts

IV.6

Multiple of 12 sts + 7.

1st row (wrong side): [K2, p1] twice, *[k1, p1] 3 times, [k2, p1] twice; rep from * to last st, k1.

2nd row: [P1, T2F] twice, p1, *[k1, p1] 3 times, [T2F, p1] twice; rep from * to end.

3rd row: K4, p1, k2, *p1, [k1, p1] twice, k4, p1, k2; rep from * to end.

4th row: P2, T2F, p3, *k1, [p1, k1] twice, p2, T2F, p3; rep from * to end.

5th row: [K3, p1] twice, [k1, p1] twice, *[k3, p1] twice, [k1, p1] twice; rep from * to last 7 sts, k3, p1, k3.

6th row: P3, T2F, p2, *k1, [p1, k1] twice, p3, T2F, p2; rep from * to end.

Rep these 6 rows.

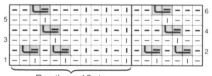

Rep these 12 sts

20th row: K4, *C2L, k4, C2R, k4; rep from * to end.

22nd row: K5, C2L, k2, C2R, *k6, C2L, k2, C2R; rep from * to last 5 sts, k5.

24th row: K6, C2L, C2R, *k8, C2L, C2R; rep from * to last 6 sts, k6.

Rep these 24 rows.

IV.5

Multiple of 12 sts + 4.

1st and every alt row (wrong side): Purl.

2nd row: K7, C2R, *k10, C2R; rep from * to last 7 sts, k7.

4th row: K6, C2R, C2L, *k8, C2R, C2L; rep from * to last 6 sts, k6.

6th row: K5, C2R, k2, C2L, *k6, C2R, k2, C2L; rep from * to last 5 sts, k5.

8th row: K4, *C2R, k4, C2L, k4; rep from * to end.

10th row: K3, *C2R, k6, C2L, k2; rep from * to last st, k1.

12th row: K2, *C2R, k8, C2L; rep from * to last 2 sts, k2.

14th row: K1, C2L, *k10, C2L; rep from * to last st, k1.

16th row: K2, *C2L, k8, C2R; rep from * to last 2 sts, k2.

18th row: K3, *C2L, k6, C2R, k2; rep from * to last st, k1.

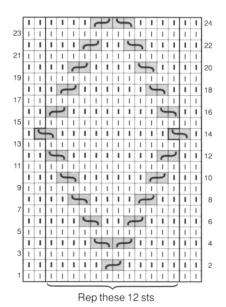

Rep these 12 sts

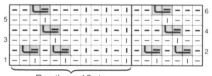 = C2R, = C2L, = T2B, = T2F.

IV.7

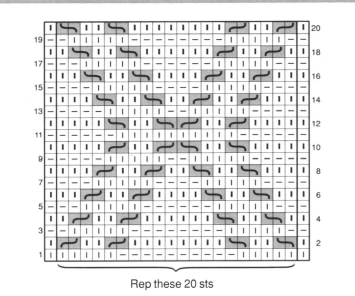

Rep these 20 sts

Multiple of 20 sts + 2.

1st row (wrong side): P6, k10, *p10, k10; rep from * to last 6 sts, p6.

2nd row: K1, *C2L, k2, C2L, k8, C2R, k2, C2R; rep from * to last st, k1.

3rd row: K2, *p5, k8, p5, k2; rep from * to end.

4th row: K2, *C2L, k2, C2L, k6, [C2R, k2] twice; rep from * to end.

5th row: K3, p5, k6, p5, *k4, p5, k6, p5; rep from * to last 3 sts, k3.

6th row: K3, C2L, k2, C2L, k4, C2R, k2, C2R, *k4, C2L, k2, C2L, k4, C2R, k2, C2R; rep from * to last 3 sts, k3.

7th row: [K4, p5] twice, *k6, p5, k4, p5; rep from * to last 4 sts, k4.

8th row: K4, [C2L, k2] twice, C2R, k2, C2R, *k6, [C2L, k2] twice, C2R, k2, C2R; rep from * to last 4 sts, k4.

9th row: K5, p5, k2, p5, *k8, p5, k2, p5; rep from * to last 5 sts, k5.

10th row: K5, C2L, k2, C2L, C2R, k2, C2R, *k8, C2L, k2, C2L, C2R, k2, C2R; rep from * to last 5 sts, k5.

11th row: K6, p10, *k10, p10; rep from * to last 6 sts, k6.

12th row: K5, C2R, k2, C2R, C2L, k2, C2L, *k8, C2R, k2, C2R, C2L, k2, C2L; rep from * to last 5 sts, k5.

13th row: As 9th row.

14th row: K4, [C2R, k2] twice, C2L, k2, C2L, *k6, [C2R, k2] twice, C2L, k2, C2L; rep from * to last 4 sts, k4.

15th row: As 7th row.

16th row: K3, C2R, k2, C2R, k4, C2L, k2, C2L, *k4, C2R, k2, C2R, k4, C2L, k2, C2L; rep from * to last 3 sts, k3.

17th row: As 5th row.

18th row: K2, *C2R, k2, C2R, k6, [C2L, k2] twice; rep from * to end.

19th row: As 3rd row.

20th row: K1, *C2R, k2, C2R, k8, C2L, k2, C2L; rep from * to last st, k1.

Rep these 20 rows.

IV.8

Multiple of 12 sts + 4.

1st row (wrong side): K7, p2, *k10, p2; rep from * to last 7 sts, k7.

2nd row: P7, C2R, *p10, C2R; rep from * to last 7 sts, p7.

3rd row: As 1st row.

4th row: P6, T2B, T2F, *p8, T2B, T2F; rep from * to last 6 sts, p6.

5th row: K6, p1, k2, p1, *k8, p1, k2, p1; rep from * to last 6 sts, k6.

6th row: P5, T2B, p2, T2F, *p6, T2B, p2, T2F; rep from * to last 5 sts, p5.

7th row: K5, p1, k4, p1, *k6, p1, k4, p1; rep from * to last 5 sts, k5.

8th row: P4, *T2B, p4, T2F, p4; rep from * to end.

9th row: K4, *p1, k6, p1, k4; rep from * to end.

10th row: P3, *T2B, p6, T2F, p2; rep from * to last st, p1.

11th row: K3, p1, k8, p1, *k2, p1, k8, p1; rep from * to last 3 sts, k3.

12th row: P2, *T2B, p8, T2F; rep from * to last 2 sts, p2.

13th row: K1, p2, *k10, p2; rep from * to last st, k1.

14th row: P1, C2L, *p10, C2L; rep from * to last st, p1.

15th row: As 13th row.

16th row: P2, *T2F, p8, T2B; rep from * to last 2 sts, p2.

17th row: As 11th row.

18th row: P3, *T2F, p6, T2B, p2; rep from * to last st, p1.

19th row: As 9th row.

20th row: P4, *T2F, p4, T2B, p4; rep from * to end.

21st row: As 7th row.

22nd row: P5, T2F, p2, T2B, *p6, T2F, p2, T2B; rep from * to last 5 sts, p5.

23rd row: As 5th row.

24th row: P6, T2F, T2B, *p8, T2F, T2B; rep from * to last 6 sts, p6.

Rep these 24 rows.

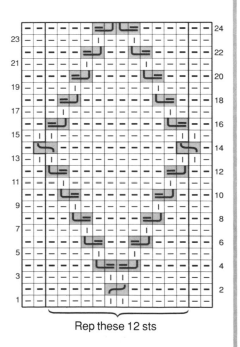

Rep these 12 sts

IV. Cross Stitch Patterns

IV.9

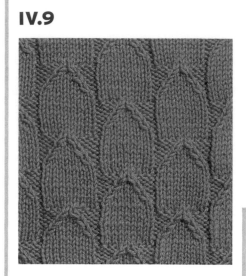

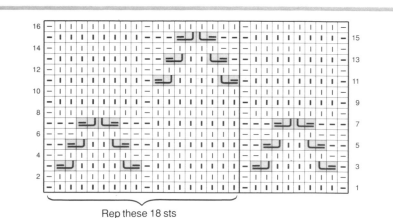

Multiple of 18 sts + 10.

1st row (right side): P1, *k8, p1; rep from * to end.

2nd row: K1, *p8, k1; rep from * to end.

3rd row: P1, T2F, k4, T2B, p1, *k8, p1, T2F, k4, T2B, p1; rep from * to end.

4th row: K2, p6, k2, *p8, k2, p6, k2; rep from * to end.

5th row: P2, T2F, k2, T2B, p2, *k8, p2, T2F, k2, T2B, p2; rep from * to end.

6th row: K3, p4, k3, *p8, k3, p4, k3; rep from * to end.

7th row: P3, T2F, T2B, p3, *k8, p3, T2F, T2B, p3; rep from * to end.

8th row: As 2nd row.

9th and 10th rows: As 1st and 2nd rows.

11th row: P1, k8, p1, *T2F, k4, T2B, p1, k8, p1; rep from * to end.

12th row: K1, p8, *k2, p6, k2, p8; rep from * to last st, k1.

13th row: P1, k8, *p2, T2F, k2, T2B, p2, k8; rep from * to last st, p1.

14th row: K1, p8, *k3, p4, k3, p8; rep from * to last st, k1.

15th row: P1, k8, *p3, T2F, T2B, p3, k8; rep from * to last st, p1.

16th row: As 2nd row.

Rep these 16 rows.

IV.11

Multiple of 18 sts + 2.

1st row (wrong side): P6, k8, *p10, k8; rep from * to last 6 sts, p6.

2nd row: K5, C2L, p6, C2R, *k8, C2L, p6, C2R; rep from * to last 5 sts, k5.

3rd row: P7, k6, *p12, k6; rep from * to last 7 sts, p7.

4th row: K1, *T2F, k3, C2L, p4, C2R, k3, T2B; rep from * to last st, k1.

5th row: K2, *p6, k4, p6, k2; rep from * to end.

6th row: P2, *T2F, k3, C2L, p2, C2R, k3, T2B, p2; rep from * to end.

7th row: K3, p6, k2, p6, *k4, p6, k2, p6; rep from * to last 3 sts, k3.

8th row: P3, T2F, k3, C2L, C2R, k3, T2B, *p4, T2F, k3, C2L, C2R, k3, T2B; rep from * to last 3 sts, p3.

9th row: K4, p12, *k6, p12; rep from * to last 4 sts, k4.

10th row: P4, T2F, k8, T2B, *p6, T2F, k8, T2B; rep from * to last 4 sts, p4.

11th row: K5, p10, *k8, p10; rep from * to last 5 sts, k5.

12th row: P4, C2R, k8, C2L, *p6, C2R, k8, C2L; rep from * to last 4 sts, p4.

13th row: As 9th row.

14th row: P3, C2R, k3, T2B, T2F, k3, C2L, *p4, C2R, k3, T2B, T2F, k3, C2L; rep from * to last 3 sts, p3.

15th row: As 7th row.

16th row: P2, *C2R, k3, T2B, p2, T2F, k3, C2L, p2; rep from * to end.

17th row: As 5th row.

18th row: K1, *C2R, k3, T2B, p4, T2F, k3, C2L; rep from * to last st, k1.

19th row: As 3rd row.

20th row: K5, T2B, p6, T2F, *k8, T2B, p6, T2F; rep from * to last 5 sts, k5.

Rep these 20 rows.

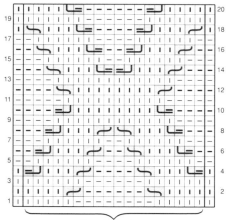

Rep these 18 sts

IV.10

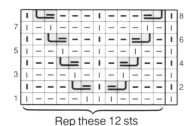

Multiple of 12 sts + 1.

1st row (wrong side): P1, *k4, p3, k4, p1; rep from * to end.

2nd row: K1, *p3, T2B, k1, T2F, p3, k1; rep from * to end.

3rd row: P1, k3, p1, [k1, p1] twice, *[k3, p1] twice, [k1, p1] twice; rep from * to last 4 sts, k3, p1.

4th row: K1, *p2, T2B, p1, k1, p1, T2F, p2, k1; rep from * to end.

5th row: P1, *k2, p1; rep from * to end.

6th row: K1, *p1, T2B, p2, k1, p2, T2F, p1, k1; rep from * to end.

7th row: P1, k1, p1, [k3, p1] twice, *[k1, p1] twice, [k3, p1] twice; rep from * to last 2 sts, k1, p1.

8th row: K1, *T2B, p3, k1, p3, T2F, k1; rep from * to end.

Rep these 8 rows.

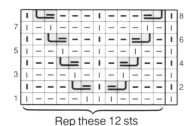

Rep these 12 sts

= C2R, = C2L, = T2B, = T2F.

IV.12

Multiple of 16 sts + 2.

1st row (wrong side): K8, p2, *k14, p2; rep from * to last 8 sts, k8.

2nd row: P7, C2R, C2L, *p12, C2R, C2L; rep from * to last 7 sts, p7.

3rd row: K7, p4, *k12, p4; rep from * to last 7 sts, k7.

4th row: P6, C2R, k2, C2L, *p10, C2R, k2, C2L; rep from * to last 6 sts, p6.

5th row: K6, p6, *k10, p6; rep from * to last 6 sts, k6.

6th row: P5, C2R, k4, C2L, *p8, C2R, k4, C2L; rep from * to last 5 sts, p5.

7th row: K5, p8, *k8, p8; rep from * to last 5 sts, k5.

8th row: P4, C2R, k1, C2R, C2L, k1, C2L, *p6, C2R, k1, C2R, C2L, k1, C2L; rep from * to last 4 sts, p4.

9th row: K4, p10, *k6, p10; rep from * to last 4 sts, k4.

10th row: P3, C2R, k1, C2R, k2, C2L, k1, C2L, *p4, C2R, k1, C2R, k2, C2L, k1, C2L; rep from * to last 3 sts, p3.

11th row: K3, p12, *k4, p12; rep from * to last 3 sts, k3.

12th row: P3, T2F, C2R, k4, C2L, T2B, *p4, T2F, C2R, k4, C2L, T2B; rep from * to last 3 sts, p3.

13th row: As 9th row.

14th row: P4, C2L, k6, C2R, *p6, C2L, k6, C2R; rep from * to last 4 sts, p4.

15th row: As 9th row.

16th row: P3, C2R, C2L, k4, C2R, C2L, *p4, C2R, C2L, k4, C2R, C2L; rep from * to last 3 sts, p3.

17th row: As 11th row.

18th row: P2, *C2R, k2, C2L, k2, C2R, k2, C2L, p2; rep from * to end.

19th row: K2, *p14, k2; rep from * to end.

20th row: P1, *C2R, k4, C2L; rep from * to last st, p1.

21st row: K1, purl to last st, k1.

22nd row: P1, *T2F, k12, T2B; rep from * to last st, p1.

23rd row: As 19th row.

24th row: P2, *T2F, k10, T2B, p2; rep from * to end.

25th row: As 11th row.

26th row: P3, T2F, k8, T2B, *p4, T2F, k8, T2B; rep from * to last 3 sts, p3.

27th row: As 9th row.

28th row: P4, T2F, k6, T2B, *p6, T2F, k6, T2B; rep from * to last 4 sts, p4.

29th row: As 7th row.

30th row: P5, T2F, k4, T2B, *p8, T2F, k4, T2B; rep from * to last 5 sts, p5.

31st row: As 5th row.

32nd row: P6, T2F, k2, T2B, *p10, T2F, k2, T2B; rep from * to last 6 sts, p6.

33rd row: As 3rd row.

34th row: P7, T2F, T2B, *p12, T2F, T2B; rep from * to last 7 sts, p7.

Rep these 34 rows.

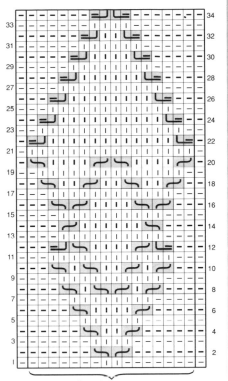

Rep these 16 sts

IV.13

Multiple of 16 sts + 1.

1st row (wrong side): K1, *p7, k1; rep from * to end.

2nd row: P1, *T2F, k5, p1, k5, T2B, p1; rep from * to end.

3rd row: K2, p6, k1, p6, *k3, p6, k1, p6; rep from * to last 2 sts, k2.

4th row: P2, T2F, k4, p1, k4, T2B, *p3, T2F, k4, p1, k4, T2B; rep from * to last 2 sts, p2.

5th row: K3, p5, k1, p5, *k5, p5, k1, p5; rep from * to last 3 sts, k3.

6th row: P3, C2L, k3, p1, k3, C2R, *p5, C2L, k3, p1, k3, C2R; rep from * to last 3 sts, p3.

7th row: As 5th row.

8th row: P2, C2R, C2L, k2, p1, k2, C2R, C2L, *p3, C2R, C2L, k2, p1, k2, C2R, C2L; rep from * to last 2 sts, p2.

9th row: As 3rd row.

10th row: P1, *C2R, k2, C2L, k1, p1, k1, C2R, k2, C2L, p1; rep from * to end.

11th row: As 1st row.

12th row: P1, *k5, C2L, p1, C2R, k5, p1; rep from * to end.

13th row: As 1st row.

14th row: P1, *k7, p1; rep from * to end.

15th row: As 1st row.

16th row: P1, *k5, T2B, p1, T2F, k5, p1; rep from * to end.

17th row: K1, *p6, k3, p6, k1; rep from * to end.

18th row: P1, *k4, T2B, p3, T2F, k4, p1; rep from * to end.

19th row: K1, *p5, k5, p5, k1; rep from * to end.

20th row: P1, *k3, C2R, p5, C2L, k3, p1; rep from * to end.

21st row: As 19th row.

22nd row: P1, *k2, C2R, C2L, p3, C2R, C2L, k2, p1; rep from * to end.

23rd row: As 17th row.

24th row: P1, *k1, C2R, k2, C2L, p1, C2R, k2, C2L, k1, p1; rep from * to end.

25th row: As 1st row.

26th row: P1, *C2R, k5, p1, k5, C2L, p1; rep from * to end.

Rep these 26 rows.

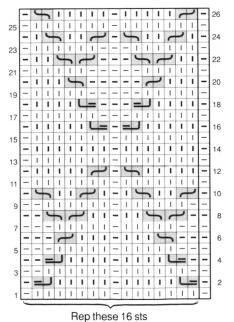

Rep these 16 sts

IV.14

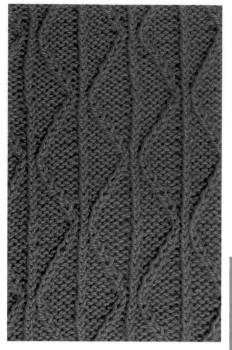

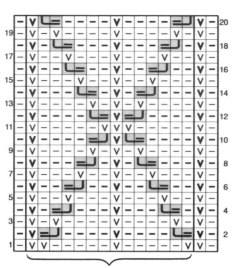

Rep these 14 sts

Multiple of 14 sts + 3.

1st row (wrong side): K1, [PB1] twice, k5, PB1, k5, *[PB1] 3 times, k5, PB1, k5; rep from * to last 3 sts, [PB1] twice, k1.

2nd row: P1, KB1, *T2F, p4, KB1, p4, T2B, KB1; rep from * to last st, p1.

3rd row: *[K1, PB1] twice, [k4, PB1] twice; rep from * to last 3 sts, k1, PB1, k1.

4th row: P1, KB1, *p1, T2F, p3, KB1, p3, T2B, p1, KB1; rep from * to last st, p1.

5th row: K1, PB1, k2, PB1, [k3, PB1] twice, *[k2, PB1] twice, [k3, PB1] twice; rep from * to last 4 sts, k2, PB1, k1.

6th row: P1, KB1, *p2, T2F, p2, KB1, p2, T2B, p2, KB1; rep from * to last st, p1.

7th row: K1, PB1, k3, PB1, [k2, PB1] twice, *[k3, PB1] twice, [k2, PB1] twice; rep from * to last 5 sts, k3, PB1, k1.

8th row: P1, KB1, *p3, T2F, p1, KB1, p1, T2B, p3, KB1; rep from * to last st, p1.

9th row: K1, PB1, k4, PB1, [k1, PB1] twice, *[k4, PB1] twice, [k1, PB1] twice; rep from * to last 6 sts, k4, PB1, k1.

10th row: P1, KB1, *p4, T2F, KB1, T2B, p4, KB1; rep from * to last st, p1.

11th row: K1, PB1, *k5, [PB1] 3 times, k5, PB1; rep from * to last st, k1.

12th row: P1, KB1, *p4, T2B, KB1, T2F, p4, KB1; rep from * to last st, p1.

13th row: As 9th row.

14th row: P1, KB1, *p3, T2B, p1, KB1, p1, T2F, p3, KB1; rep from * to last st, p1.

15th row: As 7th row.

16th row: P1, KB1, *p2, T2B, p2, KB1, p2, T2F, p2, KB1; rep from * to last st, p1.

17th row: As 5th row.

18th row: P1, KB1, *p1, T2B, p3, KB1, p3, T2F, p1, KB1; rep from * to last st, p1.

19th row: As 3rd row.

20th row: P1, KB1, *T2B, p4, KB1, p4, T2F, KB1; rep from * to last st, p1.
Rep these 20 rows.

IV.15

Multiple of 18 sts + 11.

1st row (wrong side): K4, p3, *k3, [p1, k3] 3 times, p3; rep from * to last 4 sts, k4.

2nd row: P4, k3, *p3, T2F, p2, k1, p2, T2B, p3, k3; rep from * to last 4 sts, p4.

3rd row: K4, p3, k4, *p1, [k2, p1] twice, k4, p3, k4; rep from * to end.

4th row: P4, k3, p4, *T2F, p1, k1, p1, T2B, p4, k3, p4; rep from * to end.

5th row: K4, p3, *k5, p1, [k1, p1] twice, k5, p3; rep from * to last 4 sts, k4.

6th row: P3, T2B, k1, T2F, *p4, T2F, k1, T2B, p4, T2B, k1, T2F; rep from * to last 3 sts, p3.

7th row: K3, p1, [k1, p1] twice, *k5, p3, k5, p1, [k1, p1] twice; rep from * to last 3 sts, k3.

8th row: P2, T2B, p1, k1, p1, T2F, *p4, k3, p4, T2B, p1, k1, p1, T2F; rep from * to last 2 sts, p2.

9th row: [K2, p1] 3 times, *k4, p3, k4, p1, [k2, p1] twice; rep from * to last 2 sts, k2.

10th row: P1, T2B, p2, k1, p2, T2F, *p3, k3, p3, T2B, p2, k1, p2, T2F; rep from * to last st, p1.

11th row: K1, *[p1, k3] 3 times, p3, k3; rep from * to last 10 sts, p1, [k3, p1] twice, k1.

12th row: P1, T2F, p2, k1, p2, T2B, *p3, k3, p3, T2F, p2, k1, p2, T2B; rep from * to last st, p1.

13th row: As 9th row.

14th row: P2, T2F, p1, k1, p1, T2B, *p4, k3, p4, T2F, p1, k1, p1, T2B; rep from * to last 2 sts, p2.

15th row: As 7th row.

16th row: P3, T2F, k1, T2B, *p4, T2B, k1, T2F, p4, T2F, k1, T2B; rep from * to last 3 sts, p3.

17th row: As 5th row.

18th row: P4, k3, p4, *T2B, p1, k1, p1, T2R, p4, k3, p4; rep from * to end.

19th row: As 3rd row.

20th row: P4, k3, *p3, T2B, p2, k1, p2, T2F, p3, k3; rep from * to last 4 sts, p4.

Rep these 20 rows.

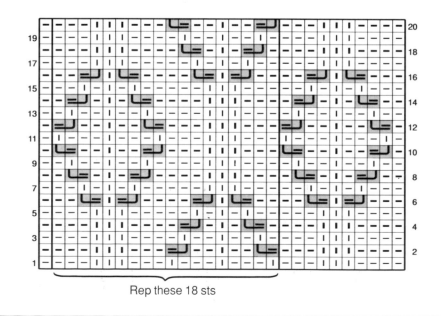

Rep these 18 sts

V = KB1, V = PB1, ⌐ = C2R, ⌐ = C2L, ⌐ = T2B, ⌐ = T2F.

IV.16

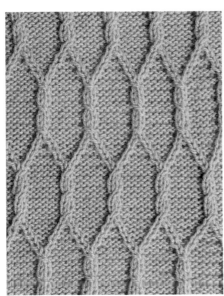

Multiple of 8 sts + 4.

1st row (wrong side): K1, p2, *k6, p2; rep from * to last st, k1.

2nd row: P1, C2R, *p6, C2R; rep from * to last st, p1.

3rd row: As 1st row.

4th row: P1, k2, *p6, k2; rep from * to last st, p1.

Rep the last 4 rows once more, then first 3 rows again.

12th row: P2, *T2F, p4, T2B; rep from * to last 2 sts, p2.

13th row: K3, p1, k4, p1, *k2, p1, k4, p1; rep from * to last 3 sts, k3.

14th row: P3, *T2F, p2, T2B, p2; rep from * to last st, p1.

15th row: K4, *p1, k2, p1, k4; rep from * to end.

16th row: P4, *T2F, T2B, p4; rep from * to end.

17th row: K5, p2, *k6, p2; rep from * to last 5 sts, k5.

18th row: P5, C2L, *p6, C2L; rep from * to last 5 sts, p5.

19th row: As 17th row.

20th row: P5, k2, *p6, k2; rep from * to last 5 sts, p5.

Rep the last 4 rows once more, then 17th, 18th and 19th rows again.

28th row: P4, *T2B, T2F, p4; rep from * to end.

29th row: As 15th row.

30th row: P3, *T2B, p2, T2F, p2; rep from * to last st, p1.

31st row: As 13th row.

32nd row: P2, *T2B, p4, T2F; rep from * to last 2 sts, p2.

Rep these 32 rows.

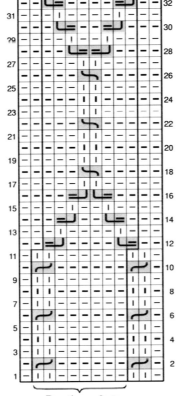

Rep these 8 sts

IV.17

Multiple of 8 sts + 2.

1st row (wrong side): P4, k2, *p6, k2; rep from * to last 4 sts, p4.

2nd row: K2, *T2B, p2, T2F, k2; rep from * to end.

3rd row: P3, k4, *p4, k4; rep from * to last 3 sts, p3.

4th row: K1, *T2B, p4, T2F; rep from * to last st, k1.

5th row: K2, *p6, k2; rep from * to end.

6th row: P2, *T2F, k2, T2B, p2; rep from * to end.

7th row: K3, p4, *k4, p4; rep from * to last 3 sts, k3.

8th row: P3, T2F, T2B, *p4, T2F, T2B; rep from * to last 3 sts, p3.

Rep these 8 rows.

IV.18

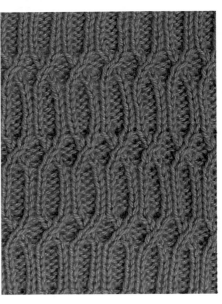

Multiple of 4 sts + 2.

1st row (right side): P1, k1, p2, *k2, p2; rep from * to last 2 sts, k1, p1.

2nd row: K1, p1, k2, *p2, k2; rep from * to last 2 sts, p1, k1.

Rep the last 2 rows once more.

5th row: P1, *T2F, T2B; rep from * to last st, p1.

6th row: K2, *p2, k2; rep from * to end.

7th row: P2, *C2R, p2; rep from * to end.

8th row: As 6th row.

9th row: P1, *T2B, T2F; rep from * to last st, p1.

10th row: As 2nd row.

11th and 12th rows: As 1st and 2nd rows.

Rep these 12 rows.

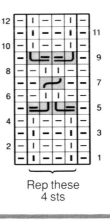

Rep these 4 sts

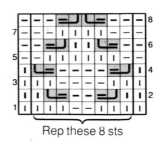

Rep these 8 sts

IV. Cross Stitch Patterns

IV.19

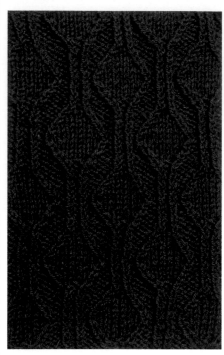

Multiple of 14 sts + 1.

1st row (wrong side): K1, *PB1, k4, PB1, k1; rep from * to end.

2nd row: P1, *KB1, p3, C2R, k1, C2L, p3, KB1, p1; rep from * to end.

3rd row: K1, *PB1, k3, PB1, p3, PB1, k3, PB1, k1; rep from * to end.

4th row: P1, *KB1, p2, C2R, k3, C2L, p2, KB1, p1; rep from * to end.

5th row: K1, *PB1, k2, PB1, p5, PB1, k2, PB1, k1; rep from * to end.

6th row: P1, *KB1, p1, C2R, k5, C2L, p1, KB1, p1; rep from * to end.

7th row: [K1, PB1] twice, p7, *PB1, [k1, PB1] 3 times, p7; rep from * to last 4 sts, [PB1, k1] twice.

8th row: P1, KB1, p1, T2F, k5, T2B, *p1, [KB1, p1] twice, T2F, k5, T2B; rep from * to last 3 sts, p1, KB1, p1.

9th row: As 5th row.

10th row: P1, *KB1, p2, T2F, k3, T2B, p2, KB1, p1; rep from * to end.

11th row: As 3rd row.

12th row: P1, *KB1, p3, T2F, k1, T2B, p3, KB1, p1; rep from * to end.

13th row: As 1st row.

14th row: K1, *C2L, p3, KB1, p1, KB1, p3, C2R, k1; rep from * to end.

15th row: P2, PB1, k3, PB1, k1, PB1, k3, PB1, *p3, PB1, k3, PB1, k1, PB1, k3, PB1; rep from * to last 2 sts, p2.

16th row: K2, C2L, p2, KB1, p1, KB1, p2, C2R, *k3, C2L, p2, KB1, p1, KB1, p2, C2R; rep from * to last 2 sts, k2.

17th row: P3, PB1, k2, PB1, k1, PB1, k2, PB1, *p5, PB1, k2, PB1, k1, PB1, k2, PB1; rep from * to last 3 sts, p3.

18th row: K3, C2L, p1, [KB1, p1] twice, C2R, *k5, C2L, p1, [KB1, p1] twice, C2R; rep from * to last 3 sts, k3.

19th row: P4, PB1, [k1, PB1] 3 times, *p7, PB1, [k1, PB1] 3 times; rep from * to last 4 sts, p4.

20th row: K3, T2B, p1, [KB1, p1] twice, T2F, *k5, T2B, p1, [KB1, p1] twice, T2F; rep from * to last 3 sts, k3.

21st row: As 17th row.

22nd row: K2, T2B, p2, KB1, p1, KB1, p2, T2F, *k3, T2B, p2, KB1, p1, KB1, p2, T2F; rep from * to last 2 sts, k2.

23rd row: As 15th row.

24th row: K1, *T2B, p3, KB1, p1, KB1, p3, T2F, k1; rep from * to end.

Rep these 24 rows.

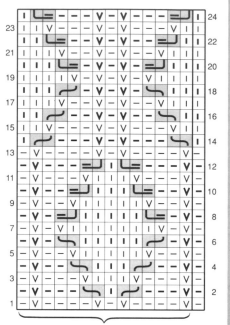

Rep these 14 sts

IV.20

Multiple of 18 sts + 1.

1st row (wrong side): K5, p1, k2, p1, k1, p1, k2, p1, *k9, p1, k2, p1, k1, p1, k2, p1; rep from * to last 5 sts, k5.

2nd row: P4, [T2B, p1] twice, T2F, p1, T2F, *p7, [T2B, p1] twice, T2F, p1, T2F; rep from * to last 4 sts, p4.

3rd row: K4, p1, k2, p1, k3, p1, k2, p1, *k7, p1, k2, p1, k3, p1, k2, p1; rep from * to last 4 sts, k4.

4th row: P3, T2B, p1, T2B, p3, T2F, p1, T2F, *p5, T2B, p1, T2B, p3, T2F, p1, T2F; rep from * to last 3 sts, p3.

5th row: K3, p1, k2, p1, *k5, p1, k2, p1; rep from * to last 3 sts, k3.

6th row: P2, T2B, p1, T2B, p5, T2F, p1, T2F, *p3, T2B, p1, T2B, p5, T2F, p1, T2F; rep from * to last 2 sts, p2.

7th row: [K2, p1] twice, k7, p1, k2, p1, *k3, p1, k2, p1, k7, p1, k2, p1; rep from * to last 2 sts, k2.

8th row: P1, *T2B, p1, T2B, p7, [T2F, p1] twice; rep from * to end.

9th row: K1, *p1, k2, p1, k9, p1, k2, p1, k1; rep from * to end.

10th row: P1, *k1, p2, k1, p9, k1, p2, k1, p1; rep from * to end.

11th row: As 9th row.

12th row: P1, *T2F, p1, T2F, p7, [T2B, p1] twice; rep from * to end.

13th row: As 7th row.

14th row: P2, T2F, p1, T2F, p5, T2B, p1, T2B, *p3, T2F, p1, T2F, p5, T2B, p1, T2B; rep from * to last 2 sts, p2.

15th row: As 5th row.

16th row: P3, T2F, p1, T2F, p3, T2B, p1, T2B, *p5, T2F, p1, T2F, p3, T2B, p1, T2B; rep from * to last 3 sts, p3.

17th row: As 3rd row.

18th row: P4, [T2F, p1] twice, T2B, p1, T2B, *p7, [T2F, p1] twice, T2B, p1, T2B; rep from * to last 4 sts, p4.

19th row: As 1st row.

20th row: P5, k1, p2, k1, p1, k1, p2, k1, *p9, k1, p2, k1, p1, k1, p2, k1; rep from * to last 5 sts, p5.

Rep these 20 rows.

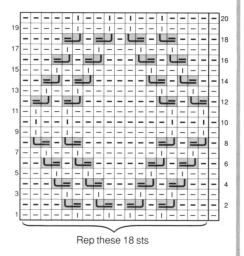

Rep these 18 sts

52

V = KB1, **V** = PB1, **⌐** = C2R, **⌐** = C2L, **⌐** = T2B, **⌐** = T2F.

IV.21

Multiple of 12 sts + 12.

1st, 3rd, 5th and 7th rows (wrong side): K2, p2, *k4, p2; rep from * to last 2 sts, k2.

2nd row: K2, C2R, k4, C2L, *k4, C2R, k4, C2L; rep from * to last 2 sts, k2.

4th row: Knit.

6th row: As 2nd row.

8th row: K3, C2L, k2, C2R, *k6, C2L, k2, C2R; rep from * to last 3 sts, k3.

9th row: [K2, p3] twice, *k4, p3, k2,.p3; rep from * to last 2 sts, k2.

10th row: K4, C2L, C2R, *k8, C2L, C2R; rep from * to last 4 sts, k4.

11th row: K2, p8, *k4, p8; rep from * to last 2 sts, k2.

12th row: K5, C2R, *k10, C2R; rep from * to last 5 sts, k5.

13th row: As 11th row.

14th row: K4, C2R, C2L, *k8, C2R, C2L; rep from * to last 4 sts, k4.

15th row: As 9th row.

16th row: K3, C2R, k2, C2L, *k6, C2R, k2, C2L; rep from * to last 3 sts, k3.

17th, 19th, 21st and 23rd rows: As 1st row.

18th row: K2, C2L, k4, C2R, *k4, C2L, k4, C2R; rep from * to last 2 sts, k2.

20th row: Knit.

22nd row: As 18th row.

24th row: K9, *C2L, k2, C2R, k6; rep from * to last 3 sts, k3.

25th row: K2, p2, k4, *p3, k2, p3, k4; rep from * to last 4 sts, p2, k2.

26th row: K10, *C2L, C2R, k8; rep from * to last 2 sts, k2.

27th row: K2, p2, k4, *p8, k4; rep from * to last 4 sts, p2, k2.

28th row: K11, *C2L, k10; rep from * to last st, k1.

29th row: As 27th row.

30th row: K10, *C2R, C2L, k8; rep from * to last 2 sts, k2.

31st row: As 25th row.

32nd row: K9, *C2R, k2, C2L, k6; rep from * to last 3 sts, k3.

Rep these 32 rows.

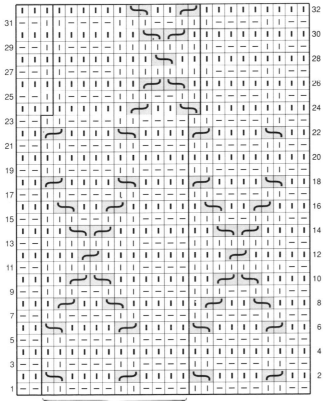

Rep these 12 sts

IV.22

Multiple of 6 sts + 1.

1st row (right side): K1, *C2L, k4; rep from * to end.

2nd row: K4, p1, *k5, p1; rep from * to last 2 sts, k2.

3rd row: K2, C2L, *k4, C2L; rep from * to last 3 sts, k3.

4th row: K3, p1, *k5, p1; rep from * to last 3 sts, k3.

5th row: K3, C2L, *k4, C2L; rep from * to last 2 sts, k2.

6th row: K2, p1, *k5, p1; rep from * to last 4 sts, k4.

7th row: *K4, C2L; rep from * to last st, k1.

8th row: K1, *p1, k5; rep from * to end.

9th row: *K4, C2R; rep from * to last st, k1.

10th row: As 6th row.

11th row: K3, C2R, *k4, C2R; rep from * to last 2 sts, k2.

12th row: As 4th row.

13th row: K2, C2R, *k4, C2R; rep from * to last 3 sts, k3.

14th row: As 2nd row.

15th row: K1, *C2R, k4; rep from * to end.

16th row: *K5, p1; rep from * to last st, k1.

Rep these 16 rows.

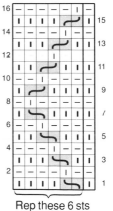

Rep these 6 sts

53

IV. Cross Stitch Patterns

IV. 23

Multiple of 26 sts + 2.

1st row (right side): P6, k16, *p10, k16; rep from * to last 6 sts, p6.

2nd row: K6, p1, k3, p8, k3, p1, *k10, p1, k3, p8, k3, p1; rep from * to last 6 sts, k6.

3rd row: K1, *C2L, p3, T2F, k2, C2L, k4, C2R, k2, T2B, p3, C2R; rep from * to last st, k1.

4th row: K2, *p1, k4, p1, k3, p6, k3, p1, k4, p1, k2; rep from * to end.

5th row: K2, *C2L, p3, T2F, k2, C2L, k2, C2R, k2, T2B, p3, C2R, k2; rep from * to end.

6th row: K3, p1, k4, p1, k3, p4, k3, p1, *[k4, p1] 3 times, k3, p4, k3, p1; rep from * to last 8 sts, k4, p1, k3.

7th row: K3, C2L, p3, T2F, k2, C2L, C2R, k2, T2B, p3, C2R, *k4, C2L, p3, T2F, k2, C2L, C2R, k2, T2B, p3, C2R; rep from * to last 3 sts, k3.

8th row: [K4, p1] twice, k8, p1, k4, *p1, k6, p1, k4, p1, k8, p1, k4; rep from * to last 5 sts, p1, k4.

9th row: K4, C2L, p3, T2F, k6, T2B, p3, C2R, *k6, C2L, p3, T2F, k6, T2B, p3, C2R; rep from * to last 4 sts, k4.

10th row: K5, p1, k4, p1, k6, p1, k4, p1, *k8, p1, k4, p1, k6, p1, k4, p1; rep from * to last 5 sts, k5.

11th row: K1, *C2L, k2, C2L, p3, T2F, k4, T2B, p3, C2R, k2, C2R; rep from * to last st, k1.

12th row: P3, k3, p1, [k4, p1] 3 times, k3, *p4, k3, p1, [k4, p1] 3 times, k3; rep from * to last 3 sts, p3.

13th row: [K2, C2L] twice, p3, T2F, k2, T2B, p3, *[C2R, k2] twice, C2L, k2, C2L, p3, T2F, k2, T2B, p3; rep from * to last 8 sts, [C2R, k2] twice.

14th row: P4, k3, p1, k4, p1, k2, p1, k4, p1, k3, *p6, k3, p1, k4, p1, k2, p1, k4, p1, k3; rep from * to last 4 sts, p4.

15th row: K3, C2L, k2, C2L, p3, T2F, T2B, p3, C2R, k2, C2R, *k4, C2L, k2, C2L, p3, T2F, T2B, p3, C2R, k2, C2R; rep from * to last 3 sts, k3.

16th row: P5, k3, p1, k10, p1, k3, *p8, k3, p1, k10, p1, k3; rep from * to last 5 sts, p5.

17th row: K9, p10, *k16, p10; rep from * to last 9 sts, k9.

18th row: As 16th row.

19th row: K3, C2R, k2, T2B, p3, C2R, C2L, p3, T2F, k2, C2L, *k4, C2R, k2, T2B, p3, C2R, C2L, p3, T2F, k2, C2L; rep from * to last 3 sts, k3.

20th row: As 14th row.

21st row: K2, *C2R, k2, T2B, p3, C2R, k2, C2L, p3, T2F, k2, C2L, k2; rep from * to end.

22nd row: As 12th row.

23rd row: K1, *C2R, k2, T2B, p3, C2R, k4, C2L, p3, T2F, k2, C2L; rep from * to last st, k1.

24th row: As 10th row.

25th row: K4, T2B, p3, C2R, k6, C2L, p3, T2F, *k6, T2B, p3, C2R, k6, C2L, p3, T2F; rep from * to last 4 sts, k4.

26th row: As 8th row.

27th row: K3, T2B, p3, C2R, k2, C2R, C2L, k2, C2L, p3, T2F, *k4, T2B, p3, C2R, k2, C2R, C2L, k2, C2L, p3, T2F; rep from * to last 3 sts, k3.

28th row: As 6th row.

29th row: K2, *T2B, p3, [C2R, k2] twice, C2L, k2, C2L, p3, T2F, k2; rep from * to end.

30th row: As 4th row.

31st row: K1, *T2B, p3, C2R, k2, C2R, k4, C2L, k2, C2L, p3, T2F; rep from * to last st, k1.

32nd row: As 2nd row.

Rep these 32 rows.

IV. 24

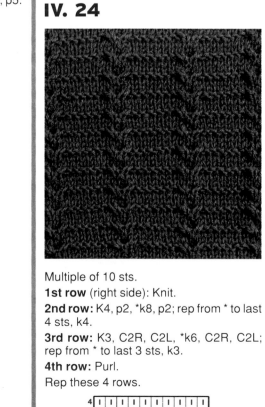

Multiple of 10 sts.

1st row (right side): Knit.

2nd row: K4, p2, *k8, p2; rep from * to last 4 sts, k4.

3rd row: K3, C2R, C2L, *k6, C2R, C2L; rep from * to last 3 sts, k3.

4th row: Purl.

Rep these 4 rows.

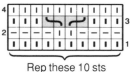

Rep these 10 sts

Rep these 26 sts

$\boxed{\text{⤵}}$ = C2R, $\boxed{\text{⤵}}$ = C2PR, $\boxed{\text{⤴}}$ = C2L, $\boxed{\text{⤴}}$ = C2PL, $\boxed{\text{⤵}}$ = T2B, $\boxed{\text{⤵}}$ = T2PR, $\boxed{\text{⤴}}$ = T2F, $\boxed{\text{⤴}}$ = T2PL.

V.1

Panel of 7 sts on a background of reverse st st.

1st row (right side): K7.
2nd row: P7.
Rep the last 2 rows once more.
5th row: C2L, k5.
6th row: P4, C2PL, p1.
7th row: K2, C2L, k3.
8th row: P2, C2PL, p1, C2PL.
9th row: K1, [C2L, k1] twice.
10th row: C2PL, p1, C2PL, p2.
11th row: C2L, k1, C2L, k2.
12th row: P1, [C2PL, p1] twice.
13th row: K2, C2L, k1, C2L.
14th row: P2, C2PL, p3.
15th row: K4, C2L, k1.
16th row: C2PL, p5.
17th row: K7.
18th row: P7.
Rep the last 2 rows 3 times more.
25th row: K5, C2R.
26th row: P1, C2PR, p4.
27th row: K3, C2R, k2.
28th row: C2PR, p1, C2PR, p2.
29th row: K1, [C2R, k1] twice.
30th row: P2, C2PR, p1, C2PR.
31st row: K2, C2R, k1, C2R.
32nd row: P1, [C2PR, p1] twice.
33rd row: C2R, k1, C2R, k2.
34th row: P3, C2PR, p2.
35th row: K1, C2R, k4.
36th row: P5, C2PR.
37th row: K7.
38th row: P7.
Rep the last 2 rows once more.
Rep these 40 rows.

7 sts

V.2

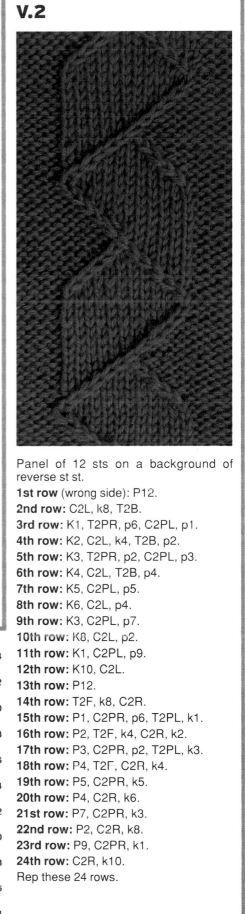

Panel of 12 sts on a background of reverse st st.

1st row (wrong side): P12.
2nd row: C2L, k8, T2B.
3rd row: K1, T2PR, p6, C2PL, p1.
4th row: K2, C2L, k4, T2B, p2.
5th row: K3, T2PR, p2, C2PL, p3.
6th row: K4, C2L, T2B, p4.
7th row: K5, C2PL, p5.
8th row: K6, C2L, p4.
9th row: K3, C2PL, p7.
10th row: K8, C2L, p2.
11th row: K1, C2PL, p9.
12th row: K10, C2L.
13th row: P12.
14th row: T2F, k8, C2R.
15th row: P1, C2PR, p6, T2PL, k1.
16th row: P2, T2F, k4, C2R, k2.
17th row: P3, C2PR, p2, T2PL, k3.
18th row: P4, T2F, C2R, k4.
19th row: P5, C2PR, k5.
20th row: P4, C2R, k6.
21st row: P7, C2PR, k3.
22nd row: P2, C2R, k8.
23rd row: P9, C2PR, k1.
24th row: C2R, k10.
Rep these 24 rows.

12 sts

V. Cross Stitch Panels

V.3

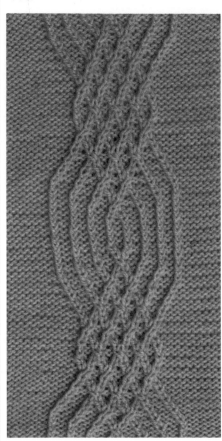

Panel of 22 sts on a background of reverse st st.

1st row (right side): KB1, [p2, KB1] 7 times.

2nd row: PB1, [k2, PB1] 7 times.

3rd row: [KB1, p2] 3 times, T2F, T2B, [p2, KB1] 3 times.

4th row: PB1, [k2, PB1] twice, k3, p2, k3, PB1, [k2, PB1] twice.

5th row: [KB1, p2] twice, T2F, p2, C2L, p2, T2B, [p2, KB1] twice.

6th row: PB1, k2, PB1, k3, PB1, k2, p2, k2, PB1, k3, PB1, k2, PB1.

7th row: KB1, [p2, T2F] twice, T2B, T2F, [T2B, p2] twice, KB1.

8th row: [PB1, k3] twice, p2, k2, p2, [k3, PB1] twice.

9th row: [T2F, p2] twice, [C2R, p2] twice, T2B, p2, T2B.

10th row: K1, PB1, k3, PB1, k2, [p2, k2] twice, PB1, k3, PB1, k1.

11th row: P1, T2F, p2, [T2F, T2B] 3 times, p2, T2B, p1.

12th row: K2, PB1, k3, p2, [k2, p2] twice, k3, PB1, k2.

13th row: P2, T2F, p2, [C2L, p2] 3 times, T2B, p2.

14th row: K3, PB1, k2, [p2, k2] 3 times, PB1, k3.

15th row: P3, [T2F, T2B] 4 times, p3.

16th row: K4, p2, [k2, p2] 3 times, k4.

17th row: P4, C2R, [p2, C2R] 3 times, p4.

18th row: As 16th row.

19th row: P3, [T2B, T2F] 4 times, p3.

20th row: As 14th row.

21st row: P3, KB1, p2, [C2L, p2] 3 times, KB1, p3.

22nd, 23rd, 24th and 25th rows: As 14th, 15th, 16th and 17th rows.

26th row: As 16th row.

27th row: As 19th row.

28th row: As 14th row.

29th row: P2, T2B, p2, [C2L, p2] 3 times, T2F, p2.

30th row: As 12th row.

31st row: P1, T2B, p2, [T2B, T2F] 3 times, p2, T2F, p1.

32nd row: As 10th row.

33rd row: [T2B, p2] twice, [C2R, p2] twice, T2F, p2, T2F.

34th row: As 8th row.

35th row: KB1, p2, T2B, p2, [T2B, T2F] twice, p2, T2F, p2, KB1.

36th row: As 6th row.

37th row: [KB1, p2] twice, T2B, p2, C2L, p2, T2F, [p2, KB1] twice.

38th row: As 4th row.

39th row: [KB1, p2] 3 times, T2B, T2F, [p2, KB1] 3 times.

40th row: As 2nd row.

41st and 42nd rows: As 1st and 2nd rows.

Rep these 42 rows.

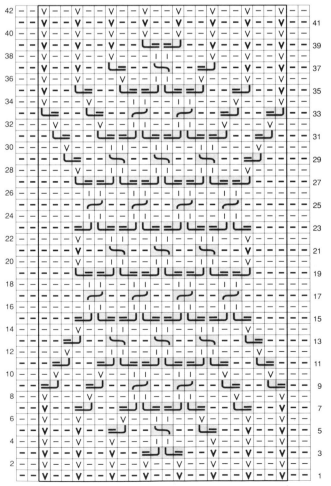

22 sts

V.4

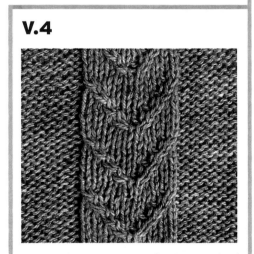

Panel of 10 sts on a background of reverse st st.

1st and every alt row (wrong side): P10.

2nd row: K3, C2R, C2L, k3.

4th row: K2, C2R, k2, C2L, k2.

6th row: K1, C2R, k4, C2L, k1.

8th row: C2R, k6, C2L.

Rep these 8 rows.

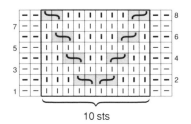

10 sts

V = KB1, V = PB1, ⤵ = C2R, ⤶ = C2L, ▱ = T2B, ▱ = T2F.

V.5

Panel of 20 sts on a background of reverse st st.

1st row (wrong side): K3, p1, [k5, p2] twice, k2.

2nd row: P2, C2L, p5, C2R, p4, T2B, p3.

3rd row: K4, p1, k4, p2, k5, p2, k2.

4th row: P1, C2R, C2L, p4, k2, p3, T2B, p4.

5th row: K5, p1, k3, p2, k4, p4, k1.

6th row: C2R, k2, C2L, p3, C2R, p2, T2B, p5.

7th row: K6, p1, k2, p2, k3, p6.

8th row: T2F, k2, T2B, p3, k2, p1, T2B, p6.

9th row: K7, p1, k1, p2, k4, p4, k1.

10th row: P1, T2F, T2B, p4, C2R, T2B, p7.

11th row: K8, p3, k5, p2, k2.

12th row: P2, T2F, p5, k1, T2B, p8.

13th row: K2, [p2, k5] twice, p1, k3.

14th row: P3, T2F, p4, C2R, p5, C2R, p2.

15th row: K2, p2, k5, p2, k4, p1, k4.

16th row: P4, T2F, p3, k2, p4, C2R, C2L, p1.

17th row: K1, p4, k4, p2, k3, p1, k5.

18th row: P5, T2F, p2, C2R, p3, C2R, k2, C2L.

19th row: P6, k3, p2, k2, p1, k6.

20th row: P6, T2F, p1, k2, p3, T2F, k2, T2B.

21st row: K1, p4, k4, p2, k1, p1, k7.

22nd row: P7, T2F, C2R, p4, T2F, T2B, p1.

23rd row: K2, p2, k5, p3, k8.

24th row: P8, T2F, k1, p5, T2B, p2.
Rep these 24 rows.

V.6

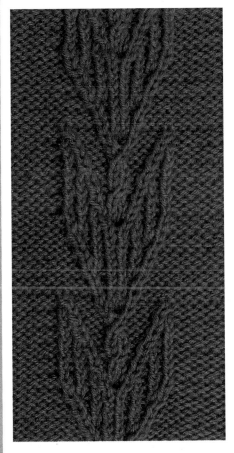

Panel of 14 sts on a background of reverse st st.

1st row (wrong side): PB1, k1, p1, k3, p2, k3, p1, k1, PB1.

2nd row: KB1, T2B, p3, C2R, p3, T2F, KB1.

3rd row: P2, [k4, p2] twice.

4th row: T2B, p3, C2R, C2L, p3, T2F.

5th row: K5, p4, k5.

6th row: P4, T2B, [KB1] twice, T2F, p4.

7th row: K4, p1, k1, [PB1] twice, k1, p1, k4.

8th row: P3, C2R, p1, [KB1] twice, p1, C2L, p3.

9th row: K3, p2, k1, [PB1] twice, k1, p2, k3.

10th row: P2, T2B, KB1, p1, [KB1] twice, p1, KB1, T2F, p2.

11th row: K2, p1, k1, PB1, k1, [PB1] twice, k1, PB1, k1, p1, k2.

12th row: P1, C2R, p1, KB1, p1, [KB1] twice, p1, KB1, p1, C2L, p1.

13th row: K1, p2, k1, PB1, k1, p2, k1, PB1, k1, p2, k1.

14th row: T2B, KB1, p1, KB1, C2R, C2L, KB1, p1, KB1, T2F.

15th row: P1, k1, PB1, k1, p6, k1, PB1, k1, p1.

16th row: [KB1, p1] twice, T2B, k2, T2F, [p1, KB1] twice.

17th row: [PB1, k1] twice, p1, k1, p2, k1, p1, [k1, PB1] twice.

18th row: KB1, p1, KB1, T2B, p1, C2R, p1, T2F, KB1, p1, KB1.

19th row: PB1, k1, p2, [k2, p2] twice, k1, PB1.

20th row: KB1, p1, T2B, p2, k2, p2, T2F, p1, KB1.
Rep these 20 rows.

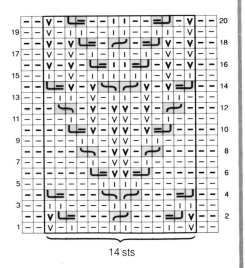

V. Cross Stitch Panels

V.7

Panel of 13 sts on a background of reverse st st.

1st row (right side): T2B, k1, [p1, k1] 5 times.

2nd row: P1, [k1, p1] 5 times, C2PL.

3rd row: K1, T2F, [p1, k1] 5 times.

4th row: P1, [k1, p1] 4 times, C2PL, k1, p1.

5th row: K1, p1, k1, T2F, [p1, k1] 4 times.

6th row: P1, [k1, p1] 3 times, C2PL, [k1, p1] twice.

7th row: K1, [p1, k1] twice, T2F, [p1, k1] 3 times.

8th row: P1, [k1, p1] twice, C2PL, [k1, p1] 3 times.

9th row: K1, [p1, k1] 3 times, T2F, [p1, k1] twice.

10th row: P1, k1, p1, C2PL, [k1, p1] 4 times.

11th row: K1, [p1, k1] 4 times, T2F, p1, k1.

12th row: P1, C2PL, [k1, p1] 5 times.

13th row: K1, [p1, k1] 5 times, T2F.

14th row: C2PR, p1, [k1, p1] 5 times.

15th row: [K1, p1] 5 times, T2B, k1.

16th row: P1, k1, C2PR, p1, [k1, p1] 4 times.

17th row: [K1, p1] 4 times, T2B, k1, p1, k1.

18th row: [P1, k1] twice, C2PR, p1, [k1, p1] 3 times.

19th row: [K1, p1] 3 times, T2B, k1, [p1, k1] twice.

20th row: [P1, k1] 3 times, C2PR, p1, [k1, p1] twice.

21st row: [K1, p1] twice, T2B, k1, [p1, k1] 3 times.

22nd row: [P1, k1] 4 times, C2PR, p1, k1, p1.

23rd row: K1, p1, T2B, k1, [p1, k1] 4 times.

24th row: [P1, k1] 5 times, C2PR, p1.
Rep these 24 rows.

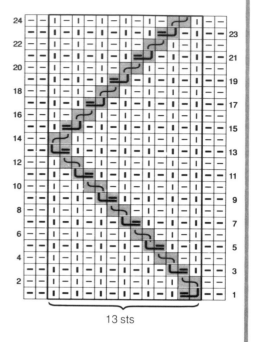

13 sts

V.8

Panel of 16 sts on a background of reverse st st.

1st row (wrong side): PB1, k6, p2, k6, PB1.

2nd row: KB1, p6, C2R, p6, KB1.

3rd row: As 1st row.

4th row: KB1, p5, C2R, C2L, p5, KB1.

5th row: PB1, k5, p4, k5, PB1.

6th row: KB1, p4, C2R, k2, C2L, p4, KB1.

7th row: PB1, k4, p6, k4, PB1.

8th row: KB1, p3, C2R, k4, C2L, p3, KB1.

9th row: PB1, k3, p8, k3, PB1.

10th row: KB1, p2, C2R, k6, C2L, p2, KB1.

11th row: PB1, k2, p10, k2, PB1.

12th row: KB1, p2, k4, C2R, k4, p2, KB1.

13th row: As 11th row.

14th row: KB1, p2, k3, C2R, C2L, k3, p2, KB1.

15th row: As 11th row.

16th row: KB1, p2, T2F, C2R, k2, C2L, T2B, p2, KB1.

17th row: As 9th row.

18th row: KB1, p3, C2R, k4, C2L, p3, KB1.

19th row: As 9th row.

20th row: KB1, p2, C2R, C2L, k2, C2R, C2L, p2, KB1.

21st row: As 11th row.

22nd row: KB1, p2, k3, C2L, C2R, k3, p2, KB1.

23rd and 24th rows: As 11th and 12th rows.

25th row: As 11th row.

26th row: KB1, p2, T2F, k6, T2B, p2, KB1.

27th row: As 9th row.

28th row: KB1, p3, T2F, k4, T2B, p3, KB1.

29th row: As 7th row.

30th row: KB1, p4, T2F, k2, T2B, p4, KB1.

31st row: As 5th row.

32nd row: KB1, p5, T2F, T2B, p5, KB1.
Rep these 32 rows.

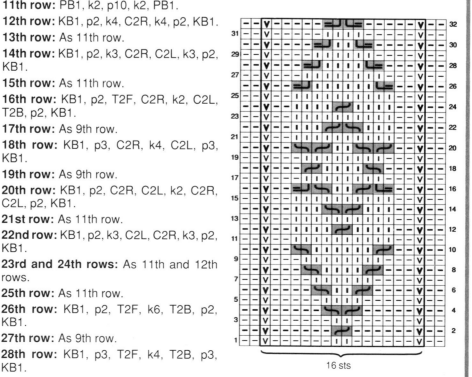

16 sts

$\boxed{V}$ = KB1, $\boxed{V}$ = PB1, = C2R, = C2PR, = C2L, = C2PL, = T2B, = T2F.

V.9

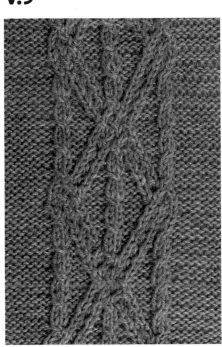

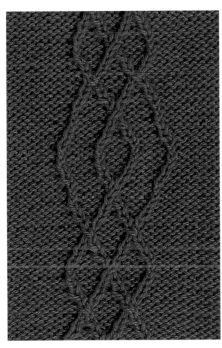

20 sts

Panel of 20 sts on a background of reverse st st.

1st row (wrong side): K1, p2, k4, p6, k4, p2, k1.

2nd row: P1, C2R, p4, [C2L] 3 times, p4, C2L, p1.

3rd row: As 1st row.

4th row: P1, k2, p3, [C2R] 3 times, C2L, p3, k2, p1.

5th row: K1, p2, k3, p8, k3, p2, k1.

6th row: P1, C2R, p2, C2R, T2B, C2L, T2F, C2L, p2, C2L, p1.

7th row: K1, p2, k2, p3, k1, p2, k1, p3, k2, p2, k1.

8th row: P1, k2, p1, C2R, T2B, p1, k2, p1, T2F, C2L, p1, k2, p1.

9th row: K1, p2, k1, p3, k2, p2, k2, p3, k1, p2, k1.

10th row: P1, [C2R] twice, T2B, p2, C2L, p2, T2F, [C2L] twice, p1.

11th row: K1, p5, k3, p2, k3, p5, k1.

12th row: [C2R] twice, T2B, p3, k2, p3, T2F, [C2L] twice.

13th row: P5, k4, p2, k4, p5.

14th row: K1, [C2R] twice, p4, C2L, p4, [C2L] twice, k1.

15th row: As 13th row.

16th row: T2F, C2R, C2L, p3, k2, p3, C2R, C2L, T2B.

17th row: As 11th row.

18th row: P1, C2R, T2F, [C2L, p2] twice, C2R, T2B, C2L, p1.

19th row: As 9th row.

20th row: P1, k2, p1, T2F, C2L, p1, k2, p1, C2R, T2B, p1, k2, p1.

21st row: As 7th row.

22nd row: P1, C2R, p2, T2F, [C2L] twice, C2R, T2B, p2, C2L, p1.

23rd row: As 5th row.

24th row: P1, k2, p3, T2F, [C2R] twice, T2B, p3, k2, p1.

Rep these 24 rows.

V.10

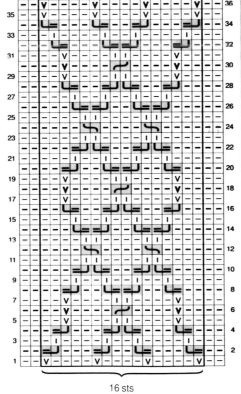

Panel of 16 sts on a background of reverse st st.

1st row (wrong side): PB1, [k4, PB1] 3 times.

2nd row: T2F, p3, T2F, p2, T2B, p3, T2B.

3rd row: K1, p1, k4, p1, k2, p1, k4, p1, k1.

4th row: P1, T2F, p3, T2F, T2B, p3, T2B, p1.

5th row: K2, PB1, k4, p2, k4, PB1, k2.

6th row: P2, KB1, p4, C2R, p4, KB1, p2.

7th row: As 5th row.

8th row: P2, [T2F, p2, T2B] twice, p2.

9th row: K3, p1, [k2, p1] 3 times, k3.

10th row: P3, T2F, T2B, p2, T2F, T2B, p3.

11th row: K4, [p2, k4] twice.

12th row: P4, [C2L, p4] twice.

13th row: As 11th row.

14th row: P3, T2B, T2F, p2, T2B, T2F, p3.

15th row: As 9th row.

16th row: P2, [T2B, p2, T2F] twice, p2.

17th and 18th rows: As 5th and 6th rows.

19th row: As 5th row.

20th to 31st rows: As 8th to 19th rows inclusive.

32nd row: P1, T2B, p3, T2B, T2F, p3, T2F, p1.

33rd row: As 3rd row.

34th row: T2B, p3, T2B, p2, T2F, p3, T2F.

35th row: As 1st row.

36th row: KB1, [p4, KB1] 3 times.

Rep these 36 rows.

16 sts

V. Cross Stitch Panels

V.11

Panel of 20 sts on a background of reverse st st.

1st row (wrong side): K7, p1, k1, p2, k1, p1, k7.

2nd row: P6, [T2B] twice, [T2F] twice, p6.

3rd row: K6, p1, k1, p1, k2, p1, k1, p1, k6.

4th row: P5, [T2B] twice, p2, [T2F] twice, p5.

5th row: K5, p1, k1, p1, k4, p1, k1, p1, k5.

6th row: P4, [T2B] twice, p4, [T2F] twice, p4.

7th row: K4, p1, k1, p1, k6, p1, k1, p1, k4.

8th row: P3, [T2B] twice, p6, [T2F] twice, p3.

9th row: K3, p1, k1, p2, k6, p2, k1, p1, k3.

10th row: P2, [T2B] twice, T2F, p4, T2B, [T2F] twice, p2.

11th row: K2, p1, k1, p1, k2, p1, k4, p1, k2, p1, k1, p1, k2.

12th row: P1, [T2B] twice, p2, T2F, p2, T2B, p2, [T2F] twice, p1.

13th row: [K1, p1] twice, k4, p1, k2, p1, k4, [p1, k1] twice.

14th row: [T2B] twice, p4, T2F, T2B, p4, [T2F] twice.

15th row: P1, k1, p1, k6, p2, k6, p1, k1, p1.

16th row: K1, p1, k1, p6, k2, p6, k1, p1, k1.

17th row: As 15th row.

18th row: [T2F] twice, p4, T2B, T2F, p4, [T2F] twice.

19th row: As 13th row.

20th row: P1, [T2F] twice, p2, T2B, p2, T2F, p2, [T2B] twice, p1.

21st row: As 11th row.

22nd row: P2, [T2F] twice, T2B, p4, T2F, [T2B] twice, p2.

23rd row: As 9th row.

24th row: P3, [T2F] twice, p6, [T2B] twice, p3.

25th row: As 7th row.

26th row: P4, [T2F] twice, p4, [T2B] twice, p4.

27th row: As 5th row.

28th row: P5, [T2F] twice, p2, [T2B] twice, p5.

29th row: As 3rd row.

30th row: P6, [T2F] twice, [T2B] twice, p6.
Rep these 30 rows.

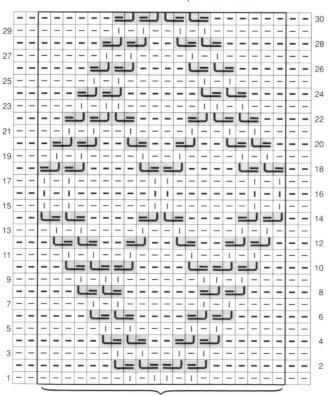

20 sts

V.12

Panel of 14 sts on a background of reverse st st.

1st row (wrong side): P3, k3, p4, C2PR, k2.

2nd row: P1, C2R, k1, T2B, k2, p3, T2F, k1.

3rd row: P2, k4, p2, k1, p3, C2PR.

4th row: K3, T2B, p1, k1, C2L, p3, T2F.

5th row: K4, C2PL, p2, k2, p4.

6th row: K2, T2B, p2, k1, [C2L] twice, p3.

7th row: K2, C2PL, p4, k3, p3.

8th row: K1, T2B, p3, k2, T2F, k1, C2L, p1.

9th row: C2PL, p3, k1, p2, k4, p2.

10th row: T2B, p3, C2R, k1, p1, T2F, k3.

11th row: P4, k2, p2, C2PR, k4.

12th row: P3, [C2R] twice, k1, p2, T2F, k2.

Rep these 12 rows.

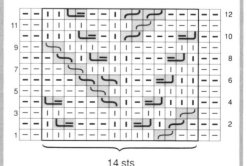

14 sts

$\boxed{}$ = C2R, $\boxed{}$ = C2PR, $\boxed{}$ = C2L, $\boxed{}$ = C2PL, $\boxed{}$ = T2B, $\boxed{}$ = T2F.

By using a cable needle one stitch or a group of stitches can be crossed over another, or sets of stitches can be moved across the background fabric. Cables are most often worked in stocking stitch on a reverse stocking stitch background. They can also be worked on a stocking stitch or garter stitch background, but however intricate a cable pattern or panel may appear, the basic techniques still apply.

Working a Basic Cable

Moving one group of stitches over another.

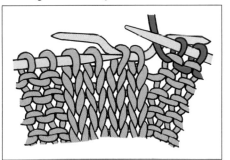

C4B (Cable 4 Back)

Here the cable panel consists of four stitches in stocking stitch against a reverse stocking stitch background.

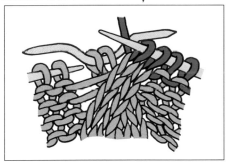

1. On a right side row, work to the position of the cable panel and slip the next two stitches onto the cable needle.

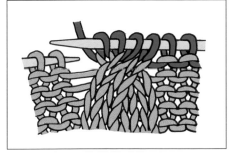

2. With the stitches on the cable needle held at the back of the work, knit the next two stitches from the left-hand needle.

3. Now knit the two stitches from the cable needle to produce the crossover.

Leaving the first set of stitches at the back of the work produces a cable that twists to the right.

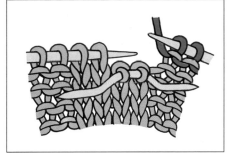

C4F (Cable 4 Front)

1. On a right side row, work to the position of the cable panel and slip the next two stitches onto the cable needle, leaving it at the **front** of the work.

2. Working behind the cable needle, knit the next two stitches from the left-hand needle.

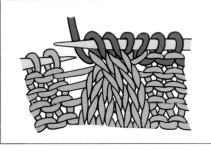

3. Now knit the two stitches from the cable needle to produce a crossover to the left.

Leaving the first set of stitches at the front of the work produces a cable that twists to the left.

Working C4B or C4F on every sixth row creates cables that look like these.

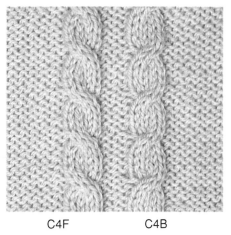

C4F   C4B

Twisting Stitches

Moving stitches across the background fabric.

Here two stitches are moved across a background of reverse stocking stitch.

T3B (Twist 3 Back)

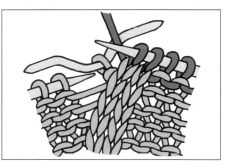

1. On a right side row, work to one stitch before the two stocking stitch stitches. Slip the next stitch onto a cable needle and leave it at the back of the work.

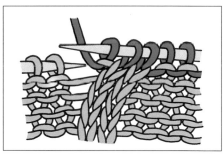

2. Knit the next two stitches on the left-hand needle.

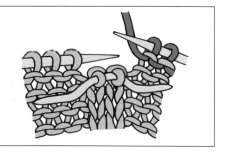

3. Now purl the stitch on the cable needle to produce a twist to the **right**.

T3F (Twist 3 Front)

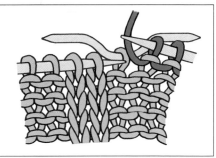

1. On a right side row, work to the two stocking stitch stitches. Slip these two stitches onto a cable needle and leave them at the front of the work.

Cable Patterns

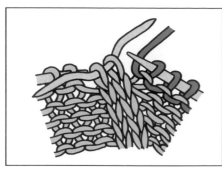

2. Purl the next stitch on the left-hand needle.

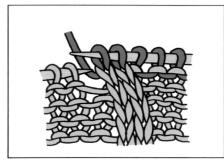

3. Knit the two stitches on the cable needle to produce a twist to the **left**.

Cable and Cross Stitch Tension

It is important to remember all cables and crossed stitches pull the fabric in like a rib and that the tension will be much tighter than for a flat fabric. This means that more stitches are required to knit a cable fabric to the same measurements as a stocking stitch fabric. Therefore, if you wish to add a cable or aran panel to a stocking stitch sweater you need to calculate the extra stitches required as follows:

1. Knit a piece of the cable panel with a few stitches extra in the background fabric at either side. The swatch should be a minimum of 5 cm (2 ins) in length, or at least one complete pattern repeat if it measures more than this.

2. Mark the edges of the cable panel with pins (inside the extra background stitches) and measure the distance between the pins without stretching.

3. Calculate how many stitches in the background fabric would be required to produce the same width as the cable panel, then subtract this number from the number of stitches in the cable panel to find the number of stitches to be increased. For example, a cable panel contains 36 sts and measures 15 cm (6 ins). The background stitch is stocking stitch with a tension of 18 sts to 10 cm (4 ins). To produce 15 cm (6 ins) of stocking stitch, 27 sts would be required. The cable panel has 9 sts more than this, therefore an extra 9 sts would have to be increased to allow for the cable panel and maintain the same width.

These stitches should be increased above the welt across the stitches to be used for the panel.

Bobbles

Bobbles are an important feature of textured knitting where they can be used either on an all-over fabric or individually.

Bobbles can be worked in stocking stitch, reverse stocking stitch or garter stitch and usually consist of three, four or five stitches. The number of rows worked over the bobble stitches varies according to the size of bobble required.

The following instructions are for a small bobble worked in stocking stitch against a reverse stocking stitch background and involves making five stitches out of one, (used in pattern VII.19).

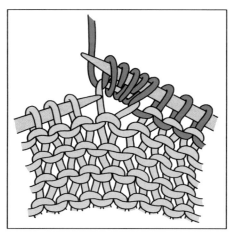

1. On a right side row, work to the position of the bobble. Work [knit, yarn forward (to make a stitch), knit , yf, knit] all into the next stitch. Slip the stitch off the left-hand needle so that five new stitches are on the right-hand needle instead of one.

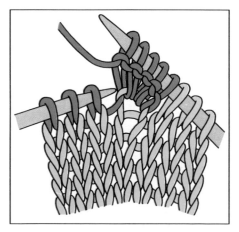

2. Turn the work so that the wrong side is facing and purl the five bobble stitches.

3. Turn the work so that the right side is facing, slip two of the bobble stitches onto the right-hand needle, knit the next three bobble stitches together. Pass the two slipped stitches over the stitch resulting from the knit three together.

4. One stitch remains and you can continue to work the remainder of the row as required. Any small gap in the fabric when you continue knitting is hidden by the bobble.

Cables with Lace

By combining lace stitches with cables some very striking designs can be produced. Holes are made by wrapping the yarn over the needle to form a stitch. These increases are combined with decreases so that the total number of stitches in a row usually remains the same.

Yarn Forward to Make a Stitch (yf)

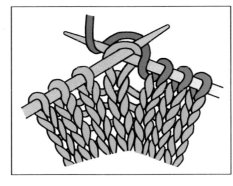

Between two knit stitches: bring the yarn forward as if to purl a stitch, but then knit the next stitch taking the yarn over the top of the needle to do so.

Yarn Forward and Round Needle (yfrn)

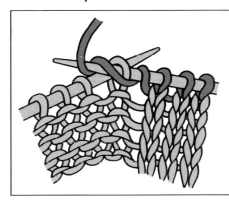

Between a knit and a purl stitch: bring the yarn forward as if to purl, then over the needle to the back, then between the needles to the front again before purling the next stitch.

Yarn Forward Twice to Make 2 Stitches ([yf] twice)

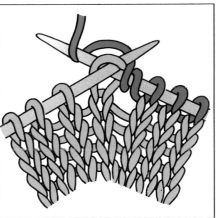

Bring the yarn forward to the front, over the needle and round to the front again, then over the needle to knit the next stitch.

Yarn Over Needle To Make a Stitch (yon)

Between a purl and a knit stitch: instead of taking the yarn back between the needles ready to knit the next stitch, take it over

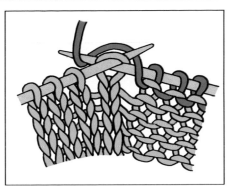

the top of the right-hand needle and knit the next stitch.

Yarn Round Needle (yrn)

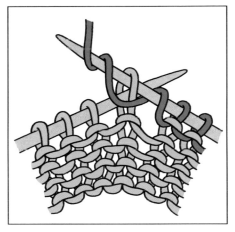

Between two purl stitches: take the yarn over the top of the needle, then between the needles to the front again before purling the next stitch.

VI.1

Multiple of 22 sts + 13.

1st row (right side): P2, *k9, p2; rep from * to end.

2nd and every alt row: K2, *p9, k2; rep from * to end.

3rd row: P2, k9, p2, *C4F, k1, C4B, p2, k9, p2; rep from * to end.

5th row: As 1st row.

7th row: P2, k9, p2, *C4B, k1, C4F, p2, k9,

p2; rep from * to end.

9th row: As 1st row.

11th row: P2, C4F, k1, C4B, p2, *k9, p2, C4F, k1, C4B, p2; rep from * to end.

13th row: As 1st row.

15th row: P2, C4B, k1, C4F, p2, *k9, p2, C4B, k1, C4F, p2; rep from * to end.

16th row: As 2nd row.

Rep these 16 rows.

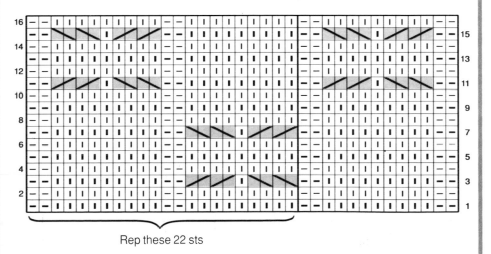

Rep these 22 sts

VI. Cable Patterns

VI.2

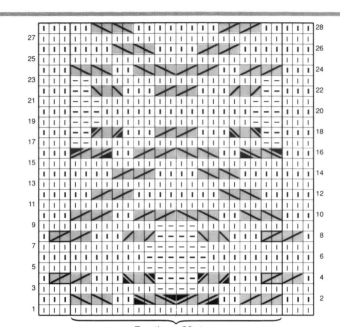

Rep these 20 sts

Multiple of 20 sts + 6.

1st row (wrong side): Purl.

2nd row: K3, *C4B, k2, T4B, T4F, k2, C4F; rep from * to last 3 sts, k3.

3rd row: P11, k4, *p16, k4; rep from * to last 11 sts, p11.

4th row: K1, C4B, *k3, T3B, p4, T3F, k3, C4B; rep from * to last st, k1.

5th row: P10, k6, *p14, k6; rep from * to last 10 sts, p10.

6th row: K10, p6, *k14, p6; rep from * to last 10 sts, k10.

7th row: As 5th row.

8th row: K1, C4B, *k3, C3F, p4, C3B, k3, C4B; rep from * to last st, k1.

9th row: As 3rd row.

10th row: K3, *C4F, k2, C4F, C4B, k2, C4B; rep from * to last 3 sts, k3.

11th row: Purl.

12th row: K5, *C4F, k8, C4B, k4; rep from * to last st, k1.

13th row: Purl.

14th row: K7, C4F, k4, C4B, *k8, C4F, k4, C4B; rep from * to last 7 sts, k7.

15th row: Purl.

16th row: K3, *T4F, k2, C4F, C4B, k2, T4B; rep from * to last 3 sts, k3.

17th row: P3, k2, p16, *k4, p16; rep from * to last 5 sts, k2, p3.

18th row: K3, p2, T3F, k3, C4B, k3, T3B, *p4, T3F, k3, C4B, k3, T3B; rep from * to last 5 sts, p2, k3.

19th row: P3, k3, p14, *k6, p14; rep from

* to last 6 sts, k3, p3.

20th row: K3, p3, k14, *p6, k14; rep from * to last 6 sts, p3, k3.

21st row: As 19th row.

22nd row: K3, p2, C3B, k3, C4B, k3, C3F, *p4, C3B, k3, C4B, k3, C3F; rep from * to last 5 sts, p2, k3.

23rd row: As 17th row.

24th row: K3, *C4B, k2, C4B, C4F, k2, C4F; rep from * to last 3 sts, k3.

25th row: Purl.

26th row: K7, C4B, k4, C4F, *k8, C4B, k4, C4F; rep from * to last 7 sts, k7.

27th row: Purl.

28th row: K5, *C4B, k8, C4F, k4; rep from * to last st, k1.

Rep these 28 rows.

VI.3

Rep these 28 sts

Multiple of 28 sts + 2.

1st row (right side): [K2, p4] twice, k6, p4, *[k2, p4] 3 times, k6, p4; rep from * to last 8 sts, k2, p4, k2.

2nd row: [P2, k4] twice, p6, k4, *[p2, k4] 3 times, p6, k4; rep from * to last 8 sts, p2, k4, p2.

3rd row: K2, *[p2, T4B] twice, k2, [T4F, p2] twice, k2; rep from * to end.

4th row: P2, k2, p2, k4, p2, *[k2, p2] twice, k4, p2; rep from * to last 4 sts, k2, p2.

5th row: K2, *[T4B, p2] twice, k2, [p2, T4F] twice, k2; rep from * to end.

6th row: P4, k4, [p2, k4] 3 times, *p6, k4, [p2, k4] 3 times; rep from * to last 4 sts, p4.

7th row: K4, p4, [k2, p4] 3 times, *k6, p4, [k2, p4] 3 times; rep from * to last 4 sts, k4.

Rep the last 2 rows once more, then 6th row again.

11th row: K2, *[T4F, p2] twice, k2, [p2, T4B] twice, k2; rep from * to end.

12th row: As 4th row.

13th row: K2, *[p2, T4F] twice, k2, [T4B, p2] twice, k2; rep from * to end.

14th row: As 2nd row.

15th and 16th rows: As 1st and 2nd rows.

Rep these 16 rows.

 = C3B, = C3F, = C4B, = C4F, =T3B, =T3F, =T4B, =T4F.

VI.4

Multiple of 16 sts + 6.

1st row (wrong side): K7, p8, *k8, p8; rep from * to last 7 sts, k7.

2nd row: P7, C4B, C4F, *p8, C4B, C4F; rep from * to last 7 sts, p7.

3rd row: As 1st row.

4th row: P6, *T3B, k4, T3F, p6; rep from * to end.

5th row: K6, *p2, k1, p4, k1, p2, k6; rep from * to end.

6th row: P5, *T3B, p1, k4, p1, T3F, p4; rep from * to last st, p1.

7th row: K5, *p2, k2, p4, k2, p2, k4; rep from * to last st, k1.

8th row: P4, *T3B, p2, k4, p2, T3F, p2; rep from * to last 2 sts, p2.

9th row: K4, *p2, k10, p2, k2; rep from * to last 2 sts, k2.

10th row: P3, *T3B, p3, k4, p3, T3F; rep from * to last 3 sts, p3.

11th row: K1, p4, *k12, p4; rep from * to last st, k1.

12th row: P1, C4F, *p4, k4, p4, C4F; rep from * to last st, p1.

13th row: K3, p2, k12, *p4, k12; rep from * to last 5 sts, p2, k3.

14th row: P3, *T3F, p3, k4, p3, T3B; rep from * to last 3 sts, p3.

15th row: As 9th row.

16th row: P4, *T3F, p2, k4, p2, T3B, p2; rep from * to last 2 sts, p2.

17th row: As 7th row.

18th row: P5, *T3F, p1, k4, p1, T3B, p4; rep from * to last st, p1.

19th row: As 5th row.

20th row: P6, *T3F, k4, T3B, p6; rep from * to end.

Rep these 20 rows.

VI.5

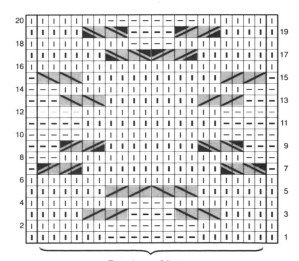

Multiple of 20 sts + 2.

1st row (right side): K7, p8, *k12, p8; rep from * to last 7 sts, k7.

2nd row: P7, k8, *p12, k8; rep from * to last 7 sts, p7.

3rd row: K5, C4F, p4, C4B, *k8, C4F, p4, C4B; rep from * to last 5 sts, k5.

4th row: P9, k4, *p16, k4; rep from * to last 9 sts, p9.

5th row: K7, C4F, C4B, *k12, C4F, C4B; rep from * to last 7 sts, k7.

6th row: Purl.

7th row: P1, *T4F, k12, T4B; rep from * to last st, p1.

8th row: K3, p16, *k4, p16; rep from * to last 3 sts, k3.

9th row: P3, T4F, k8, T4B, *p4, T4F, k8, T4B; rep from * to last 3 sts, p3.

10th row: K5, p12, *k8, p12; rep from * to last 5 sts, k5.

11th row: P5, k12, *p8, k12; rep from * to last 5 sts, p5.

12th row: As 10th row.

13th row: P3, C4B, k8, C4F, *p4, C4B, k8, C4F; rep from * to last 3 sts, p3.

14th row: As 8th row.

15th row: P1, *C4B, k12, C4F; rep from * to last st, p1.

16th row: Purl.

17th row: K7, T4B, T4F, *k12, T4B, T4F; rep from * to last 7 sts, k7.

18th row: As 4th row.

19th row: K5, T4B, p4, T4F, *k8, T4B, p4, T4F; rep from * to last 5 sts, k5.

20th row: As 2nd row.

Rep these 20 rows.

Rep these 16 sts

Rep these 20 sts

VI. Cable Patterns

VI.6

Multiple of 26 sts + 18.

Special Abbreviations

C5B (Cross 5 Back) = slip next 3 sts onto cable needle and hold at back of work, knit next 2 sts from left-hand needle, then knit sts from cable needle.

C5F (Cross 5 Front) = slip next 2 sts onto cable needle and hold at front of work, knit next 3 sts from left-hand needle, then knit sts from cable needle.

1st row (wrong side): K1, p5, k6, p5, *k3, p4, k3, p5, k6, p5; rep from * to last st, k1.

2nd row: P1, k3, T3F, p4, T3B, k3, *p2, T3B, T3F, p2, k3, T3F, p4, T3B, k3; rep from * to last st, p1.

3rd row: K1, p3, k1, p2, k4, p2, k1, p3, *k2, [p2, k2] twice, p3, k1, p2, k4, p2, k1, p3; rep from * to last st, k1.

4th row: P1, k3, p1, T3F, p2, T3B, p1, k3, *p1, T3B, p2, T3F, p1, k3, p1, T3F, p2, T3B, p1, k3; rep from * to last st, p1.

5th row: K1, p3, k2, [p2, k2] twice, p3, *k1, p2, k4, p2, k1, p3, k2, [p2, k2] twice, p3; rep from * to last st, k1.

6th row: P1, k3, p2, T3F, T3B, p2, k3, *T3B, p4, T3F, k3, p2, T3F, T3B, p2, k3; rep from * to last st, p1.

7th row: K1, p3, k3, p4, k3, *p5, k6, p5, k3, p4, k3; rep from * to last 4 sts, p3, k1.

8th row: P1, k3, p3, C4B, p3, *C5F, p6, C5B, p3, C4B, p3; rep from * to last 4 sts, k3, p1.

9th row: As 7th row.

10th row: P1, k3, p2, T3B, T3F, p2, k3, *T3F, p4, T3B, k3, p2, T3B, T3F, p2, k3; rep from * to last st, p1.

11th row: As 5th row.

12th row: P1, k3, p1, T3B, p2, T3F, p1, k3, *p1, T3F, p2, T3B, p1, k3, p1, T3B, p2, T3F, p1, k3; rep from * to last st, p1.

13th row: As 3rd row.

14th row: P1, k3, T3B, p4, T3F, k3, *p2, T3F, T3B, p2, k3, T3B, p4, T3F, k3; rep from * to last st, p1.

15th row: As 1st row.

16th row: P1, C5F, p6, C5B, *p3, C4B, p3, C5F, p6, C5B; rep from * to last st, p1.
Rep these 16 rows.

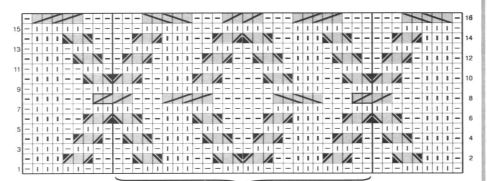

Rep these 26 sts

VI.7

Multiple of 20 sts + 12.

Special Abbreviations

T4LX (Twist 4 Left X) = slip next 2 sts onto cable needle and hold at front of work, purl next 2 sts from left-hand needle, then yon, sl 1, k1, psso from cable needle.

T4RX (Twist 4 Right X) = slip next 2 sts onto cable needle and hold at back of work, k2tog from left-hand needle, then yfrn and purl sts from cable needle.

1st row (right side): P2, k1, p6, k1, p2, *k2, p4, k2, p2, k1, p6, k1, p2; rep from * to end.

2nd and 4th rows: K2, *p2, k4, p2, k2; rep from * to end.

3rd row: P2, *k2, p4, k2, p2; rep from * to end.

5th row: P2, k2, p4, k2, p2, *T4LX, T4RX, p2, k2, p4, k2, p2; rep from * to end.

6th row: K2, p2, k4, p2, *k12, p2, k4, p2; rep from * to last 2 sts, k2.

7th row: P2, k2, p4, k2, p2, *k1, p6, k1, p2, k2, p4, k2, p2; rep from * to end.

8th and 10th rows: As 2nd row.

9th row: As 3rd row.

11th row: P2, T4LX, T4RX, p2, *k2, p4, k2, p2, T4LX, T4RX, p2; rep from * to end.

12th row: K12, *p2, k4, p2, k12; rep from * to end.

Rep these 12 rows.

Rep these 20 sts

N N = C3F, = C4B, = C4F, = C6B, = C6F.

VI.8

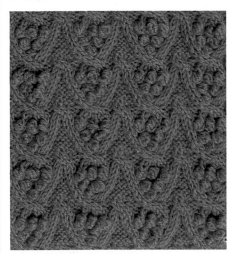

Multiple of 13 sts + 15.

Special Abbreviation

● **MB (Make Bobble)** = work [k1, p1, k1, p1, k1, p1, k1] all into next st, then pass 2nd, 3rd, 4th, 5th, 6th and 7th sts over first st.

1st row (wrong side): P3, k2, p2, k1, p2, k2, *p4, k2, p2, k1, p2, k2; rep from * to last 3 sts, p3.

2nd row: K3, p2, T5L, p2, *C4F, p2, T5L, p2; rep from * to last 3 sts, k3.

3rd row: K5, p2, k1, p2, *k8, p2, k1, p2; rep from * to last 5 sts, k5.

4th row: P4, T3B, MB, T3F, *p6, T3B, MB, T3F; rep from * to last 4 sts, p4.

5th row: K4, p2, k3, p2, *k6, p2, k3, p2; rep from * to last 4 sts, k4.

6th row: P3, T3B, MB, p1, MB, T3F, *p4, T3B, MB, p1, MB, T3F; rep from * to last 3 sts, p3.

7th row: K3, p2, k5, p2, *k4, p2, k5, p2; rep from * to last 3 sts, k3.

8th row: P2, *T3B, MB, [p1, MB] twice, T3F, p2; rep from * to end.

9th row: K2, *p2, [k1, p2] 3 times, k2; rep from * to end.

10th row: K1, *T3B, p1, [k2, p1] twice, T3F; rep from * to last st, k1.

Rep these 10 rows.

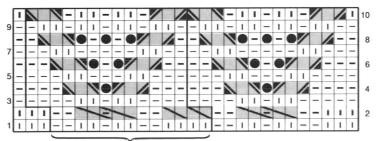

Rep these 13 sts

VI.9

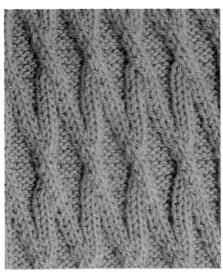

Multiple of 8 sts + 4.

1st row (wrong side): K1, p2, *k6, p2; rep from * to last st, k1.

2nd row: P1, *C3F, p5; rep from * to last 3 sts, k2, p1.

3rd row: K1, p2, *k5, p3; rep from * to last st, k1.

4th row: P1, *k1, C3F, p4; rep from * to last 3 sts, k2, p1.

5th row: K1, p2, *k4, p4; rep from * to last st, k1.

6th row: P1, k2, *T3F, p3, k2; rep from * to last st, p1.

7th row: K1, p2, *k3, p2, k1, p2; rep from * to last st, k1.

8th row: P1, k2, p1, *T3F, p2, k2, p1; rep from * to end.

9th row: K1, p2, *k2, p2; rep from * to last st, k1.

10th row: P1, k2, *p2, T3F, p1, k2; rep from * to last st, p1.

11th row: [K1, p2] twice, k3, p2, *k1, p2, k3, p2; rep from * to last st, k1.

12th row: P1, k2, *p3, T3F, k2; rep from * to last st, p1.

13th row: K1, *p4, k4; rep from * to last 3 sts, p2, k1.

14th row: P1, k2, *p4, T3F, k1; rep from * to last st, p1.

15th row: K1, *p3, k5; rep from * to last 3 sts, p2, k1.

16th row: P1, k2, *p5, T3F; rep from * to last st, p1.

Rep these 16 rows.

VI.10

Multiple of 14 sts + 2.

1st row (right side): P2, k1, p2, [k2, p2] twice, *[k1, p2] twice, [k2, p2] twice; rep from * to last 3 sts, k1, p2.

2nd row: K2, p1, k2, [p2, k2] twice, *[p1, k2] twice, [p2, k2] twice; rep from * to last 3 sts, p1, k2.

Rep the last 2 rows once more.

5th row: P2, *k12, p2; rep from * to end.

6th row: K2, *p12, k2; rep from * to end.

7th row: P2, *C6B, C6F, p2; rep from * to end.

8th row: As 6th row.

9th and 10th rows: As 1st and 2nd rows.

Rep these 10 rows.

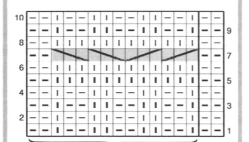

Rep these 14 sts

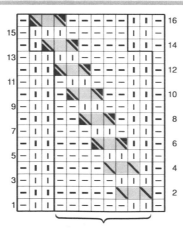

Rep these 8 sts

=T3B. =T3F. =T5L.

VI. Cable Patterns

VI.11

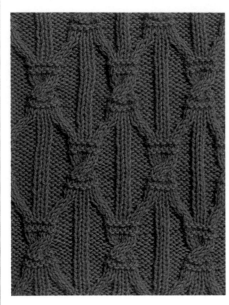

Multiple of 16 sts + 8.

1st row (right side): P1, k6, *p4, k2, p4, k6; rep from * to last st, p1.

2nd row: K11, p2, *k14, p2; rep from * to last 11 sts, k11.

Rep the last 2 rows once more, then 1st row again.

6th row: K1, p6, *k4, p2, k4, p6; rep from * to last st, k1.

7th row: P3, k2, *T4F, p2, k2, p2, T4B, k2; rep from * to last 3 sts, p3.

8th row: K3, p2, *k2, p2; rep from * to last 3 sts, k3.

9th row: P3, k2, *p2, T4F, k2, T4B, p2, k2; rep from * to last 3 sts, p3.

10th row: K3, p2, *k4, p6, k4, p2; rep from * to last 3 sts, k3.

11th row: P3, k2, *p4, k6, p4, k2; rep from * to last 3 sts, p3.

12th row: K3, p2, *k14, p2; rep from * to last 3 sts, k3.

Rep the last 2 rows once more, then 11th row again.

16th row: As 10th row.

17th row: P3, k2, *p4, C6B, p4, k2; rep from * to last 3 sts, p3.

18th row: As 10th row.

19th, 20th, 21st, 22nd and 23rd rows: Rep 11th and 12th rows twice more, then 11th row again.

24th row: As 10th row.

25th row: P3, k2, *p2, T4B, k2, T4F, p2, k2; rep from * to last 3 sts, p3.

26th row: As 8th row.

27th row: P3, k2, *T4B, p2, k2, p2, T4F, k2; rep from * to last 3 sts, p3.

28th row: As 6th row.

29th, 30th, 31st, 32nd and 33rd rows: Rep 1st and 2nd rows twice more, then 1st row again.

34th row: As 6th row.

35th row: P1, C6B, *p4, k2, p4, C6B; rep from * to last st, p1.

36th row: As 6th row.

Rep these 36 rows.

VI.12

Multiple of 15 sts + 5.

1st row (right side): Knit.

2nd and every alt row: K2, p1, *k4, p6, k4, p1; rep from * to last 2 sts, k2.

3rd row: Knit.

5th row: K7, C6B, *k9, C6B; rep from * to last 7 sts, k7.

7th row: Knit.

9th row: As 5th row.

11th row: Knit.

13th row: As 5th row.

15th, 17th, 19th, 21st and 23rd rows: Knit.

24th row: As 2nd row.

Rep these 24 rows.

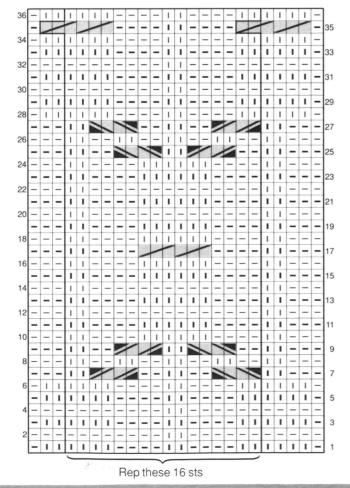

Rep these 16 sts

Rep these 15 sts

⌐⌐ =T2F, ⌐⌐ =T2B, ◥◣ =T4L, ◸◹ =T4R, ◥◣ =T4F.

VI.13

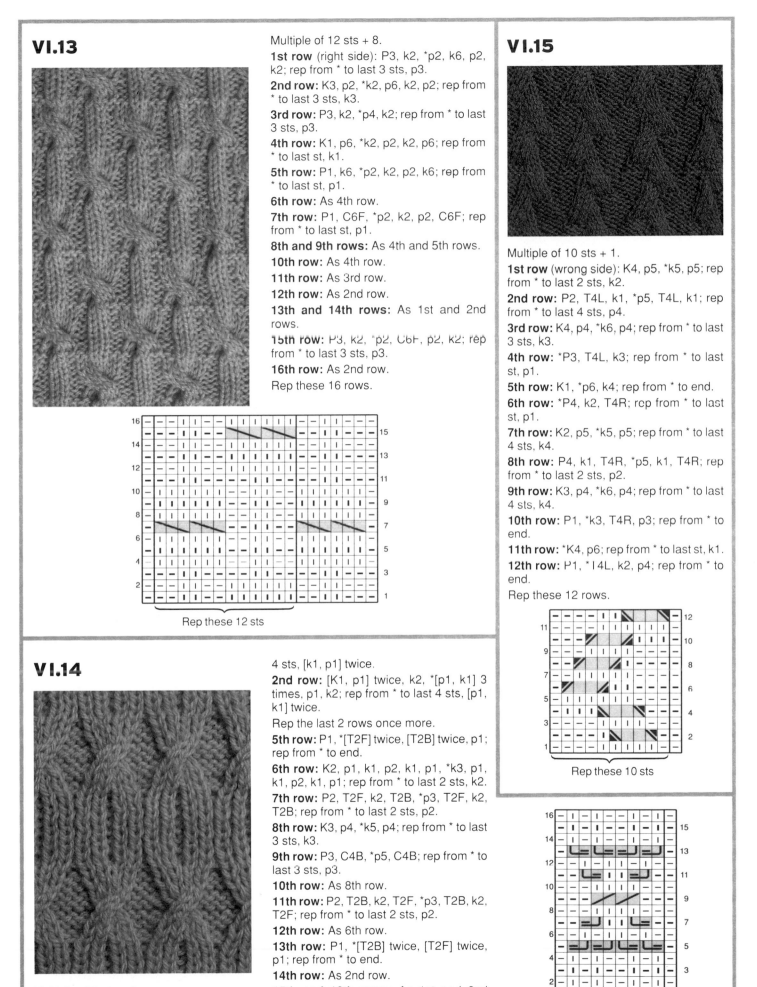

Multiple of 12 sts + 8.

1st row (right side): P3, k2, *p2, k6, p2, k2; rep from * to last 3 sts, p3.

2nd row: K3, p2, *k2, p6, k2, p2; rep from * to last 3 sts, k3.

3rd row: P3, k2, *p4, k2; rep from * to last 3 sts, p3.

4th row: K1, p6, *k2, p2, k2, p6; rep from * to last st, k1.

5th row: P1, k6, *p2, k2, p2, k6; rep from * to last st, p1.

6th row: As 4th row.

7th row: P1, C6F, *p2, k2, p2, C6F; rep from * to last st, p1.

8th and 9th rows: As 4th and 5th rows.

10th row: As 4th row.

11th row: As 3rd row.

12th row: As 2nd row.

13th and 14th rows: As 1st and 2nd rows.

15th row: P3, k2, *p2, C6F, p2, k2; rep from * to last 3 sts, p3.

16th row: As 2nd row.

Rep these 16 rows.

Rep these 12 sts

VI.14

Multiple of 9 sts + 1.

1st row (right side): [P1, k1] twice, p2, *[k1, p1] 3 times, k1, p2; rep from * to last 4 sts, [k1, p1] twice.

2nd row: [K1, p1] twice, k2, *[p1, k1] 3 times, p1, k2; rep from * to last 4 sts, [p1, k1] twice.

Rep the last 2 rows once more.

5th row: P1, *[T2F] twice, [T2B] twice, p1; rep from * to end.

6th row: K2, p1, k1, p2, k1, p1, *k3, p1, k1, p2, k1, p1; rep from * to last 2 sts, k2.

7th row: P2, T2F, k2, T2B, *p3, T2F, k2, T2B; rep from * to last 2 sts, p2.

8th row: K3, p4, *k5, p4; rep from * to last 3 sts, k3.

9th row: P3, C4B, *p5, C4B; rep from * to last 3 sts, p3.

10th row: As 8th row.

11th row: P2, T2B, k2, T2F, *p3, T2B, k2, T2F; rep from * to last 2 sts, p2.

12th row: As 6th row.

13th row: P1, *[T2B] twice, [T2F] twice, p1; rep from * to end.

14th row: As 2nd row.

15th and 16th rows: As 1st and 2nd rows.

Rep these 16 rows.

VI.15

Multiple of 10 sts + 1.

1st row (wrong side): K4, p5, *k5, p5; rep from * to last 2 sts, k2.

2nd row: P2, T4L, k1, *p5, T4L, k1; rep from * to last 4 sts, p4.

3rd row: K4, p4, *k6, p4; rep from * to last 3 sts, k3.

4th row: *P3, T4L, k3; rep from * to last st, p1.

5th row: K1, *p6, k4; rep from * to end.

6th row: *P4, k2, T4R; rep from * to last st, p1.

7th row: K2, p5, *k5, p5; rep from * to last 4 sts, k4.

8th row: P4, k1, T4R, *p5, k1, T4R; rep from * to last 2 sts, p2.

9th row: K3, p4, *k6, p4; rep from * to last 4 sts, k4.

10th row: P1, *k3, T4R, p3; rep from * to end.

11th row: *K4, p6; rep from * to last st, k1.

12th row: P1, *T4L, k2, p4; rep from * to end.

Rep these 12 rows.

Rep these 10 sts

=T4B, = C4B, = C6B, = C6F.

69

V1. Cable Patterns

VI.16

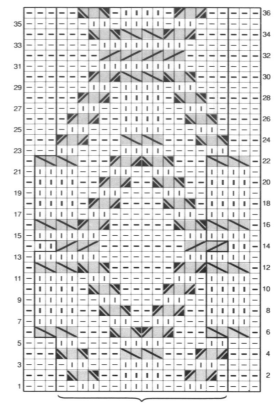

Rep these 16 sts

Multiple of 16 sts + 6.

1st row (wrong side): K5, *p2, k2, p4, k2, p2, k4; rep from * to last st, k1.

2nd row: P4, *T3B, p2, k4, p2, T3F, p2; rep from * to last 2 sts, p2.

3rd row: K4, *p2, k3, p4, k3, p2, k2; rep from * to last 2 sts, k2.

4th row: P3, *T3B, p3, C4F, p3, T3F; rep from * to last 3 sts, p3.

5th row: K3, p2, k4, *p4, k4; rep from * to last 5 sts, p2, k3.

6th row: P1, C4F, *p3, T3B, T3F, p3, C4F; rep from * to last st, p1.

7th row: K1, p4, *k3, p2, k2, p2, k3, p4; rep from * to last st, k1.

8th row: P1, k4, *p2, T3B, p2, T3F, p2, k4; rep from * to last st, p1.

9th row: K1, p4, *k2, p2, k4, p2, k2, p4; rep from * to last st, k1.

10th row: P1, k4, p1, *T3B, p4, T3F, p1, k4, p1; rep from * to end.

11th row: K1, p4, k1, *p2, k6, p2, k1, p4, k1; rep from * to end.

12th row: P1, C4F, *T3B, p6, T3F, C4F; rep from * to last st, p1.

13th row: K1, p6, k8, *p8, k8; rep from * to last 7 sts, p6, k1.

14th row: P1, k2, C4B, p8, *[C4B] twice, p8; rep from * to last 7 sts, C4B, k2, p1.

15th row: As 13th row.

16th row: P1, C4F, *T3F, p6, T3B, C4F; rep from * to last st, p1.

17th row: As 11th row.

18th row: P1, k4, p1, *T3F, p4, T3B, p1, k4, p1; rep from * to end.

19th row: As 9th row.

20th row: P1, k4, *p2, T3F, p2, T3B, p2, k4; rep from * to last st, p1.

21st row: As 7th row.

22nd row: P1, C4F, *p3, T3F, T3B, p3, C4F; rep from * to last st, p1.

23rd row: As 5th row.

24th row: P3, *T3F, p3, C4F, p3, T3B; rep from * to last 3 sts, p3.

25th row: As 3rd row.

26th row: P4, *T3F, p2, k4, p2, T3B, p2; rep from * to last 2 sts, p2.

27th row: As 1st row.

28th row: P5, *T3F, p1, k4, p1, T3B, p4; rep from * to last st, p1.

29th row: K6, *p2, k1, p4, k1, p2, k6; rep from * to end.

30th row: P6, *T3F, C4F, T3B, p6; rep from * to end.

31st row: K7, p8, *k8, p8; rep from * to last 7 sts, k7.

32nd row: P7, [C4B] twice, *p8, [C4B] twice; rep from * to last 7 sts, p7.

33rd row: As 31st row.

34th row: P6, *T3B, C4F, T3F, p6; rep from * to end.

35th row: As 29th row.

36th row: P5, *T3B, p1, k4, p1, T3F, p4; rep from * to last st, p1.

Rep these 36 rows.

VI.17

Multiple of 16 sts + 8.

1st row (right side): P8, *k8, p8; rep from * to end.

2nd row: K8, *p8, k8; rep from * to end.

3rd row: P8, *C8F, p8; rep from * to end.

4th row: As 2nd row.

5th row: As 1st row.

6th row: Purl.

7th row: K8, *p8, k8; rep from * to end.

8th row: P8, *k8, p8; rep from * to end.

Rep the last 2 rows once more, then 7th row again.

12th row: Purl.

Rep these 12 rows.

Rep these 16 sts

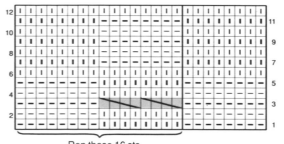

= C4B, = C4F, = C8F, = T3B, = T3F.

VI.18

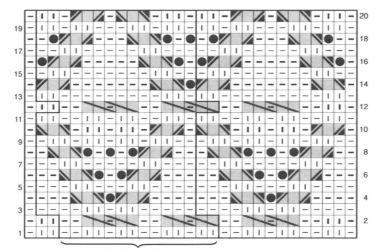

Rep these 14 sts

Multiple of 14 sts + 15.

Special Abbreviation

● **MB (Make Bubble)** = work [k1, p1, k1, p1, k1, p1, k1] all into next st, then pass 2nd, 3rd, 4th, 5th, 6th and 7th sts over first st.

1st row (wrong side): K1, *p2, k2, p2, k1; rep from * to end.

2nd row: P1, k2, p2, *T5L, p2; rep from * to last 3 sts, k2, p1.

3rd row: K5, p2, k1, p2, *k9, p2, k1, p2; rep from * to last 5 sts, k5.

4th row: P4, T3B, MB, T3F, *p7, T3B, MB, T3F; rep from * to last 4 sts, p4.

5th row: K4, p2, k3, p2, *k7, p2, k3, p2; rep from * to last 4 sts, k4.

6th row: P3, T3B, MB, p1, MB, T3F, *p5, T3B, MB, p1, MB, T3F; rep from * to last 3 sts, p3.

7th row: K3, p2, *k5, p2; rep from * to last 3 sts, k3.

8th row: P2, T3B, MB, [p1, MB] twice, T3F, *p3, T3B, MB, [p1, MB] twice, T3F; rep from * to last 2 sts, p2.

9th row: K2, p2, [k1, p2] 3 times, *k3, p2, [k1, p2] 3 times; rep from * to last 2 sts, k2.

10th row: P1, *T3B, p1, [k2, p1] twice, T3F, p1; rep from * to end.

11th and 12th rows: As 1st and 2nd rows.

13th row: K1, p2, k9, *p2, k1, p2, k9; rep from * to last 3 sts, p2, k1.

14th row: P1, T3F, p7, T3B, *MB, T3F, p7, T3B; rep from * to last st, p1.

15th row: K2, p2, k7, *p2, k3, p2, k7; rep from * to last 4 sts, p2, k2.

16th row: P1, MB, T3F, p5, T3B, *MB, p1, MB, T3F, p5, T3B; rep from * to last 2 sts, MB, p1.

17th row: As 7th row.

18th row: P2, MB, T3F, p3, T3B, *MB, [p1, MB] twice, T3F, p3, T3B; rep from * to last 3 sts, MB, p2.

19th row: [K1, p2] twice, k3, p2, *[k1, p2] 3 times, k3, p2; rep from * to last 4 sts, k1, p2, k1.

20th row: P1, k2, p1, T3F, p1, T3B, p1, *[k2, p1] twice, T3F, p1, T3B, p1; rep from * to last 3 sts, k2, p1.

Rep these 20 rows.

VI.19

Multiple of 20 sts + 2.

1st row (right side): K2, p2, k4, *p2, k2, p2, k4; rep from * to last 4 sts, p2, k2.

2nd row: P2, k2, p4, *k2, p2, k2, p4; rep from * to last 4 sts, k2, p2.

3rd row: K2, *p2, C4F, p2, k2, p2, C4B, p2, k2; rep from * to end.

4th row: As 2nd row.

5th row: K2, p2, k2, C4F, k2, C4B, k2, *[p2, k2] twice, C4F, k2, C4B, k2; rep from * to last 4 sts, p2, k2.

6th row: P2, *k2, p14, k2, p2; rep from * to end.

7th row: K2, *p2, k4, T3F, T3B, k4, p2, k2; rep from * to end.

8th row: P2, *k2, p4, [k1, p4] twice, k2, p2; rep from * to end.

9th row: K2, *p2, k4, p1, T2F, T2B, p1, k4, p2, k2; rep from * to end.

10th, 12th and 14th rows: As 2nd row.

11th row: As 1st row.

13th row: K2, *p2, C4B, p2, k2, p2, C4F, p2, k2; rep from * to end.

15th row: K2, *C4B, k2, [p2, k2] twice, C4F, k2; rep from * to end.

16th row: P8, k2, p2, k2, *p14, k2, p2, k2; rep from * to last 8 sts, p8.

17th row: K1, *T3B, k4, p2, k2, p2, k4, T3F; rep from * to last st, k1.

18th row: P3, k1, p4, k2, p2, k2, p4, *[k1, p4] twice, k2, p2, k2, p4; rep from * to last 4 sts, k1, p3.

19th row: K1, *T2B, p1, k4, p2, k2, p2, k4, p1, T2F; rep from * to last st, k1.

20th row: As 2nd row.

Rep these 20 rows.

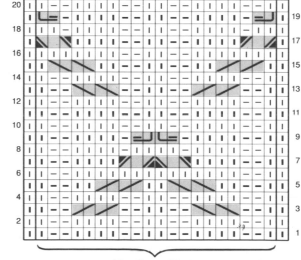

Rep these 20 sts

VI. Cable Patterns

VI.20

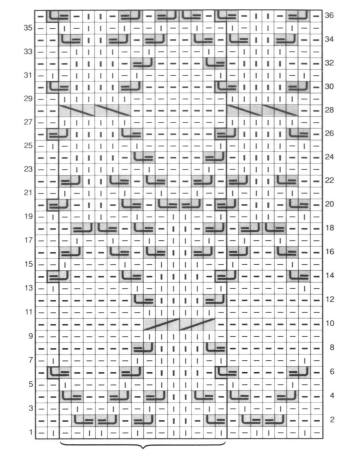

Rep these 14 sts

Multiple of 14 sts + 10.

1st row (wrong side): K1, p1, *k2, p2, k2, p1; rep from * to last st, k1.

2nd row: P3, T2B, *[T2F, p1] twice, k2, [p1, T2B] twice; rep from * to last 5 sts, T2F, p3.

3rd row: K3, p1, [k2, p1] twice, k1, p2, k1, p1, *[k2, p1] 3 times, k1, p2, k1, p1; rep from * to last 9 sts, [k2, p1] twice, k3.

4th row: P2, T2B, p2, T2F, *p1, T2F, k2, T2B, p1, T2B, p2, T2F; rep from * to last 2 sts, p2.

5th row: K2, p1, k4, p1, k2, *p4, k2, p1, k4, p1, k2; rep from * to end.

6th row: P1, T2B, p4, T2F, *p1, k4, p1, T2B, p4, T2F; rep from * to last st, p1.

7th row: K1, p1, k6, p1, k1, *p4, k1, p1, k6, p1, k1; rep from * to end.

8th row: P8, *T2F, k4, T2B, p6; rep from * to last 2 sts, p2.

9th row: K9, *p6, k8; rep from * to last st, k1.

10th row: P9, *C6B, p8; rep from * to last st, p1.

11th row: As 9th row.

12th row: P8, *T2B, k4, T2F, p6; rep from * to last 2 sts, p2.

13th row: As 7th row.

14th row: P1, T2F, p4, T2B, *p1, k4, p1, T2F, p4, T2B; rep from * to last st, p1.

15th row: As 5th row.

16th row: P2, T2F, p2, T2B, *p1, T2B, k2, T2F, p1, T2F, p2, T2B; rep from * to last 2 sts, p2.

17th row: As 3rd row.

18th row: P3, T2F, *[T2B, p1] twice, k2, [p1, T2F] twice; rep from * to last 5 sts, T2B, p3.

19th row: As 1st row.

20th row: P1, T2F, p1, k2, *[p1, T2B] twice, [T2F, p1] twice, k2; rep from * to last 4 sts, p1, T2B, p1.

21st row: K2, p1, k1, p2, k1, p1, *[k2, p1] 3 times, k1, p2, k1, p1; rep from * to last 2 sts, k2.

22nd row: P2, T2F, k2, T2B, *p1, T2B, p2, T2F, p1, T2F, k2, T2B; rep from * to last 2 sts, p2.

23rd row: K3, p4, *k2, p1, k4, p1, k2, p4; rep from * to last 3 sts, k3.

24th row: P3, k4, *p1, T2B, p4, T2F, p1, k4; rep from * to last 3 sts, p3.

25th row: K1, p1, k1, p4, k1, p1, *k6, p1, k1, p4, k1, p1; rep from * to last st, k1.

26th row: P1, T2F, k4, T2B, *p6, T2F, k4, T2B; rep from * to last st, p1.

27th row: K2, p6, *k8, p6; rep from * to last 2 sts, k2.

28th row: P2, C6F, *p8, C6F; rep from * to last 2 sts, p2.

29th row: As 27th row.

30th row: P1, T2B, k4, T2F, *p6, T2B, k4, T2F; rep from * to last st, p1.

31st row: As 25th row.

32nd row: P3, k4, *p1, T2F, p4, T2B, p1, k4; rep from * to last 3 sts, p3.

33rd row: As 23rd row.

34th row: P2, T2B, k2, T2F, *p1, T2F, p2, T2B, p1, T2B, k2, T2F; rep from * to last 2 sts, p2.

35th row: As 21st row.

36th row: P1, T2B, p1, k2, *[p1, T2F] twice, [T2B, p1] twice, k2; rep from * to last 4 sts, p1, T2F, p1.

Rep these 36 rows.

VI.21

Multiple of 12 sts + 2.

1st row (right side): Knit.

2nd and every alt row: Purl.

3rd row: K1, *C4B, k4, C4F; rep from * to last st, k1.

5th row: Knit.

7th row: K3, C4F, C4B, *k4, C4F, C4B; rep from * to last 3 sts, k3.

8th row: Purl.

Rep these 8 rows.

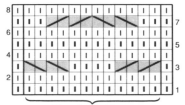

Rep these 12 sts

  = C4B, = C4F, = C6B, = C6F.

VI.22

Multiple of 28 sts + 2.

1st row (right side): P1, k3, p4, [k1, p2] twice, k2, [p2, k1] twice, p4, *k6, p4, [k1, p2] twice, k2, [p2, k1] twice, p4; rep from * to last 4 sts, k3, p1.

2nd row: K1, p3, k4, [p1, k2] twice, p2, [k2, p1] twice, k4, *p6, k4, [p1, k2] twice, p2, [k2, p1] twice, k4; rep from * to last 4 sts, p3, k1.

3rd row: P1, *T4L, p2, T2B, [p1, T2B] twice, T2F, [p1, T2F] twice, p2, T4R; rep from * to last st, p1.

4th row: K2, *p3, k2, [p1, k2] 6 times, p3, k2; rep from * to end.

5th row: P2, *T4L, T2B, [p1, T2B] twice, p2, T2F, [p1, T2F] twice, T4R, p2; rep from * to end.

6th row: K3, p4, [k2, p1] twice, k4, [p1, k2] twice, p4, *k4, p4, [k2, p1] twice, k4, [p1, k2] twice, p4; rep from * to last 3 sts, k3.

7th row: P3, T4L, [p1, T2B] twice, p4, [T2F, p1] twice, T4R, *p4, T4L, [p1, T2B] twice, p4, [T2F, p1] twice, T4R; rep from * to last 3 sts, p3.

8th row: K4, p3, k1, p1, k2, p1, k6, p1, k2, p1, k1, p3, *k6, p3, k1, p1, k2, p1, k6, p1, k2, p1, k1, p3; rep from * to last 4 sts, k4.

9th row: P4, T4L, k1, p1, T2B, p6, T2F, p1, k1, T4R, *p6, T4L, k1, p1, T2B, p6, T2F, p1, k1, T4R; rep from * to last 4 sts, p4.

10th row: K5, p4, k1, p1, k8, p1, k1, p4, *k8, p4, k1, p1, k8, p1, k1, p4; rep from * to last 5 sts, k5.

11th row: P5, T4L, T2B, p8, T2F, T4R, *p8, T4L, T2B, p8, T2F, T4R; rep from * to last 5 sts, p5.

12th row: K6, p4, *k10, p4; rep from * to last 6 sts, k6.

13th row: P6, T4L, p10, T4R, *p10, T4L, p10, T4R; rep from * to last 6 sts, p6.

14th row: K7, p3, k10, p3, *k12, p3, k10, p3; rep from * to last 7 sts, k7.

15th row: P7, T4L, p8, T4R, *p12, T4L, p8, T4R; rep from * to last 7 sts, p7.

16th row: [K8, p3] twice, *k14, p3, k8, p3; rep from * to last 8 sts, k8.

17th row: P8, T4L, p6, T4R, *p14, T4L, p6, T4R; rep from * to last 8 sts, p8.

18th row: K9, p3, k6, p3, *k16, p3, k6, p3; rep from * to last 9 sts, k9.

19th row: P9, T4L, p4, T4R, *p16, T4L, p4, T4R; rep from * to last 9 sts, p9.

20th row: K10, p3, k4, p3, *k18, p3, k4, p3; rep from * to last 10 sts, k10.

21st row: P10, T4L, p2, T4R, *p18, T4L, p2, T4R; rep from * to last 10 sts, p10.

22nd row: K11, p3, k2, p3, *k20, p3, k2, p3; rep from * to last 11 sts, k11.

23rd row: P11, T4L, T4R, *p20, T4L, T4R; rep from * to last 11 sts, p11.

24th row: K12, p6, *k22, p6; rep from * to last 12 sts, k12.

Rep these 24 rows.

VI.23

Multiple of 10 sts + 8.

1st row (right side): Knit.

2nd row: P7, *k4, p6; rep from * to last st, p1.

Rep the last 2 rows twice more.

7th row: K1, C6F, *k4, C6F; rep from * to last st, k1.

8th row: As 2nd row.

9th row: Knit.

Rep the last 2 rows twice more.

14th row: P2, k4, *p6, k4; rep from * to last 2 sts, p2.

15th row: Knit.

Rep the last 2 rows once more, then 14th row again.

19th row: K6, *C6B, k4; rep from * to last 2 sts, k2.

20th row: As 14th row.

21st row: Knit.

Rep the last 2 rows once more, then 14th row again.

Rep these 24 rows.

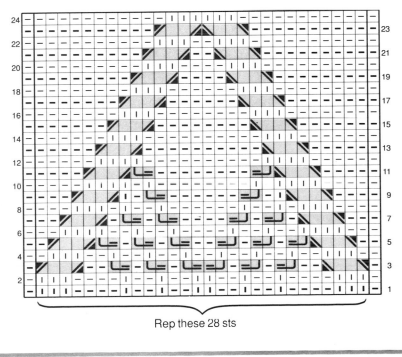

Rep these 28 sts

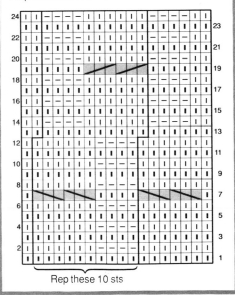

Rep these 10 sts

= T2B, = T2F, = T4L, = T4R.

VI. Cable Patterns

VI.24

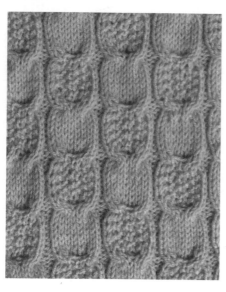

Multiple of 20 sts + 12.

1st row (right side): P2, k8, p2, *[k1, p1] 3 times, k2, p2, k8, p2; rep from * to end.

2nd row: K2, p8, k2, *[p1, k1] 3 times, p2, k2, p8, k2; rep from * to end.

Rep the last 2 rows 3 times more.

9th row: P2, *C4B, C4F, p2; rep from * to end.

10th row: K2, [p1, k1] 3 times, p2, k2, *p8, k2, [p1, k1] 3 times, p2, k2; rep from * to end.

11th row: P2, [k1, p1] 3 times, k2, p2, *k8, p2, [k1, p1] 3 times, k2, p2; rep from * to end.

Rep the last 2 rows 3 times more, then 10th row again.

19th row: As 9th row.

20th row: As 2nd row.

Rep these 20 rows.

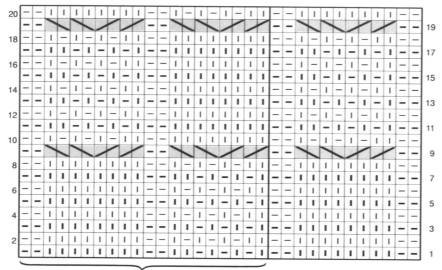

Rep these 20 sts

VI.25

Multiple of 24 sts + 2.

1st row (right side): P2, *k10, p2; rep from * to end.

2nd and every alt row: K2, *p10, k2; rep from * to end.

3rd row: As 1st row.

5th row: P2, *C6R, k4, p2, k4, C6L, p2; rep from * to end.

7th and 9th rows: As 1st row.

11th row: P2, *k4, C6R, p2, C6L, k4, p2; rep from * to end.

12th row: As 2nd row.

Rep these 12 rows.

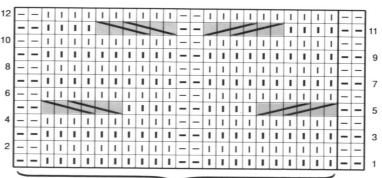

Rep these 24 sts

VI.26

Multiple of 14 sts + 2.

1st row (right side): K2, *p4, k4, p4, k2; rep from * to end.

2nd row: P2, *k4, p4, k4, p2; rep from * to end.

3rd row: K2, *p4, C4B, p4, k2; rep from * to end.

4th row: As 2nd row.

5th row: K2, *p3, T3B, T3F, p3, k2; rep from * to end.

6th row: P2, k3, p2, k2, p2, *[k3, p2] twice, k2, p2; rep from * to last 5 sts, k3, p2.

7th row: K2, *p2, T3B, p2, T3F, p2, k2; rep from * to end.

8th row: P2, k2, p2, k4, *[p2, k2] twice, p2, k4; rep from * to last 6 sts, p2, k2, p2.

9th row: K2, *p1, T3B, p4, T3F, p1, k2; rep from * to end.

10th row: [P2, k1] twice, p4, k1, *[p2, k1] 3 times, p4, k1; rep from * to last 5 sts, p2, k1, p2.

Rep these 10 rows.

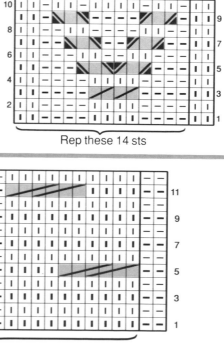

Rep these 14 sts

= C4B,   = C4F,   = C6L,   = C6R.

VI.27

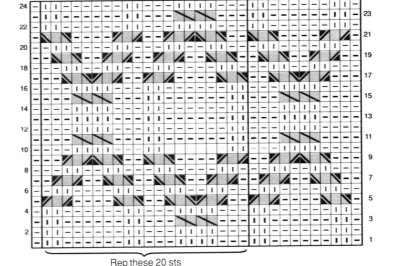

Rep these 20 sts

Multiple of 20 sts + 12.

1st row (right side): P1, k2, p6, k2, *p3, k4, p3, k2, p6, k2; rep from * to last st, p1.

2nd row: K1, p2, k6, p2, *k3, p4, k3, p2, k6, p2; rep from * to last st, k1.

3rd row: P1, k2, p6, k2, *p3, C4F, p3, k2, p6, k2; rep from * to last st, p1.

4th row: As 2nd row.

5th row: P1, T3F, p4, T3B, *p2, T3B, T3F, p2, T3F, p4, T3B; rep from * to last st, p1.

6th row: K2, p2, k4, p2, *k3, p2, k2, p2, k3, p2, k4, p2; rep from * to last 2 sts, k2.

7th row: P2, T3F, *[p2, T3B] twice, [p2, T3F] twice; rep from * to last 7 sts, p2, T3B, p2.

8th row: K3, p2, k2, p2, k3, *p2, k4, p2, k3, p2, k2, p2, k3; rep from * to end.

9th row: P3, T3F, T3B, *p2, T3B, p4, T3F, p2, T3F, T3B; rep from * to last 3 sts, p3.

10th, 12th, 14th and 16th rows: K4, p4, *k3, p2, k6, p2, k3, p4; rep from * to last 4 sts, k4.

11th row: P4, C4F, *p3, k2, p6, k2, p3, C4F; rep from * to last 4 sts, p4.

13th row: P4, k4, *p3, k2, p6, k2, p3, k4; rep from * to last 4 sts, p4.

15th row: As 11th row.

17th row: P3, T3B, T3F, *p2, T3F, p4, T3B, p2, T3B, T3F; rep from * to last 3 sts, p3.

18th row: As 8th row.

19th row: P2, T3B, p2, *[T3F, p2] twice, [T3B, p2] twice; rep from * to last 5 sts, T3F, p2.

20th row: As 6th row.

21st row: P1, T3B, p4, T3F, *p2, T3F, T3B, p2, T3B, p4, T3F; rep from * to last st, p1.

22nd and 23rd rows: As 2nd and 3rd rows.

24th row: As 2nd row.

Rep these 24 rows.

VI.28

Multiple of 20 sts + 10.

1st row (right side): Knit.

2nd row: K1, p2, k4, p2, k1, *p10, k1, p2, k4, p2, k1; rep from * to end.

3rd row: P1, T3F, p2, T3B, p1, *k10, p1, T3F, p2, T3B, p1; rep from * to end.

4th row: K2, [p2, k2] twice, *p10, k2, [p2, k2] twice; rep from * to end.

5th row: P2, T3F, T3B, p2, *k10, p2, T3F, T3B, p2; rep from * to end.

6th row: K3, p4, *k16, p4; rep from * to last 3 sts, k3.

7th row: P3, C4B, p3, *k10, p3, C4B, p3; rep from * to end.

8th row: As 6th row.

9th row: P2, T3B, T3F, p2, *k10, p2, T3B, T3F, p2; rep from * to end.

10th row: As 4th row.

11th row: P1, T3B, p2, T3F, p1, *k10, p1, T3B, p2, T3F, p1; rep from * to end.

12th row: As 2nd row.

13th row: Knit.

14th row: P10, *k1, p2, k4, p2, k1, p10; rep from * to end.

15th row: K10, *p1, T3F, p2, T3B, p1, k10; rep from * to end.

16th row: P10, *k2, [p2, k2] twice, p10; rep from * to end.

17th row: K10, *p2, T3F, T3B, p2, k10; rep from * to end.

18th row: K13, p4, *k16, p4; rep from * to last 13 sts, k13.

19th row: K10, *p3, C4B, p3, k10; rep from * to end.

20th row: As 18th row.

21st row: K10, *p2, T3B, T3F, p2, k10; rep from * to end.

22nd row: As 16th row.

23rd row: K10, *p1, T3B, p2, T3F, p1, k10; rep from * to end.

24th row: As 14th row.

Rep these 24 rows.

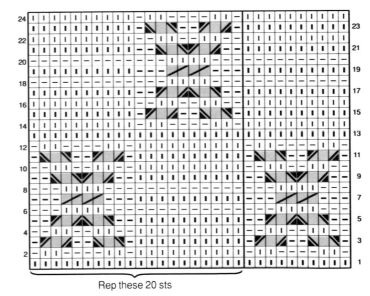

Rep these 20 sts

=T3B. =T3F.

VI. Cable Patterns

VI.29

Multiple of 24 sts + 13.

Special Abbreviation

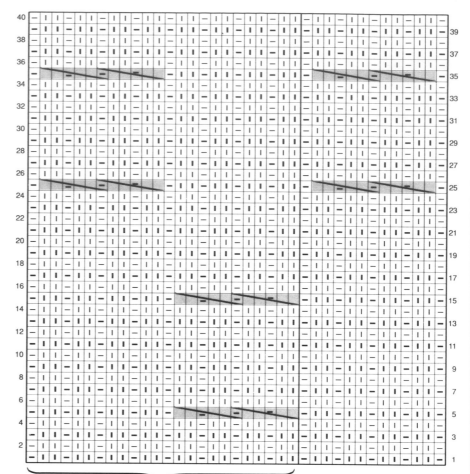

Rep these 24 sts

T11F Rib (Twist 11 Front Rib) = slip next 5 sts onto cable needle and hold at front of work, [k2, p1] twice from left-hand needle, then k2, p1, k2 from cable needle.

1st row (right side): P1, *k2, p1; rep from * to end.

2nd and every alt row: K1, *p2, k1; rep from * to end.

3rd row: As 1st row.

5th row: P1, [k2, p1] 4 times, *T11F Rib, [p1, k2] 4 times, p1; rep from * to end.

7th, 9th, 11th and 13th rows: As 1st row.

15th row: As 5th row.

17th, 19th, 21st and 23rd rows: As 1st row.

25th row: P1, T11F Rib, p1, *[k2, p1] 4 times, T11F Rib, p1; rep * to end.

27th, 29th, 31st and 33rd rows: As 1st row.

35th row: As 25th row.

37th and 39th rows: As 1st row.

40th row: As 2nd row.

Rep these 40 rows.

VI.30

Multiple of 16 sts + 10.

1st row (right side): P2, *k6, p2; rep from * to end.

2nd row: K2, *p6, k2; rep from * to end.

3rd row: P2, C6F, p2, *k6, p2, C6F, p2; rep from * to end.

4th row: As 2nd row.

5th and 6th rows: As 1st and 2nd rows.

Work 3 rows in reverse st st, starting purl.

10th row: As 2nd row.

11th and 12th rows: As 1st and 2nd rows.

13th row: P2, k6, p2, *C6F, p2, k6, p2; rep from * to end.

14th row: As 2nd row.

15th and 16th rows: As 1st and 2nd rows.

Work 3 rows in reverse st st, starting purl.

20th row: As 2nd row.

Rep these 20 rows.

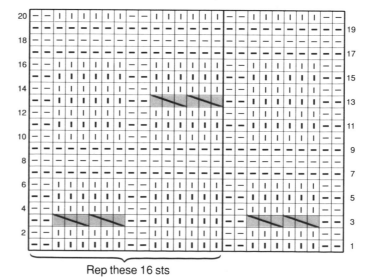

Rep these 16 sts

 = C4B, = C4F, = C6B, = C6F.

VI.31

Multiple of 24 sts + 15.

1st row (right side): K14, *p2, [k1, p2] 3 times, k13; rep from * to last st, k1.

2nd row: P14, *k2, [p1, k2] 3 times, p13; rep from * to last st, p1.

Rep the last 2 rows twice more.

7th row: [K1, C6B] twice, *p2, [k1, p2] 3 times, C6B, k1, C6B; rep from * to last st, k1.

8th row: As 2nd row.

Rep 1st and 2nd rows twice more.

13th row: K2, p2, [k1, p2] 3 times, *k13, p2, [k1, p2] 3 times; rep from * to last 2 sts, k2.

14th row: P2, k2, [p1, k2] 3 times, *p13, k2, [p1, k2] 3 times; rep from * to last 2 sts, p2.

Rep the last 2 rows twice more.

19th row: K2, p2, [k1, p2] 3 times, *C6B, k1, C6B, p2, [k1, p2] 3 times; rep from * to last 2 sts, k2.

20th row: As 14th row.

Rep 13th and 14th rows twice more.

Rep these 24 rows.

VI.32

Multiple of 8 sts + 6.

1st row (right side): K5, *p4, k4; rep from * to last st, k1.

2nd row: P5, *k4, p4; rep from * to last st, p1.

Rep the last 2 rows once more.

5th row: K1, C4F, *k4, C4F; rep from * to last st, k1.

6th row: K5, *p4, k4; rep from * to last st, k1.

7th row: P5, *k4, p4; rep from * to last st, p1.

Rep the last 2 rows once more, then 6th row again.

11th row: K5, *C4F, k4; rep from * to last st, k1.

12th row: As 2nd row.

Rep these 12 rows.

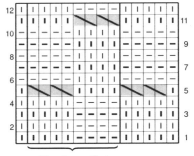

Rep these 8 sts

VI.33

Multiple of 16 sts + 2.

1st row (wrong side): P3, k2, p8, k2, *p4, k2, p8, k2; rep from * to last 3 sts, p3.

2nd row: K3, p2, C4B, C4F, p2, *k4, p2, C4B, C4F, p2; rep from * to last 3 sts, k3.

3rd row: As 1st row.

4th row: K3, p1, T3B, k4, T3F, p1, *k4, p1, T3B, k4, T3F, p1; rep from * to last 3 sts, k3.

5th row: P3, k1, p2, k1, *p4, k1, p2, k1; rep from * to last 3 sts, p3.

6th row: K3, T3B, p1, k4, p1, T3F, *k4, T3B, p1, k4, p1, T3F; rep from * to last 3 sts, k3.

7th row: P5, k2, p4, k2, *p8, k2, p4, k2; rep from * to last 5 sts, p5.

8th row: K1, *C4F, p2, k4, p2, C4B; rep from * to last st, k1.

9th row: As 7th row.

10th row: K3, T3F, p1, k4, p1, T3B, *k4, T3F, p1, k4, p1, T3B; rep from * to last 3 sts, k3.

11th row: As 5th row.

12th row: K3, p1, T3F, k4, T3B, p1, *k4, p1, T3F, k4, T3B, p1; rep from * to last 3 sts, k3.

Rep these 12 rows.

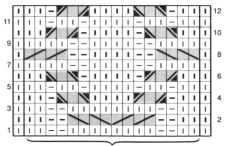

Rep these 16 sts

 =T3B, =T3F.

VI. Cable Patterns

VI.34

Multiple of 18 sts + 2.

1st row (wrong side): K6, p8, *k10, p8; rep from * to last 6 sts, k6.

2nd row: P6, T4B, T4F, *p10, T4B, T4F; rep from * to last 6 sts, p6.

3rd row: K6, p2, k4, p2, *k10, p2, k4, p2; rep from * to last 6 sts, k6.

4th row: P5, T3B, p4, T3F, *p8, T3B, p4, T3F; rep from * to last 5 sts, p5.

5th row: K5, p2, k6, p2, *k8, p2, k6, p2; rep from * to last 5 sts, k5.

6th row: P4, T3B, p6, T3F, *p6, T3B, p6, T3F; rep from * to last 4 sts, p4.

7th row: K4, p2, k8, p2, *k6, p2, k8, p2; rep from * to last 4 sts, k4.

8th row: P3, T3B, p8, T3F, *p4, T3B, p8, T3F; rep from * to last 3 sts, p3.

9th row: K3, p2, k10, p2, *k4, p2, k10, p2; rep from * to last 3 sts, k3.

10th row: P1, *T4B, p10, T4F; rep from * to last st, p1.

11th row: K1, p4, k10, *p8, k10; rep from * to last 5 sts, p4, k1.

12th row: P1, k2, T3F, p8, T3B, *k4, T3F, p8, T3B; rep from * to last 3 sts, k2, p1.

13th row: [K1, p2] twice, k8, p2, k1, *p4, k1, p2, k8, p2, k1; rep from * to last 3 sts, p2, k1.

14th row: P1, k2, p1, T3F, p6, T3B, p1, *k4, p1, T3F, p6, T3B, p1; rep from * to last 3 sts, k2, p1.

15th row: K1, p2, k2, p2, k6, p2, k2, *p4, k2, p2, k6, p2, k2; rep from * to last 3 sts, p2, k1.

16th row: P1, k2, p1, T3B, p6, T3F, p1, *k4, p1, T3B, p6, T3F, p1; rep from * to last 3 sts, k2, p1.

17th row: As 13th row.

18th row: P1, k2, T3B, p8, T3F, *k4, T3B, p8, T3F; rep from * to last 3 sts, k2, p1.

19th row: As 11th row.

20th row: P1, *T4F, p10, T4B; rep from * to last st, p1.

21st row: As 9th row.

22nd row: P3, T3F, p8, T3B, *p4, T3F, p8, T3B; rep from * to last 3 sts, p3.

23rd row: As 7th row.

24th row: P4, T3F, p6, T3B, *p6, T3F, p6, T3B; rep from * to last 4 sts, p4.

25th row: As 5th row.

26th row: P5, T3F, p4, T3B, *p8, T3F, p4, T3B; rep from * to last 5 sts, p5.

27th row: As 3rd row.

28th row: P6, T4F, T4B, *p10, T4F, T4B; rep from * to last 6 sts, p6.

29th row: As 1st row.

30th row: P5, T3B, k4, T3F, *p8, T3B, k4, T3F; rep from * to last 5 sts, p5.

31st row: K5, p2, k1, p4, k1, p2, *k8, p2, k1, p4, k1, p2; rep from * to last 5 sts, k5.

32nd row: P4, T3B, p1, k4, p1, T3F, *p6, T3B, p1, k4, p1, T3F; rep from * to last 4 sts, p4.

33rd row: K4, p2, k2, p4, k2, p2, *k6, p2, k2, p4, k2, p2; rep from * to last 4 sts, k4.

34th row: P4, T3F, p1, k4, p1, T3B, *p6, T3F, p1, k4, p1, T3B; rep from * to last 4 sts, p4.

35th row: As 31st row.

36th row: P5, T3F, k4, T3B, *p8, T3F, k4, T3B; rep from * to last 5 sts, p5.

Rep these 36 rows.

VI.35

Multiple of 17 sts + 3.

1st row (right side): K3, *p4, k6, p4, k3; rep from * to end.

2nd row: K7, p6, *k11, p6; rep from * to last 7 sts, k7.

Rep the last 2 rows twice more.

7th row: K3, *p1, T5B, k2, T5F, p1, k3; rep from * to end.

8th row: K4, p2, [k3, p2] twice, *k5, p2, [k3, p2] twice; rep from * to last 4 sts, k4.

Rep these 8 rows.

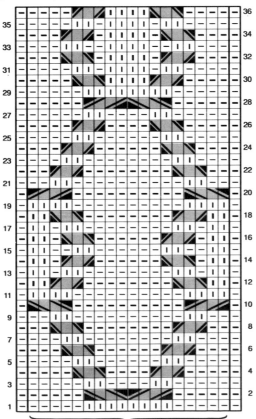

Rep these 18 sts

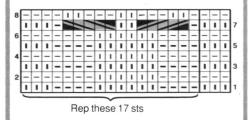

Rep these 17 sts

=T3B, =T3F, =T4B, =T4F, =T5B, =T5L.

VI.36

Multiple of 18 sts + 14.

1st row (right side): K4, p6, *k12, p6; rep from * to last 4 sts, k4.

2nd row: P4, k6, *p12, k6; rep from * to last 4 sts, p4.

Rep the last 2 rows 5 times more.

13th row: K4, p6, *C6F, C6B, p6; rep from * to last 4 sts, k4.

14th row: As 2nd row.

15th and 16th rows: As 1st and 2nd rows.

17th row: K4, p6, *k3, C6F, k3, p6; rep from * to last 4 sts, k4.

18th row: As 2nd row.

19th and 20th rows: As 1st and 2nd rows.

21st row: K4, p6, *T6B, T6F, p6; rep from * to last 4 sts, k4.

22nd row: K1, p12, *k6, p12; rep from * to last st, k1.

23rd row: P1, k12, *p6, k12; rep from * to last st, p1.

Rep the last 2 rows 5 times more, then 22nd row again.

35th row: P1, C6F, C6B, *p6, C6F, C6B; rep from * to last st, p1.

36th and 37th rows: As 22nd and 23rd rows.

38th row: As 22nd row.

39th row: P1, k3, C6F, k3, *p6, k3, C6F, k3; rep from * to last st, p1.

40th and 41st rows: As 22nd and 23rd rows.

42nd row: As 22nd row.

43rd row: P1, T6B, T6F, *p6, T6B, T6F; rep from * to last st, p1.

44th row: As 2nd row.

Rep these 44 rows.

VI.37

Multiple of 8 sts + 10.

1st row (right side): P1, k2, p4, *k4, p4; rep from * to last 3 sts, k2, p1.

2nd row: K1, p2, k4, *p4, k4; rep from * to last 3 sts, p2, k1.

3rd row: P1, k2, p4, *C4B, p4; rep from * to last 3 sts, k2, p1.

4th row: As 2nd row.

5th row: P1, *T4F, T4B; rep from * to last st, p1.

6th row: K3, p4, *k4, p4; rep from * to last 3 sts, k3.

7th row: P3, C4B, *p4, C4B; rep from * to last 3 sts, p3.

8th row: As 6th row.

9th row: P3, k4, *p4, k4; rep from * to last 3 sts, p3.

Rep the last 4 rows twice more, then 6th, 7th and 8th rows again.

21st row: P1, *T4B, T4F; rep from * to last st, p1.

22nd and 23rd rows: As 2nd and 3rd rows.

24th row: As 2nd row.

Rep these 24 rows.

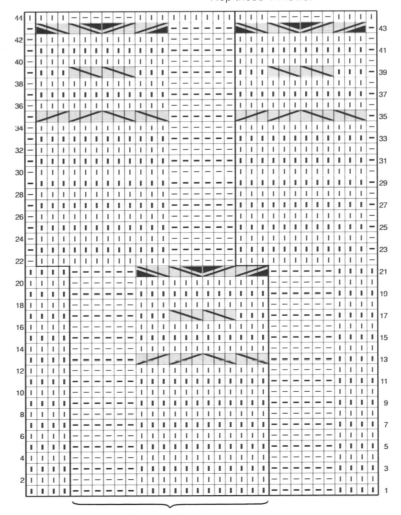

Rep these 18 sts

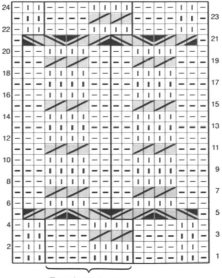

Rep these 8 sts

=T6B,　　=T6F,　　= C4B,　　= C6B,　　= C6F.

79

VI. Cable Patterns

VI.38

Multiple of 12 sts + 12

1st row (right side): K3, p2, k2, p2, *k6, p2, k2, p2; rep from * to last 3 sts, k3.

2nd row: P3, k2, p2, k2, *p6, k2, p2, k2; rep from * to last 3 sts, p3.

3rd row: K3, p2, k2, p2, *C4F, [k2, p2] twice; rep from * to last 3 sts, k3.

4th row: As 2nd row.

5th row: K1, T3F, p1, k2, p1, T3B, *k2, T3F, p1, k2, p1, T3B; rep from * to last st, k1.

6th row: P1, k1, *p2, k1; rep from * to last st, p1.

7th row: K1, p1, T3F, k2, T3B, p1, *k2, p1, T3F, k2, T3B, p1; rep from * to last st, k1.

8th row: P1, k2, p6, k2, *p2, k2, p6, k2; rep from * to last st, p1.

9th row: K1, p2, k2, C4B, *[p2, k2] twice, C4B; rep from * to last 3 sts, p2, k1.

10th row: As 8th row.

11th row: K1, p2, k6, p2, *k2, p2, k6, p2; rep from * to last st, k1.

12th row: As 8th row.

13th row: K1, p2, C4F, *[k2, p2] twice, C4F; rep from * to last 5 sts, k2, p2, k1.

14th row: As 8th row.

15th row: K1, p1, T3B, k2, T3F, p1, *k2, p1, T3B, k2, T3F, p1; rep from * to last st, k1.

16th row: As 6th row.

17th row: K1, T3B, p1, k2, p1, T3F, *k2, T3B, p1, k2, p1, T3F; rep from * to last st, k1.

18th row: As 2nd row.

19th row: K3, [p2, k2] twice, *C4B, [p2, k2] twice; rep from * to last st, k1.

20th row: As 2nd row.

Rep these 20 rows.

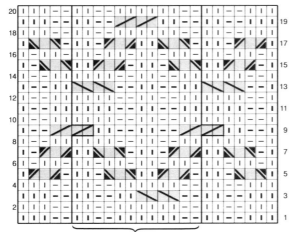

Rep these 12 sts

VI.39

Multiple of 12 sts + 2.

1st row (right side): Knit.

2nd row: P3, k6, *p6, k6; rep from * to last 5 sts, p5.

3rd row: Knit.

4th row: P1, *k6, p6; rep from * to last st, k1.

5th row: K1, *C6B, k6; rep from * to last st, k1.

6th row: K5, p6, *k6, p6; rep from * to last 3 sts, k3.

7th row: Knit.

8th row: K3, p6, *k6, p6; rep from * to last 5 sts, k5.

9th row: Knit.

10th row: K1, *p6, k6; rep from * to last st, p1.

11th row: K7, C6B, *k6, C6B; rep from * to last st, k1.

12th row: P5, k6, *p6, k6; rep from * to last 3 sts, p3.

Rep these 12 rows.

VI.40

Multiple of 12 sts + 4.

1st row (wrong side): *[K1, p2] twice, k4, p2; rep from * to last 4 sts, k1, p2, k1.

2nd row: P1, C2L, p1, *k8, p1, C2L, p1; rep from * to end.

3rd row: As 1st row.

4th row: P1, C2L, p1, *T3F, k2, T3B, p1, C2L, p1; rep from * to end.

5th row: K1, p2, *k2, p2; rep from * to last st, k1.

6th row: P1, C2L, *p2, T3F, T3B, p2, C2L; rep from * to last st, p1.

7th row: K1, p2, *k3, p4, k3, p2; rep from * to last st, k1.

8th row: P1, C2L, *p3, C4F, p3, C2L; rep from * to last st, p1.

9th row: As 7th row.

10th row: P1, C2L, *p2, C3B, C3F, p2, C2L; rep from * to last st, p1.

11th row: As 5th row.

12th row: P1, C2L, p1, *C3B, k2, C3F, p1, C2L, p1; rep from * to end.

13th row: As 1st row.

14th row: As 2nd row.

Rep these 14 rows.

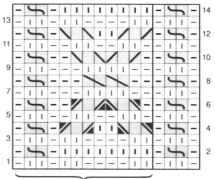

Rep these 12 sts

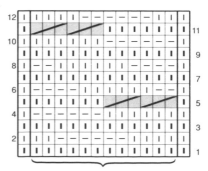

Rep these 12 sts

 = C2L, = C3B, = C3F, = C4B, = C4F, = C4L, = C4R.

VI.41

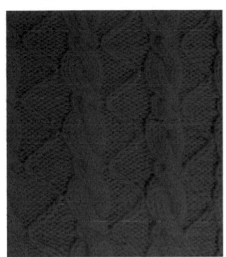

Multiple of 16 sts + 10.

1st row (right side): P1, k8, *T2B, p6, k8; rep from * to last st, p1.

2nd row: K1, p8, *k6, T2PL, p8; rep from * to last st, k1.

3rd row: P1, k8, *p1, T2F, p5, k8; rep from * to last st, p1.

4th row: K1, p8, *k4, T2PL, k2, p8; rep from * to last st, k1.

5th row: P1, k8, *p3, T2F, p3, k8; rep from * to last st, p1.

6th row: K1, p8, *k2, T2PL, k4, p8; rep from * to last st, k1.

7th row: P1, C8F, *p5, T2F, p1, C8F; rep from * to last st, p1.

8th row: K1, p8, *T2PL, k6, p8; rep from * to last st, k1.

9th row: P1, k8, *p6, T2B, k8; rep from * to last st, p1.

10th row: K1, p8, *k1, T2PR, k5, p8; rep from * to last st, k1.

11th row: P1, C8F, *p4, T2B, p2, C8F; rep from * to last st, p1.

12th row: K1, p8, *k3, T2PR, k3, p8; rep from * to last st, k1.

13th row: P1, k8, *p2, T2B, p4, k8; rep from * to last st, p1.

14th row: K1, p8, *k5, T2PR, k1, p8; rep from * to last st, k1.

Rep these 14 rows.

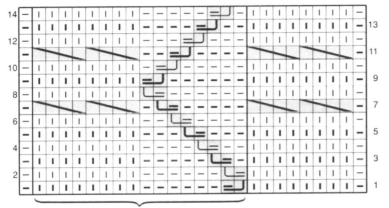

Rep these 16 sts

VI.42

Multiple of 16 sts + 2.

1st row (wrong side): K5, p8, *k8, p8; rep from * to last 5 sts, k5.

2nd row: P5, C4F, C4B, *p8, C4F, C4B; rep from * to last 5 sts, p5.

3rd row: As 1st row.

4th row: P5, k8, *p8, k8; rep from * to last 5 sts, p5.

Rep the last 4 rows once more then 1st and 2nd rows again.

11th row: K5, p2, k4, p2, *k8, p2, k4, p2; rep from * to last 5 sts, k5.

12th row: P4, T3B, p4, T3F, *p6, T3B, p4, T3F; rep from * to last 4 sts, p4.

13th row: K4, p2, *k6, p2; rep from * to last 4 sts, k4.

14th row: P3, T3B, p6, T3F, *p4, T3B, p6, T3F; rep from * to last 3 sts, p3.

15th row: K1, p4, k8, *p8, k8; rep from * to last 5 sts, p4, k1.

16th row: P1, *C4B, p8, C4F; rep from * to last st, p1.

17th row: As 15th row.

18th row: P1, k4, p8, *k8, p8; rep from * to last 5 sts, k4, p1.

Rep the last 4 rows once more, then 15th and 16th rows again.

25th row: K3, p2, k8, p2, *k4, p2, k8, p2; rep from * to last 3 sts, k3.

26th row: P3, T3F, p6, T3B, *p4, T3F, p6, T3B; rep from * to last 3 sts, p3.

27th row: As 13th row.

28th row: P4, T3F, p4, T3B, *p6, T3F, p4, T3B; rep from * to last 4 sts, p4.

Rep these 28 rows.

VI.43

Multiple of 13 sts + 2.

1st row (wrong side): K2, *p3, k10; rep from * to end.

2nd row: K3, C4R, k3, C4L, *k2, C4R, k3, C4L; rep from * to last st, k1.

3rd row: K9, p3, *k10, p3; rep from * to last 3 sts, k3.

4th row: K2, *C4R, k9; rep from * to end.

5th row: *K10, p3; rep from * to last 2 sts, k2.

6th row: K1, *C4R, k3, C4L, k2; rep from * to last st, k1.

7th row: K3, p3, *k10, p3; rep from * to last 9 sts, k9.

8th row: *K9, C4L; rep from * to last 2 sts, k2.

Rep these 8 rows.

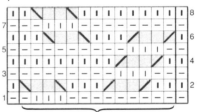

Rep these 13 sts

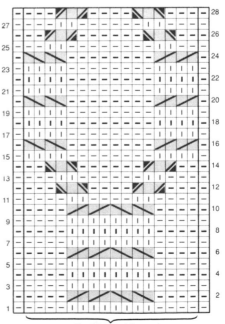

Rep these 16 sts

= T2B, = T2F, = T2PR, = T2PL, = T3B, = T3F, = C8F.

VII.1

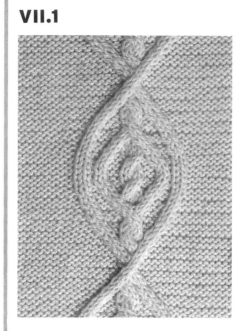

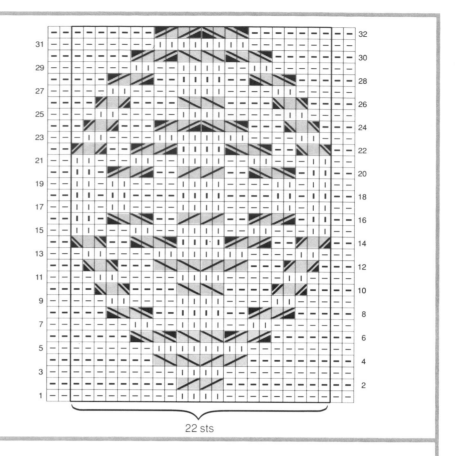

22 sts

Panel of 22 sts on a background of reverse st st.

1st row (wrong side): K9, p4, k9.

2nd row: P9, C4B, p9.

3rd row: As 1st row.

4th row: P7, C4B, C4F, p7.

5th row: K7, p8, k7.

6th row: P5, T4B, C4F, T4F, p5.

7th row: K5, p2, k2, p4, k2, p2, k5.

8th row: P3, T4B, p2, k4, p2, T4F, p3.

9th row: K3, p2, k4, p4, k4, p2, k3.

10th row: P2, T3B, p4, C4F, p4, T3F, p2.

11th row: K2, p2, k5, p4, k5, p2, k2.

12th row: P1, T3B, p3, C4B, C4F, p3, T3F, p1.

13th row: K1, p2, k4, p8, k4, p2, k1.

14th row: T3B, p2, T4B, k4, T4F, p2, T3F.

15th row: P2, k3, p2, k2, p4, k2, p2, k3, p2.

16th row: K2, p1, T4B, p2, C4B, p2, T4F, p1, k2.

17th row: P2, k1, p2, k4, p4, k4, p2, k1, p2.

18th row: K2, p1, k2, p4, k4, p4, k2, p1, k2.

19th row: As 17th row.

20th row: K2, p1, T4F, p2, C4B, p2, T4B, p1, k2.

21st row: As 15th row.

22nd row: T3F, p2, T4F, k4, T4B, p2, T3B.

23rd row: As 13th row.

24th row: P1, T3F, p3, T4F, T4B, p3, T3B, p1.

25th row: As 11th row.

26th row: P2, T3F, p4, C4F, p4, T3B, p2.

27th row: As 9th row.

28th row: P3, T4F, p2, k4, p2, T4B, p3.

29th row: As 7th row.

30th row: P5, T4F, C4F, T4B, p5.

31st row: As 5th row.

32nd row: P7, T4F, T4B, p7.

Rep these 32 rows.

VII.2

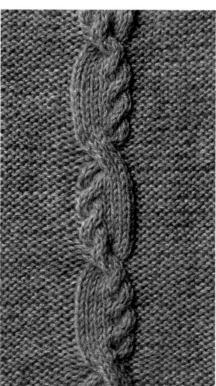

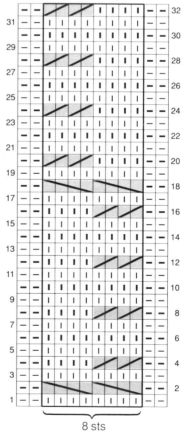

8 sts

Panel of 8 sts on a background of reverse st st.

1st row (wrong side): P8.

2nd row: C8F.

3rd row: P8.

4th row: C4B, k4.

5th row: P8.

6th row: K8.

Rep the last 4 rows twice more, then 3rd, 4th and 5th rows again.

18th row: C8F.

19th row: P8.

20th row: K4, C4B.

21st row: P8.

22nd row: K8.

Rep the last 4 rows twice more, then 19th and 20th rows again.

Rep these 32 rows.

◪◪ = C3B, ◩◩ = C3F, ◪◪◪ = C4B, ◩◩◩ = C4F, ▨▨▨▨ = C8B, ▨▨▨▨ = C8F.

VII.3

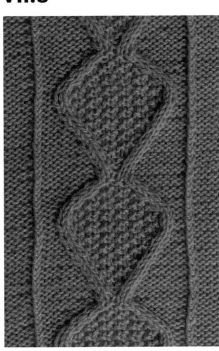

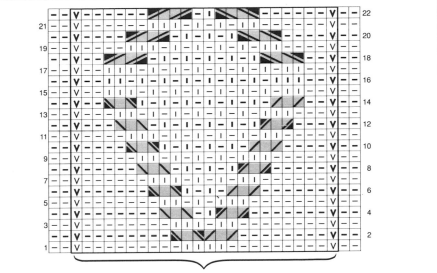

24 sts

Panel of 24 sts on a background of reverse st st.

1st row (wrong side): PB1, k9, p4, k9, PB1.

2nd row: KB1, p8, C3B, T3F, p8, KB1.

3rd row: PB1, k8, p3, k1, p2, k8, PB1.

4th row: KB1, p7, T3B, k1, p1, C3F, p7, KB1.

5th row: PB1, k7, p2, k1, p1, k1, p3, k7, PB1.

6th row: KB1, p6, C3B, [p1, k1] twice, T3F, p6, KB1.

7th row: PB1, k6, p3, k1, [p1, k1] twice, p2, k6, PB1.

8th row: KB1, p5, T3B, [k1, p1] 3 times, C3F, p5, KB1.

9th row: PB1, k5, p2, k1, [p1, k1] 3 times, p3, k5, PB1.

10th row: KB1, p4, C3B, [p1, k1] 4 times, T3F, p4, KB1.

11th row: PB1, k4, p3, k1, [p1, k1] 4 times, p2, k4, PB1.

12th row: KB1, p3, T3B, [k1, p1] 5 times, C3F, p3, KB1.

13th row: PB1, k3, p2, k1, [p1, k1] 5 times, p3, k3, PB1.

14th row: KB1, p2, C3B, [p1, k1] 6 times, T3F, p2, KB1.

15th row: PB1, k2, p3, k1, [p1, k1] 6 times, p2, k2, PB1.

16th row: KB1, p2, k3, p1, [k1, p1] 6 times, k2, p2, KB1.

17th row: As 15th row.

18th row: KB1, p2, T4F, [k1, p1] 5 times, T4B, p2, KB1.

19th row: As 11th row.

20th row: KB1, p4, T4F, [k1, p1] 3 times, T4B, p4, KB1.

21st row: As 7th row.

22nd row: KB1, p6, T4F, k1, p1, T4B, p6, KB1.

Rep these 22 rows.

VII.4

Panel of 16 sts on a background of garter st.

1st row (right side): K4, p3, k2, p3, k4.

2nd row: P4, k3, p2, k3, p4.

Rep the last 2 rows 4 times more.

11th row: C8F, C8B.

12th row: P16.

Rep these 12 rows.

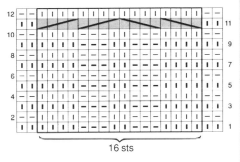

16 sts

VII.5

Panel of 14 sts on a background of reverse st st.

1st row (wrong side): K4, p6, k4.

2nd row: P4, C4B, T4F, p2.

3rd row: K2, p2, k2, p4, k4.

4th row: P4, k4, p2, T4F.

5th and 7th rows: P2, k4, p4, k4.

6th row: P4, C4B, p4, k2.

8th row: P4, k4, p2, T4B.

9th row: K2, p2, k2, p4, k4.

10th row: P4, C4B, T4B, p2.

11th row: As 1st row.

12th row: P2, T4B, C4F, p4.

13th row: K4, p4, k2, p2, k2.

14th row: T4B, p2, k4, p4.

15th and 17th rows: K4, p4, k4, p2.

16th row: K2, p4, C4F, p4.

18th row: T4F, p2, k4, p4.

19th row: As 13th row.

20th row: P2, T4F, C4F, p4.

Rep these 20 rows.

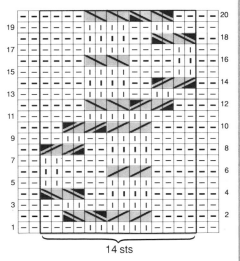

14 sts

VII. Cable Panels

VII.6

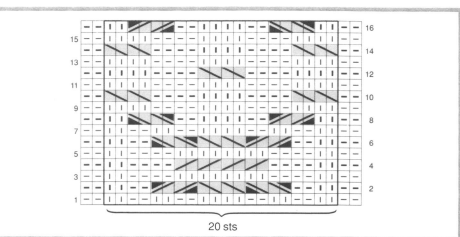

20 sts

Panel of 20 sts on a background of reverse st st.

1st row (wrong side): [P2, k2] twice, p4, [k2, p2] twice.

2nd row: K2, p2, T4F, C4F, T4B, p2, k2.

3rd row: P2, k4, p8, k4, p2.

4th row: K2, p4, [C4B] twice, p4, k2.

5th row: As 3rd row.

6th row: K2, p2, T4B, C4F, T4F, p2, k2.

7th row: As 1st row.

8th row: K2, T4B, p2, k4, p2, T4F, k2.

9th, 11th, 13th and 15th rows: P4, [k4, p4] twice.

10th row: C4F, p4, k4, p4, C4F.

12th row: K4, p4, C4F, p4, k4.

14th row: As 10th row.

16th row: K2, T4F, p2, k4, p2, T4B, k2.

Rep these 16 rows.

VII.7

VII.8

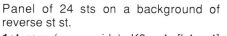

10 sts

Panel of 10 sts on a background of reverse st st.

1st and 3rd rows (right side): KB1, p2, k4, p2, KB1.

2nd and every alt row: PB1, k2, p4, k2, PB1.

5th, 7th, 9th, 11th and 13th rows: KB1, p2, C4F, p2, KB1.

15th and 17th rows: As 1st row.

18th row: As 2nd row.

Rep these 18 rows.

Panel of 24 sts on a background of reverse st st.

1st row (wrong side): K2, p4, [k4, p4] twice, k2.

2nd row: P2, C4B, [p4, C4B] twice, p2.

3rd row: As 1st row.

4th row: P1, T3B, [T4F, T4B] twice, T3F, p1.

5th row: K1, p2, k3, p4, k4, p4, k3, p2, k1.

6th row: T3B, p3, C4F, p4, C4B, p3, T3F.

7th row: P2, k4, [p4, k4] twice, p2.

8th row: K2, p3, T3B, T4F, T4B, T3F, p3, k2.

9th and 11th rows: [P2, k3] twice, p4, [k3, p2] twice.

10th row: [K2, p3] twice, C4B, [p3, k2] twice.

12th row: K2, p3, T3F, T4B, T4F, T3B, p3, k2.

13th row: As 7th row.

14th row: T3F, p3, C4F, p4, C4B, p3, T3B.

15th row: As 5th row.

16th row: P1, T3F, [T4B, T4F] twice, T3B, p1.

Rep these 16 rows.

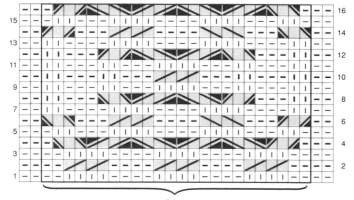

24 sts

84

$\boxed{V}$ = KB1, $\boxed{v}$ = PB1, $\diagdown$ = C2L, $\diagup$ = C4B, $\diagdown$ = C4F.

VII.9

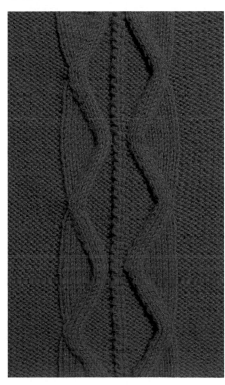

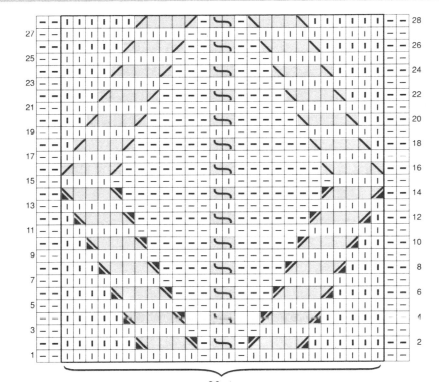

26 sts

Panel of 26 sts on a background of reverse st st.

Special Abbreviations

Cr5R (Cross 5 Right) = slip next st onto cable needle and hold at back of work, knit next 4 sts from left-hand needle, then knit st from cable needle.

Cr5L (Cross 5 Left) = slip next 4 sts onto cable needle and hold at front of work, knit next st from left-hand needle, then knit sts from cable needle.

Tw5R (Twist 5 Right) = slip next st onto cable needle and hold at back of work, knit next 4 sts from left-hand needle, then purl st from cable needle.

Tw5L (Twist 5 Left) = slip next 4 sts onto cable needle and hold at front of work, purl next st from left-hand needle, then knit sts from cable needle.

1st row (wrong side): P11, k1, p2, k1, p11.

2nd row: K6, Tw5R, p1, C2L, p1, Tw5L, k6.

3rd row: P10, k2, p2, k2, p10.

4th row: K5, Tw5R, p2, C2L, p2, Tw5L, k5.

5th row: P9, k3, p2, k3, p9.

6th row: K4, Tw5R, p3, C2L, p3, Tw5L, k4.

7th row: P8, k4, p2, k4, p8.

8th row: K3, Tw5R, p4, C2L, p4, Tw5L, k3.

9th row: P7, k5, p2, k5, p7.

10th row: K2, Tw5R, p5, C2L, p5, Tw5L, k2.

11th row: P6, k6, p2, k6, p6.

12th row: K1, Tw5R, p6, C2L, p6, Tw5L, k1.

13th row: P5, k7, p2, k7, p5.

14th row: Tw5R, p7, C2L, p7, Tw5L.

15th row: P4, k8, p2, k8, p4.

16th row: Cr5L, p7, C2L, p7, Cr5R.

17th row: As 13th row.

18th row: K1, Cr5L, p6, C2L, p6, Cr5R, k1.

19th row: As 11th row.

20th row: K2, Cr5L, p5, C2L, p5, Cr5R, k2.

21st row: As 9th row.

22nd row: K3, Cr5L, p4, C2L, p4, Cr5R, k3.

23rd row: As 7th row.

24th row: K4, Cr5L, p3, C2L, p3, Cr5R, k4.

25th row: As 5th row.

26th row: K5, Cr5L, p2, C2L, p2, Cr5R, k5.

27th row: As 3rd row.

28th row: K6, Cr5L, p1, C2L, p1, Cr5R, k6.

Rep these 28 rows.

VII.10

Panel of 14 sts on a background of reverse st st.

Special Abbreviation

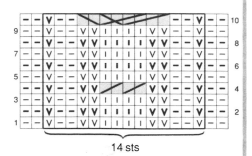 **C8RL (Cross 8 Right/ Left)** = slip next 4 sts onto cable needle and hold at back of work, knit next 2 sts from left-hand needle, knit first 2 sts from cable needle and hold remaining 2 sts at front of work, knit next 2 sts from left-hand needle, then knit sts from cable needle.

1st and every alt row (wrong side): PB1, k2, [PB1] twice, p4, [PB1] twice, k2, PB1.

2nd row: KB1, p2, [KB1] twice, k4, [KB1] twice, p2, KB1.

4th row: KB1, p2, [KB1] twice, C4B, [KB1] twice, p2, KB1.

6th and 8th rows: As 2nd row.

10th row: KB1, p2, C8RL, p2, KB1.

Rep these 10 rows.

14 sts

=T3B, =T3F, =T4B, =T4F.

VII. Cable Panels

VII.11

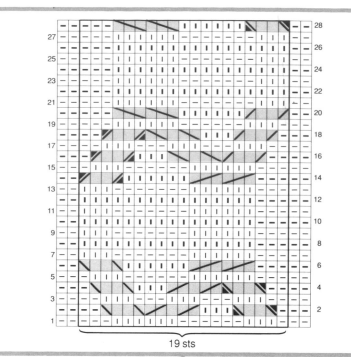

19 sts

Panel of 19 sts on a background of reverse st st.

Special Abbreviations

 **Cr5BR (Cross 5 Back Right)** = slip next 2 sts onto cable needle and hold at back of work, knit next 3 sts from left-hand needle, then knit sts from cable needle.

Cr5FL (Cross 5 Front Left) = slip next 3 sts onto cable needle and hold at front of work, knit next 2 sts from left-hand needle, then knit sts from cable needle.

1st row (wrong side): K3, p6, k6, p3, k1.
2nd row: P1, T4L, k3, Cr5BR, C4L, p2.
3rd row: K2, p3, [k3, p3] twice, k2.
4th row: P2, T4L, Cr5BR, k3, C4L, p1.
5th row: K1, p3, k6, p6, k3.
6th row: P3, C6B, k6, C4L.
7th row: P3, k7, p6, k3.
8th row: P3, k16.
Rep the last 2 rows twice more, then 7th row again.
14th row: P3, C6B, k6, T4R.
15th row: As 5th row.
16th row: P2, C4R, Cr5FL, k3, T4R, p1.
17th row: As 3rd row.
18th row: P1, C4R, k3, Cr5FL, T4R, p2.
19th row: As 1st row.
20th row: C4R, k6, C6F, p3.
21st row: K3, p6, k7, p3.
22nd row: K16, p3.
Rep the last 2 rows twice more, then 21st row again.
28th row: T4L, k6, C6F, p3.
Rep these 28 rows.

VII.12

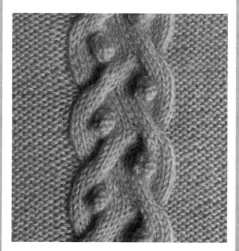

Panel of 16 sts on a background of reverse st st.

Special Abbreviation

● **MB (Make Bobble)** = [k1, yf, k1, yf, k1] all into next st, turn and k5, turn and p5, turn and k5, turn and sl 2, k3tog, p2sso.

Work 4 rows in st st, starting knit (1st row is right side).
5th row: C8F, k3, MB, k4.
Work 5 rows in st st, starting purl.
11th row: K4, MB, k3, C8B.
12th row: P16.
Rep these 12 rows.

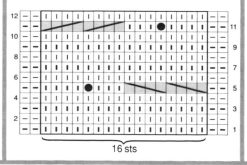

16 sts

VII.13

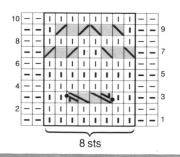

Panel of 8 sts on a background of reverse st st.

Special Abbreviation

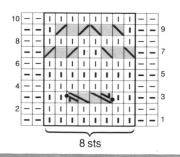 **C4FX (Cable 4 Front X)** = yf, slip next 2 sts onto cable needle and hold at front of work, k2tog from left-hand needle, then sl 1, k1, psso from cable needle, yf.

1st row (right side): K8.
2nd and every alt row: P8.
3rd row: K2, C4FX, k2.
5th row: K8.
7th row: C3F, k2, C3B.
9th row: K1, C3F, C3B, k1.
10th row: P8.
Rep these 10 rows.

8 sts

 = C4L,  = C4R, ⟍ = C6B, ⟋ = C6F, ⟍ = C8B, ⟋ = C8F,

VII.14

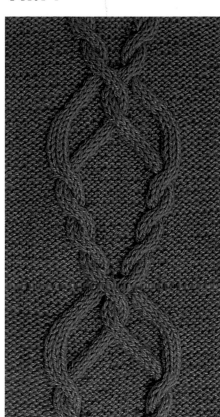

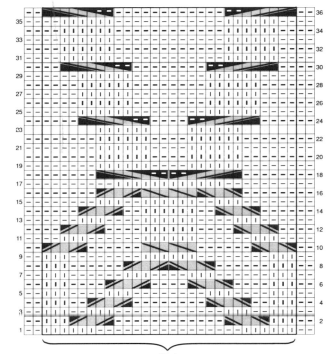

28 sts

Panel of 28 sts on a background of reverse st st.

Special Abbreviations

T5BR (Twist 5 Back/Right) = slip next 2 sts onto cable needle and hold at back of work, knit next 3 sts from left-hand needle, then purl sts from cable needle.

T5FL (Twist 5 Front/Left) = slip next 3 sts onto cable needle and hold at front of work, purl next 2 sts from left-hand needle, then knit sts from cable needle.

T8BR (Twist 8 Back/Right) = slip next 5 sts onto cable needle and hold at back of work, knit next 3 sts from left-hand needle, then k3, p2 from cable needle.

T8FL (Twist 8 Front/Left) = slip next 3 sts onto cable needle and hold at front of work, p2, k3 from left-hand needle, then knit sts from cable needle.

1st row (wrong side): P6, k16, p6.
2nd row: K3, T5FL, p12, T5BR, k3.
3rd row: P3, k2, p3, k12, p3, k2, p3.
4th row: K3, p2, T5FL, p8, T5BR, p2, k3.
5th row: P3, k4, p3, k8, p3, k4, p3.
6th row: K3, p4, T5FL, p4, T5BR, p4, k3.
7th row: P3, k6, p3, k4, p3, k6, p3.
8th row: K3, p6, T5FL, T5BR, p6, k3.
9th row: P3, k8, p6, k8, p3.
10th row: T5FL, p6, C6F, p6, T5BR.
11th row: K2, p3, k6, p6, k6, p3, k2.
12th row: P2, T5FL, p4, k6, p4, T5BR, p2.

13th row: K4, p3, k4, p6, k4, p3, k4.
14th row: P4, T5FL, p2, k6, p2, T5BR, p4.
15th row: K6, p3, k2, p6, k2, p3, k6.
16th row: P6, T5FL, C6F, T5BR, p6.
17th row: K8, p12, k8.
18th row: P6, T8BR, T8FL, p6.
19th row: K6, p6, k4, p6, k6.
20th row: P6, k6, p4, k6, p6.
Rep the last 2 rows once more, then 19th row again.
24th row: P4, T8BR, p4, T8FL, p4.
25th row: K4, p6, k8, p6, k4.
26th row: P4, k6, p8, k6, p4.
Rep the last 2 rows once more, then 25th row again.
30th row: P2, T8BR, p8, T8FL, p2.
31st row: K2, p6, k12, p6, k2.
32nd row: P2, k6, p12, k6, p2.
Rep the last 2 rows once more, then 31st row again.
36th row: T8BR, p12, T8FL.
Rep these 36 rows.

VII.15

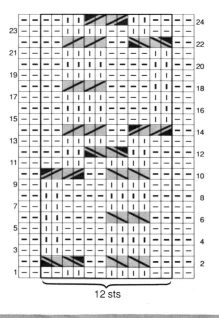

Panel of 12 sts on a background of reverse st st.

1st row (wrong side): K2, p2, k2, p4, k2.
2nd row: P2, C4F, p2, T4F.
3rd, 4th and 5th rows: P2, k4, p4, k2.
6th row: P2, C4F, p4, k2.
7th, 8th and 9th rows: As 3rd row.
10th row: P2, C4F, p2, T4B.
11th row: As 1st row.
12th row: P2, k2, T4F, k2, p2.
13th row: K2, p4, k2, p2, k2.
14th row: T4B, p2, C4B, p2.
15th, 16th and 17th rows: K2, p4, k4, p2.
18th row: K2, p4, C4B, p2.
19th, 20th and 21st rows: As 15th row.
22nd row: T4F, p2, C4B, p2.
23rd row: As 13th row.
24th row: P2, k2, T4B, k2, p2.
Rep these 24 rows.

12 sts

= C4B, = C4F, = C3B, = C3F, = T4L, = T4R, = T4B, = T4F.

VII. Cable Panels

VII.16

Panel of 18 sts on a background of reverse st st.

1st row (wrong side): P6, k6, p6.
2nd row: K3, T4L, p4, T4R, k3.
3rd row: P3, k1, p3, k4, p3, k1, p3.
4th row: K3, p1, T4L, p2, T4R, p1, k3.
5th row: P3, [k2, p3] 3 times.
6th row: K3, p2, T4L, T4R, p2, k3.
7th, 9th, 11th, 13th and 15th rows: P3, k3, p6, k3, p3.
8th row: K3, p3, C6B, p3, k3.
10th and 12th rows: K3, p3, k6, p3, k3.
14th row: As 8th row.
16th row: K3, p2, T4R, T4L, p2, k3.
17th row: As 5th row.
18th row: K3, p1, T4R, p2, T4L, p1, k3.
19th row: As 3rd row.
20th row: K3, T4R, p4, T4L, k3.
21st, 23rd, 25th and 27th rows: As 1st row.
22nd row: C6B, p6, C6F.
24th and 26th rows: K6, p6, k6.
28th row: As 22nd row.
Rep these 28 rows.

VII.18

Panel of 28 sts on a background of reverse st st.

1st row (right side): C2L, p2, k20, p2, C2L.
2nd and every alt row: P2, k2, p20, k2, p2.
3rd row: C2R, p2, k20, p2, C2R.
5th row: As 1st row.
7th row: C2R, p2, C10B, C10F, p2, C2R.
9th row: As 1st row.
11th row: As 3rd row.
12th row: As 2nd row.
Rep these 12 rows.

Key to Symbols

(symbol)	= C10B
(symbol)	= C10F

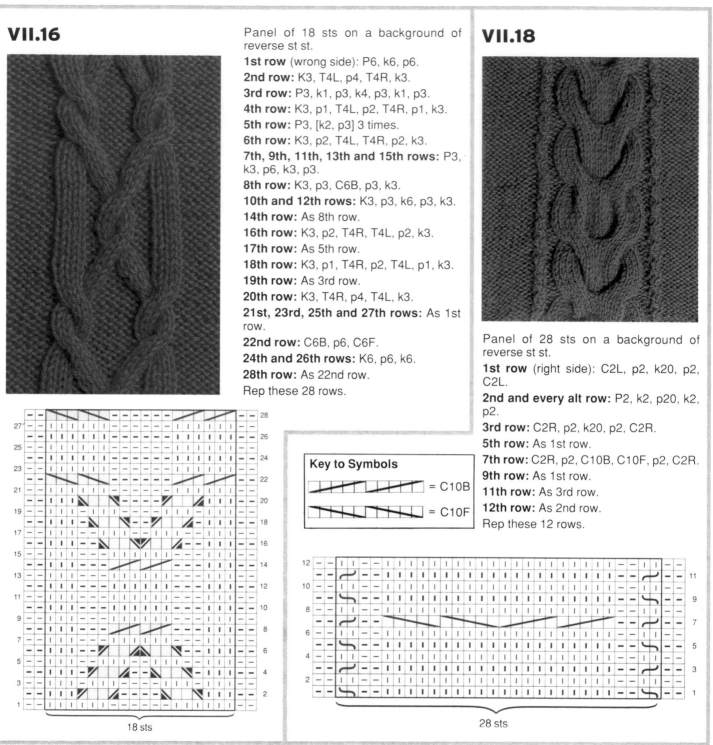

18 sts

28 sts

VII.17

Panel of 26 sts on a background of reverse st st.

1st row (right side): C2R, p2, k18, p2, C2L.
2nd and every alt row: P2, k2, p18, k2, p2.

3rd row: C2R, p2, C12F, k6, p2, C2L.
5th and 7th rows: As 1st row.
9th row: C2R, p2, k6, C12B, p2, C2L.
11th row: As 1st row.
12th row: As 2nd row.
Rep these 12 rows.

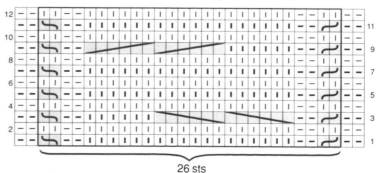

26 sts

(symbol) = C2R, (symbol) = C2L, (symbol) = C4B, (symbol) = C4F, (symbol) = C6B, (symbol) = C6F, (symbol) = T4L

VII.19

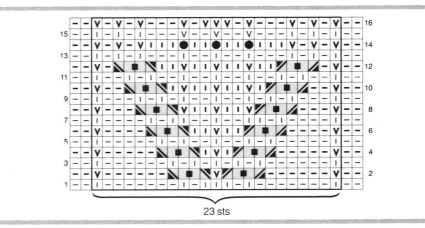

23 sts

Panel of 23 sts on a background of reverse st st.

Special Abbreviations

 **T4Rtbl (Twist 4 Right through back of loops)** = slip next st onto cable needle and hold at back of work, KB1, p1, KB1 from left-hand needle, then knit st from cable needle.

T4Ltbl (Twist 4 Left through back of loops) = slip next 3 sts onto cable needle and hold at front of work, knit next st from left-hand needle, then KB1, p1, KB1 from cable needle.

● **MB (Make Bobble)** = [k1, yf, k1, yf, k1] all into next st, turn and p5, turn and sl 2, k3tog, p2sso.

1st row (wrong side): P1, k7, p1, k1, p3, k1, p1, k7, p1.

2nd row: KB1, p6, T4Rtbl, KB1, T4Ltbl, p6, KB1.

3rd row: P1, k6, p1, [k1, p1] 4 times, k6, p1.

4th row: KB1, p5, T4Rtbl, k1, KB1, k1, T4Ltbl, p5, KB1.

5th row: P1, k5, p1, k1, p1, [k2, p1] twice, k1, p1, k5, p1.

6th row: KB1, p4, T4Rtbl, k2, KB1, k2, T4Ltbl, p4, KB1.

7th row: P1, k4, p1, k1, p2, k2, p1, k2, p2, k1, p1, k4, p1.

8th row: KB1, p3, T4Rtbl, KB1, [k2, KB1] twice, T4Ltbl, p3, KB1.

9th row: P1, k3, p1, [k1, p1] twice, [k2, p1] twice, [k1, p1] twice, k3, p1.

10th row: KB1, p2, T4Rtbl, k1, KB1, [k2, KB1] twice, k1, T4Ltbl, p2, KB1.

11th row: P1, k2, p1, k1, p1, [k2, p1] 4 times, k1, p1, k2, p1.

12th row: KB1, p1, T4Rtbl, k2, [KB1, k2] 3 times, T4Ltbl, p1, KB1.

13th row: P1, [k1, p1] twice, k3, p1, [k2, p1] twice, k3, p1, [k1, p1] twice.

14th row: KB1, [p1, KB1] twice, k3, MB, [k2, MB] twice, k3, KB1, [p1, KB1] twice.

15th row: P1, [k1, p1] twice, k3, PB1, [k2, PB1] twice, k3, p1, [k1, p1] twice.

16th row: KB1, [p1, KB1] twice, p3, KB1, p1, [KB1] 3 times, p1, KB1, p3, KB1, [p1, KB1] twice.

Rep these 16 rows.

VII.20

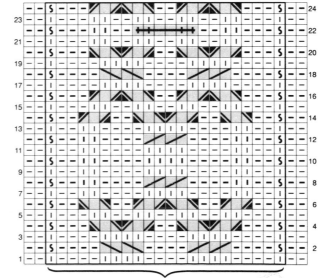

Panel of 22 sts on a background of reverse st st.

Special Abbreviation

Cluster 6 = k2, p2, k2, slip the last 6 sts just worked onto cable needle and wrap yarn anticlockwise 4 times round these 6 sts, then slip sts back onto right-hand needle.

Note: Slip sts purlwise with yarn at back of work (wrong side), = **S** on diagram.

1st row (wrong side): P1, k4, [p4, k4] twice, p1.

2nd row: Sl 1, p4, C4B, p4, C4F, p4, sl 1.

3rd row: As 1st row.

4th row: Sl 1, p3, T3B, T3F, p2, T3B, T3F, p3, sl 1.

5th row: P1, k3, p2, [k2, p2] 3 times, k3, p1.

6th row: Sl 1, p2, [T3B, p2, T3F] twice, p2, sl 1.

7th row: P1, k2, p2, k4, p4, k4, p2, k2, p1.

8th row: Sl 1, p2, k2, p4, C4B, p4, k2, p2, sl 1.

9th row: As 7th row.

10th row: Sl 1, p2, k2, p4, k4, p4, k2, p2, sl 1.

11th and 12th rows: As 7th and 8th rows.

13th row: As 7th row.

14th row: Sl 1, p2, [T3F, p2, T3B] twice, p2, sl 1.

15th row: As 5th row.

16th row: Sl 1, p3, T3F, T3B, p2, T3F, T3B, p3, sl 1.

17th and 18th rows: As 1st and 2nd rows.

19th row: As 1st row.

20th and 21st rows: As 4th and 5th rows.

22nd row: Sl 1, p3, k2, p2, Cluster 6, p2, k2, p3, sl 1.

23rd row: As 5th row.

24th row: As 16th row.

Rep these 24 rows.

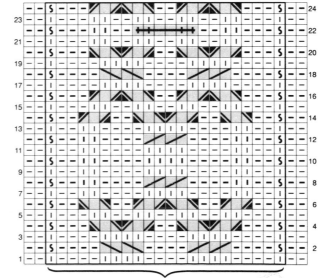

= C12F, = C12B, = T3B, = T3F, = T4R, **v** = KB1.

89

VII. Cable Panels

VII.21

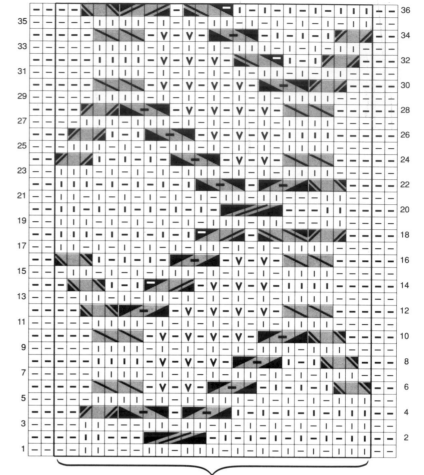

25 sts

Panel of 25 sts on a background of reverse st st.

Special Abbreviations

T5R (Twist 5 Right) = slip next 3 sts onto cable needle and hold at back of work, knit next 2 sts from left-hand needle, then p1, k2 from cable needle.

T4BP (Twist 4 Back Purl) = slip next 2 sts onto cable needle and hold at back of work, knit next 2 sts from left-hand needle, then p1, k1 from cable needle.

T4FP (Twist 4 Front Purl) = slip next 2 sts onto cable needle and hold at front of work, k1, p1 from left-hand needle, then knit sts from cable needle.

T4RP (Twist 4 Right Purl) = slip next 2 sts onto cable needle and hold at back of work, knit next 2 sts from left-hand needle, then k1, p1 from cable needle.

T4LP (Twist 4 Left Purl) = slip next 2 sts onto cable needle and hold at front of work, p1, k1 from left-hand needle, then knit sts from cable needle.

1st row (wrong side): K2, p2, k3, p2, k1, p3, k1, [p1, k1] 4 times, p3.

2nd row: K2, p1, [k1, p1] 5 times, T5R, p3, k2, p2.

3rd row: K2, p2, k3, [p2, k1] twice, [p1, k1] 5 times, p2.

4th row: K3, [p1, k1] 4 times, T4BP, p1, T4FP, T3B, p2.

5th row: K3, p4, k1, [p1, k1] twice, p3, k1, [p1, k1] 3 times, p3.

6th row: T3F, [k1, p1] 3 times, T4BP, p1, [KB1, p1] twice, C4F, p3.

7th row: K3, p4, k1, [p1, k1] 3 times, p2, k1, [p1, k1] twice, p3, k1.

8th row: P1, T3F, k1, p1, k1, T4BP, p1, [KB1, p1] 3 times, k4, p3.

9th row: K3, p4, k1, [p1, k1] 4 times, p3, k1, p3, k2.

10th row: P2, T3F, T4BP, p1, [KB1, p1] 4 times, C4F, p3.

11th row: K3, p4, k1, [p1, k1] 5 times, p4, k3.

12th row: P3, C4F, p1, [KB1, p1] 4 times, T4BP, T3F, p2.

13th row: K2, p2, k1, p1, k1, p2, k1, [p1, k1] 4 times, p4, k3.

14th row: P3, k4, p1, [KB1, p1] 3 times, T4RP, k1, p1, k1, T3F, p1.

15th row: K1, p2, k1, [p1, k1] twice, p3, k1, [p1, k1] 3 times, p4, k3.

16th row: P3, C4F, p1, [KB1, p1] twice, T4BP, [p1, k1] 3 times, T3F.

17th row: P2, k1, [p1, k1] 4 times, p2, k1, [p1, k1] twice, p4, k3.

18th row: P2, T3B, T4F, p1, T4RP, [k1, p1] 4 times, k3.

19th row: P3, k1, [p1, k1] 4 times, p3, k1, p2, k3, p2, k2.

20th row: P2, k2, p3, T5R, p1, [k1, p1] 5 times, k2.

21st row: P2, k1, [p1, k1] 5 times, p2, k1, p2, k3, p2, k2.

22nd row: P2, T3F, T4BP, p1, T4FP, [k1, p1] 4 times, k3.

23rd row: P3, k1, [p1, k1] 3 times, p3, k1, [p1, k1] twice, p4, k3.

24th row: P3, C4F, p1, [KB1, p1] twice, T4FP, [p1, k1] 3 times, T3B.

25th row: K1, p3, k1, [p1, k1] twice, p2, k1, [p1, k1] 3 times, p4, k3.

26th row: P3, k4, p1, [KB1, p1] 3 times, T4FP, k1, p1, k1, T3B, p1.

27th row: K2, [p3, k1] twice, [p1, k1] 4 times, p4, k3.

28th row: P3, C4F, p1, [KB1, p1] 4 times, T4FP, T3B, p2.

29th row: K3, p4, k1, [p1, k1] 5 times, p4, k3.

30th row: P2, T3B, T4FP, p1, [KB1, p1] 4 times, C4F, p3.

31st row: K3, p4, k1, [p1, k1] 4 times, p2, k1, p1, k1, p2, k2.

32nd row: P1, T3B, k1, p1, k1, T4LP, p1, [KB1, p1] 3 times, k4, p3.

33rd row: K3, p4, k1, [p1, k1] 3 times, p3, k1, [p1, k1] twice, p2, k1.

34th row: T3B, [k1, p1] 3 times, T4FP, p1, [KB1, p1] twice, C4F, p3.

35th row: K3, p4, k1, [p1, k1] twice, p2, k1, [p1, k1] 4 times, p2.

36th row: K3, [p1, k1] 4 times, T4LP, p1, T4B, T3F, p2.

Rep these 36 rows.

V = KB1, ⟋ = T3B, ⟍ = T3F, ⟋ = T4B, ⟍ = T4F, ⟋ = C3B, ⟍ = C3F.

VII.22

Panel of 40 sts on a background of st st.

Special Abbreviations

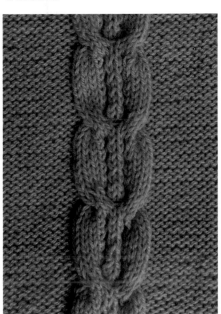

T4RP (Twist 4 Right Purl) = slip next 2 sts onto cable needle and hold at back of work, knit next 2 sts from left-hand needle, then k1, p1 from cable needle.

T4LP (Twist 4 Left Purl) = slip next 2 sts onto cable needle and hold at front of work, p1, k1 from left-hand needle, then knit sts from cable needle.

1st row (right side): P2, KB1, [p1, KB1] 7 times, p2, k2, p2, KB1, [p1, KB1] 7 times, p2.

2nd row: K2, p1, [k1, p1] 7 times, k2, p2, k2, p1, [k1, p1] 7 times, k2.

Rep the last 2 rows twice more.

7th row: P2, KB1, [p1, KB1] 4 times, C4B, p1, KB1, p2, k2, p2, KB1, p1, C4F, KB1, [p1, KB1] 4 times, p2.

8th row: K2, [p1, k1] 4 times, p5, k1, p1, k2, p2, k2, p1, k1, p5, [k1, p1] 4 times, k2.

9th row: P2, KB1, [p1, KB1] 3 times, T4B, T3F, KB1, p2, k2, p2, KB1, T3B, T4F, KB1, [p1, KB1] 3 times, p2.

10th row: K2, [p1, k1] 3 times, p3, k3, p3, k2, p2, k2, p3, k3, p3, [k1, p1] 3 times, k2.

11th row: P2, KB1, [p1, KB1] twice, T4B, p3, T3F, p2, k2, p2, T3B, p3, T4F, KB1, [p1, KB1] twice, p2.

12th row: K2, [p1, k1] twice, p3, k6, p2, [k2, p2] twice, k6, p3, [k1, p1] twice, k2.

13th row: P2, KB1, p1, KB1, T4B, p6, k2, [p2, k2] twice, p6, T4F, KB1, p1, KB1, p2.

14th row: K2, p1, k1, p3, k8, p2, [k2, p2] twice, k8, p3, k1, p1, k2.

15th row: P2, KB1, T4B, p7, C3B, p2, k2, p2, C3F, p7, T4F, KB1, p2.

16th row: K2, p3, k9, p3, k2, p2, k2, p3, k9, p3, k2.

17th row: P2, T3B, p7, T4RP, KB1, p2, k2, p2, KB1, T4LP, p7, T3F, p2.

18th row: K2, p2, k8, p3, k1, p1, k2, p2, k2, p1, k1, p3, k8, p2, k2.

19th row: P2, k2, p6, T4RP, KB1, p1, KB1, p2, k2, p2, KB1, p1, KB1, T4LP, p6, k2, p2.

20th row: K2, p2, k6, p3, [k1, p1] twice, k2, p2, k2, [p1, k1] twice, p3, k6, p2, k2.

21st row: P2, C3B, p3, T4RP, KB1, [p1, KB1] twice, p2, k2, p2, KB1, [p1, KB1] twice, T4LP, p3, C3F, p2.

22nd row: K2, p3, k3, p3, [k1, p1] 3 times, k2, p2, k2, [p1, k1] 3 times, p3, k3, p3, k2.

23rd row: P2, KB1, T3F, T4RP, KB1, [p1, KB1] 3 times, p2, k2, p2, KB1, [p1, KB1] 3 times, T4LP, T3B, KB1, p2.

24th row: K2, p1, k1, p5, [k1, p1] 4 times, k2, p2, k2, [p1, k1] 4 times, p5, k1, p1, k2.

25th row: P2, KB1, p1, C4F, KB1, [p1, KB1] 4 times, p2, k2, p2, KB1, [p1, KB1] 4 times, C4B, p1, KB1, p2.

26th row: As 2nd row.

Rep these 26 rows.

VII.23

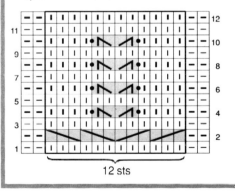

Panel of 12 sts on a background of reverse st st.

1st and every alt row (wrong side): P12.

2nd row: C6B, C6F.

4th, 6th, 8th and 10th rows: K4, yf, k2tog, sl 1, k1, psso, yf, k4.

12th row: K12.

Rep these 12 rows.

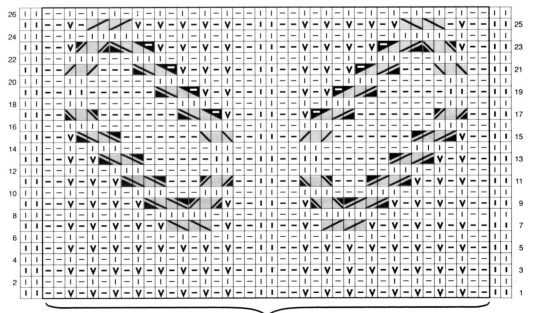

40 sts

= C4B, = C4F, = C6B, = C6F, • = yf, = k2tog, = sl 1, k1, psso.

VII. Cable Panels

VII.24

Panel of 21 sts on a background of reverse st st.

Special Abbreviations

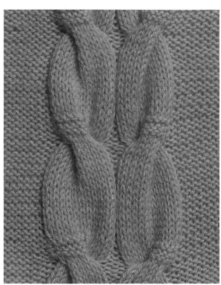 **T5BR (Twist 5 Back Right)** = slip next 2 sts onto cable needle and hold at back of work, knit next 3 sts from left-hand needle, then purl sts from cable needle.

T5FL (Twist 5 Front Left) = slip next 3 sts onto cable needle and hold at front of work, purl next 2 sts from left-hand needle, then knit sts from cable needle.

1st row (wrong side): K4, p3, [k2, p3] twice, k4.
2nd row: P4, k3, T5BR, p2, T5FL, p2.
3rd row: K2, p3, k6, p6, k4.
4th row: P4, C6F, p4, C2R, k3, p2.
5th row: K2, p3, k1, p1, k4, p6, k4.
6th row: P4, k6, p3, T2B, k1, T5FL.
7th row: P3, k1, p1, k1, p2, k3, p6, k4.
8th row: P4, k6, p2, C2R, p1, k1, p1, k4.
9th row: P3, [k1, p1] 3 times, k2, p6, k4.
10th row: P4, C6F, p2, k2, p1, k1, p1, k4.
11th row: As 9th row.
12th row: P4, k6, p2, T2F, p1, k1, p1, k4.
13th row: As 7th row.
14th row: P4, k6, p3, T2F, k1, T5BR.
15th row: As 5th row.
16th row: P4, C6F, p4, T2F, k3, p2.
17th row: K2, p4, k5, p6, k4.
18th row: P4, k3, T5FL, p2, T5BR, p2.
19th row: As 1st row.
20th row: P2, T5BR, p2, T5FL, k3, p4.
21st row: K4, p6, k6, p3, k2.
22nd row: P2, k3, C2L, p4, C6B, p4.
23rd row: K4, p6, k4, p1, k1, p3, k2.
24th row: T5BR, k1, T2F, p3, k6, p4.

25th row: K4, p6, k3, p2, k1, p1, k1, p3.
26th row: K4, p1, k1, p1, C2L, p2, k6, p4.
27th row: K4, p6, k2, [p1, k1] 3 times, p3.
28th row: K4, p1, k1, p1, k2, p2, C6B, p4.
29th row: As 27th row.
30th row: K4, p1, k1, p1, T2B, p2, k6, p4.
31st row: As 25th row.
32nd row: T5FL, k1, T2B, p3, k6, p4.
33rd row: As 23rd row.
34th row: P2, k3, T2B, p4, C6B, p4.
35th row: K4, p6, k5, p4, k2.
36th row: P2, T5FL, p2, T5BR, k3, p4.
Rep these 36 rows.

VII.25

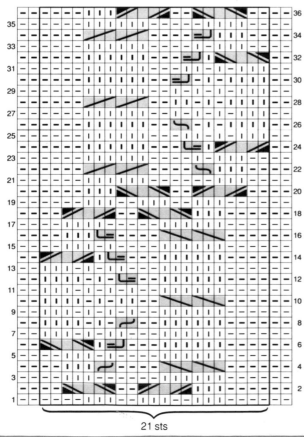

Panel of 26 sts on a background of reverse st st.

1st row (right side): K12, p2, k12.
2nd row: P12, k2, p12.
Rep the last 2 rows 3 times more.
9th row: C12B, p2, C12F.
10th row: K6, p6, k2, p6, k6.
11th row: P6, k6, p2, k6, p6.
12th row: As 10th row.
13th and 14th rows: As 1st and 2nd rows.
Rep the last 2 rows 3 times more.
Rep these 20 rows.

 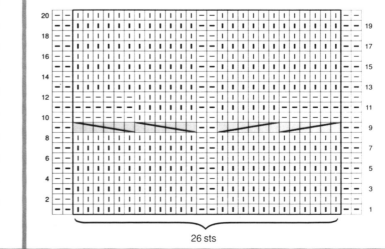 = C2R, = C2L, = C6B, = C6F, = k2tog, = sl 1, k1, psso, ♦ = yf.

VIII. Cable and Lace Patterns

VIII.1

Multiple of 14 sts + 8.

1st and every alt row (wrong side): K1, *p6, k1; rep from * to end.

2nd row: P1, C6F, p1, *k6, p1, C6F, p1; rep from * to end.

4th row: P1, k6, p1, *C6F, p1, k6, p1; rep from * to end.

6th row: P1, k6, p1, *sl 1, k1, psso, yf, k2, yf, k2tog, p1, k6, p1; rep from * to end.

8th row: P1, k6, p1, *sl 1, k1, psso, yf, C2L, yf, k2tog, p1, k6, p1; rep from * to end.

10th row: As 6th row.

12th row: P1, C6F, p1, *sl 1, k1, psso, yf, C2L, yf, k2tog, p1, C6F, p1; rep from * to end.

14th row: As 6th row.

16th row: As 8th row.

18th row: P1, *k6, p1; rep from * to end.

20th row: As 4th row.

22nd row: As 2nd row.

24th row: P1, sl 1, k1, psso, yf, k2, yf, k2tog, p1, *k6, p1, sl 1, k1, psso, yf, k2, yf, k2tog, p1; rep from * to end.

26th row: P1, sl 1, k1, psso, yf, C2L, yf, k2tog, p1, *k6, p1, sl 1, k1, psso, yf, C2L, yf, k2tog, p1; rep from * to end.

28th row: As 24th row.

30th row: P1, sl 1, k1, psso, yf, C2L, yf, k2tog, p1, *C6F, p1, sl 1, k1, psso, yf, C2L, yf, k2tog, p1; rep from * to end.

32nd row: As 24th row.

34th row: As 26th row.

36th row: As 18th row.

Rep these 36 rows.

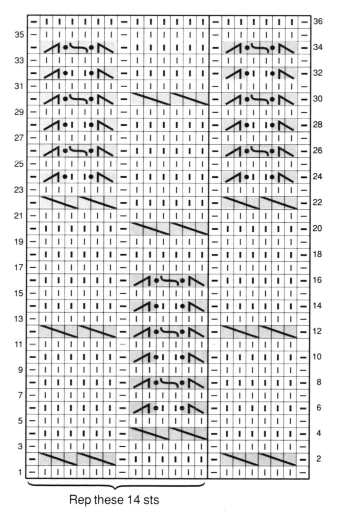

Rep these 14 sts

VIII.2

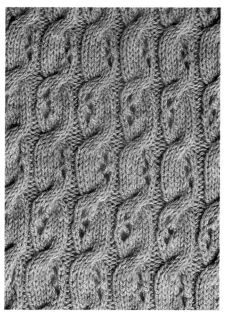

Multiple of 8 sts + 2.

1st and every alt row (wrong side): K2, *p6, k2; rep from * to end.

2nd row: P2, *k6, p2; rep from * to end.

4th row: P2, *C6B, p2; rep from * to end.

6th row: As 2nd row.

8th row: P2, *k1, yf, k2tog, k3, p2; rep from * to end.

10th row: P2, *sl 1, k1, psso, yf, k4, p2; rep from * to end.

12th row: As 8th row.

14th row: As 2nd row.

16th row: As 4th row.

18th row: As 2nd row.

20th row: P2, *k3, sl 1, k1, psso, yf, k1, p2; rep from * to end.

22nd row: P2, *k4, yf, k2tog, p2; rep from * to end.

24th row: As 20th row.

Rep these 24 rows.

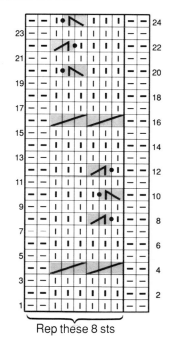

Rep these 8 sts

= C12B, = C12F, = T2B, = T2F.

VIII. Cable and Lace Patterns

VIII.3

VIII.4

Multiple of 30 sts + 9.

Special Abbreviation

C7B (Cross 7 Back) = slip next 4 sts onto cable needle and hold at back of work, knit next 3 sts from left-hand needle, then knit sts from cable needle.

1st and every alt row (wrong side): Purl.

2nd row: K2, k2tog, yf, KB1, yf, sl 1, k1, psso, k2, *yf, k3, p3, k3, sl 2tog knitwise, k1, p2sso, k3, p3, k3, yf, k2, k2tog, yf, KB1, yf, sl 1, k1, psso, k2; rep from * to end.

4th row: K1, k2tog, yf, k3, *yf, [sl 1, k1, psso] twice, yf, k3, p3, C7B, p3, k3, yf, [k2tog] twice, yf, k3; rep from * to last 3 sts, yf, sl 1, k1, psso, k1.

6th row: K3, yf, sl 2tog knitwise, k1, p2sso, yf, *k2, sl 1, k1, psso, yf, k3, p3, k7, p3, k3, yf, k2tog, k2, yf, sl 2tog knitwise, k1, p2sso, yf; rep from * to last 3 sts, k3.

8th row: K1, k2tog, yf, k3, *yf, [sl 1, k1, psso] twice, yf, k3, p3, k7, p3, k3, yf, [k2tog] twice, yf, k3; rep from * to last 3 sts, yf, sl 1, k1, psso, k1.

10th row: As 6th row.

12th row: As 4th row.

14th row: K3, yf, sl 2tog knitwise, k1, p2sso, yf, *k1, sl 1, k1, psso, yf, k2tog, k2, p3, k3, yf, k1, yf, k3, p3, k2, sl 1, k1, psso, yf, k2tog, k1, yf, sl 2tog knitwise, k1, p2sso, yf; rep from * to last 3 sts, k3.

16th row: K6, *sl 1, k1, psso, yf, k2tog, k2, p3, k3, [yf, k3] twice, p3, k2, sl 1, k1, psso, yf, k2tog, k3; rep from * to last 3 sts, k3.

18th row: K2, yf, k2tog, k1, sl 1, k1, psso, yf, *k2tog, k2, p3, k3, yf, k5, yf, k3, p3, k2, sl 1, k1, psso, yf, k2tog, k1, sl 1, k1, psso, yf; rep from * to last 2 sts, k2.

20th row: K3, yf, sl 2tog knitwise, k1, p2sso, yf, *k2tog, k2, p3, k3, yf, k2, k2tog, [yf, k3] twice, p3, k2, sl 1, k1, psso, yf, sl 2tog knitwise, k1, p2sso, yf; rep from * to last 3 sts, k3.

22nd row: K1, yf, k2, sl 2tog knitwise, k1, p2sso, *k3, p3, k3, yf, k2, k2tog, yf, KB1, yf, sl 1, k1, psso, k2, yf, k3, p3, k3, sl 2tog knitwise, k1, p2sso; rep from * to last 3 sts, k2, yf, k1.

24th row: K1, C7B, *p3, k3, yf, [k2tog] twice, yf, k3, yf, [sl 1, k1, psso] twice, yf, k3, p3, C7B; rep from * to last st, k1.

26th row: K8, *p3, k3, yf, k2tog, k2, yf, sl 2tog knitwise, k1, p2sso, yf, k2, sl 1, k1, psso, yf, k3, p3, k7; rep from * to last st, k1.

28th row: K8, *p3, k3, yf, [k2tog] twice, yf, k3, yf, [sl 1, k1, psso] twice, yf, k3, p3, k7; rep from * to last st, k1.

30th row: As 26th row.

32nd row: As 24th row.

34th row: K5, *yf, k3, p3, k2, sl 1, k1, psso, yf, k2tog, k1, yf, sl 2tog knitwise, k1, p2sso, yf, k1, sl 1, k1, psso, yf, k2tog, k2, p3, k3, yf, k1; rep from * to last 4 sts, k4.

36th row: K6, yf, k3, p3, k2, sl 1, k1, psso, yf, k2tog, k3, sl 1, k1, psso, yf, k2tog, k2, p3, *k3, [yf, k3] twice, p3, k2, sl 1, k1, psso, yf, k2tog, k3, sl 1, k1, psso, yf, k2tog, k2, p3; rep from * to last 9 sts, k3, yf, k6.

38th row: K7, *yf, k3, p3, k2, sl 1, k1, psso, yf, k2tog, k1, sl 1, k1, psso, yf, k2tog, k2, p3, k3, yf, k5; rep from * to last 2 sts, k2.

40th row: K3, *k2tog, [yf, k3] twice, p3, k2, sl 1, k1, psso, yf, sl 2tog knitwise, k1, p2sso, yf, k2tog, k2, p3, k3, yf, k2; rep from * to last 6 sts, k2tog, yf, k4.

Rep these 40 rows.

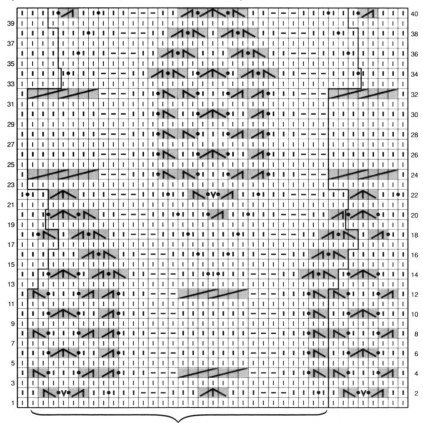

Rep these 30 sts

Multiple of 10 sts + 1.

Special Abbreviation

C5F (Cross 5 Front) = slip next 2 sts onto cable needle and hold at front of work, knit next 3 sts from left-hand needle, then knit sts from cable needle.

1st and every alt row (wrong side): K3, p5, *k5, p5; rep from * to last 3 sts, k3.

2nd row: P3, C5F, *p5, C5F; rep from * to last 3 sts, p3.

4th, 6th and 8th rows: P3, k1, yf, sl 2tog knitwise, k1, p2sso, yf, k1, *p5, k1, yf, sl 2tog knitwise, k1, p2sso, yf, k1; rep from * to last 3 sts, p3.

Rep these 8 rows.

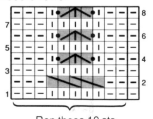

Rep these 10 sts

= sl 2tog knitwise, k1, p2sso, • = yf, ⟋ = k2tog, ⟍ = sl 1, k1, psso.

VIII.5

Multiple of 14 sts + 8.

1st and every alt row (wrong side): K1, *p6, k1; rep from * to end.

2nd row: P1, k6, p1, *k1, yf, sl 1, k1, psso, k2tog, yf, k1, p1, k6, p1; rep from * to end.

4th row: As 2nd row.

6th row: P1, C6B, p1, *k1, yf, sl 1, k1, psso, k2tog, yf, k1, p1, C6B, p1; rep from * to end.

8th row: As 2nd row.

10th row: P1, k1, yf, sl 1, k1, psso, k2tog, yf, k1, p1, *k6, p1, k1, yf, sl 1, k1, psso, k2tog, yf, k1, p1; rep from * to end.

12th row: As 10th row.

14th row: P1, k1, yf, sl 1, k1, psso, k2tog, yf, k1, p1, *C6B, p1, k1, yf, sl 1, k1, psso, k2tog, yf, k1, p1; rep from * to end.

16th row: As 10th row.

Rep these 16 rows.

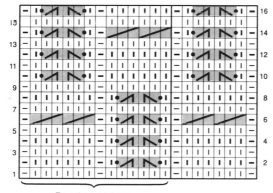

Rep these 14 sts

VIII.6

Multiple of 10 sts + 13.

Special Abbreviation

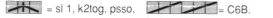 **C7F (Cross 7 Front)** = slip next 3 sts onto cable needle and hold at front of work, knit next 4 sts from left-hand needle, then knit sts from cable needle.

1st row (right side): K6, yf, sl 1, k1, psso, *k8, yf, sl 1, k1, psso; rep from * to last 5 sts, k5.

2nd and every alt row: Purl.

3rd row: K4, k2tog, yf, k1, yf, sl 1, k1, psso, *k5, k2tog, yf, k1, yf, sl 1, k1, psso; rep from * to last 4 sts, k4.

5th row: K3, *k2tog, yf, k3, yf, sl 1, k1, psso, k3; rep from * to end.

7th row: K2, *k2tog, yf, k5, yf, sl 1, k1, psso, k1; rep from * to last st, k1.

9th row: K1, k2tog, yf, k7, *yf, sl 1, k2tog, psso, yf, k7; rep from * to last 3 sts, yf, sl 1, k1, psso, k1.

11th row: K3, *C7F, k3; rep from * to end.

12th row: Purl.

Rep these 12 rows.

Rep these 10 sts

VIII.7

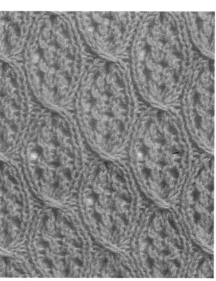

Multiple of 14 sts + 8.

Special Abbreviation

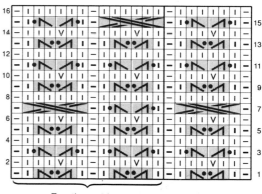 **C6FR (Cross 6 Front Right)** = slip next st onto cable needle and hold at front of work, slip next 4 sts onto 2nd cable needle and hold at back of work, knit next st from left-hand needle, knit sts from 2nd cable needle, then knit st from first cable needle.

●● **[Yf] twice** = 2 loops made.

1st row (right side): P1, *k1, k2tog, [yf] twice, sl 1, k1, psso, k1, p1; rep from * to end.

2nd row: K1, *p2, [p1, PB1] into [yf] twice of previous row, p2, k1; rep from * to end.

3rd row: P1, *k1, yf, k2tog, sl 1, k1, psso, yf, k1, p1; rep from * to end.

4th row: K1, *p6, k1; rep from * to end.

5th and 6th rows: As 1st and 2nd rows.

7th row: P1, C6FR, p1, *k1, yf, k2tog, sl 1, k1, psso, yf, k1, p1, C6FR, p1; rep from * to end.

8th row: As 4th row.

9th, 10th, 11th and 12th rows: As 1st, 2nd, 3rd and 4th rows.

13th and 14th rows: As 1st and 2nd rows.

15th row: P1, k1, yf, k2tog, sl 1, k1, psso, yf, k1, p1, *C6FR, p1, k1, yf, k2tog, sl 1, k1, psso, yf, k1, p1; rep from * to end.

16th row: As 4th row.

Rep these 16 rows.

Rep these 14 sts

VIII. Cable and Lace Patterns

VIII.8

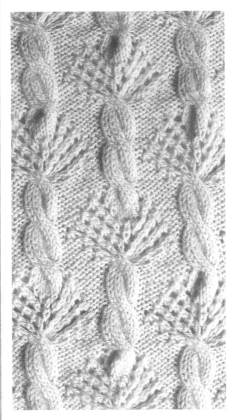

Multiple of 28 sts + 21.

Special Abbreviation

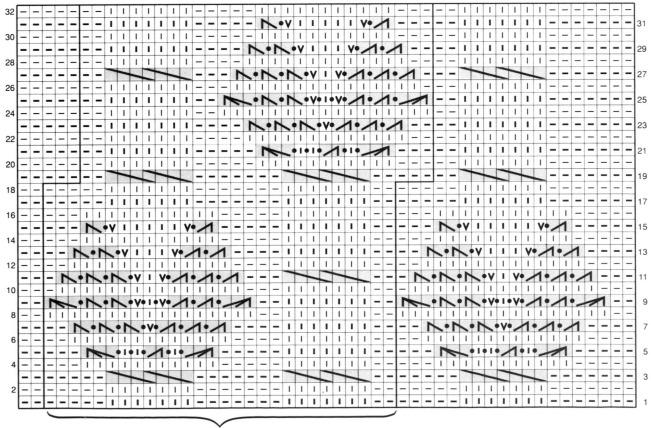 **C7F (Cross 7 Front)** = slip next 3 sts onto cable needle and hold at front of work, knit next 4 sts from left-hand needle, then knit sts from cable needle.

1st row (right side): P7, *k7, p7; rep from * to end.

2nd row: K7, *p7, k7; rep from * to end.

3rd row: P7, *C7F, p7; rep from * to end.

4th row: K5, p11, k5, *p7, k5, p11, k5; rep from * to end.

5th row: P5, k3tog, yf, k1, yf, k2tog, yf, [k1, yf] twice, k3tog tbl, p5, *k7, p5, k3tog, yf, k1, yf, k2tog, yf, [k1, yf] twice, k3tog tbl, p5; rep from * to end.

6th row: K4, p13, k4, *p7, k4, p13, k4; rep from * to end.

7th row: P4, [k2tog, yf] 3 times, KB1, [yf, sl 1, k1, psso] 3 times, p4, *k7, p4, [k2tog, yf] 3 times, KB1, [yf, sl 1, k1, psso] 3 times, p4; rep from * to end.

8th row: K2, p17, k2, *p7, k2, p17, k2; rep from * to end.

9th row: P2, k3tog, yf, [k2tog, yf] twice, KB1, yf, k1, yf, KB1, [yf, sl 1, k1, psso] twice, yf, k3tog tbl, p2, *k7, p2, k3tog, yf, [k2tog, yf] twice, KB1, yf, k1, yf, KB1, [yf, sl 1, k1, psso] twice, yf, k3tog tbl, p2; rep from * to end.

10th row: K3, p15, k3, *p7, k3, p15, k3; rep from * to end.

11th row: P3, [k2tog, yf] 3 times, KB1, k1, KB1, [yf, sl 1, k1, psso] 3 times, p3, *C7F, p3, [k2tog, yf] 3 times, KB1, k1, KB1, [yf, sl 1, k1, psso] 3 times, p3; rep from * to end.

12th row: As 6th row.

13th row: P4, [k2tog, yf] twice, KB1, k3, KB1, [yf, sl 1, k1, psso] twice, p4, *k7, p4, [k2tog, yf] twice, KB1, k3, KB1, [yf, sl 1, k1, psso] twice, p4; rep from * to end.

14th row: As 4th row.

15th row: P5, k2tog, yf, KB1, k5, KB1, yf, sl 1, k1, psso, p5, *k7, p5, k2tog, yf, KB1, k5, KB1, yf, sl 1, k1, psso, p5; rep from * to end.

16th row: As 4th row.

17th, 18th and 19th rows: As 1st, 2nd and 3rd rows.

20th row: K7, p7, *k5, p11, k5, p7; rep from * to last 7 sts, k7.

21st row: P7, k7, *p5, k3tog, yf, k1, yf, k2tog, yf, [k1, yf] twice, k3tog tbl, p5, k7; rep from * to last 7 sts, p7.

22nd row: K7, p7, *k4, p13, k4, p7; rep from * to last 7 sts, k7.

23rd row: P7, k7, *p4, [k2tog, yf] 3 times, KB1, [yf, sl 1, k1, psso] 3 times, p4, k7; rep from * to last 7 sts, p7.

24th row: K7, p7, *k2, p17, k2, p7; rep from * to last 7 sts, k7.

25th row: P7, k7, *p2, k3tog, yf, [k2tog, yf] twice, KB1, yf, k1, yf, KB1, [yf, sl 1, k1, psso] twice, yf, k3tog tbl, p2, k7; rep from * to last 7 sts, p7.

26th row: K7, p7, *k3, p15, k3, p7; rep from * to last 7 sts, k7.

27th row: P7, C7F, *p3, [k2tog, yf] 3 times, KB1, k1, KB1, [yf, sl 1, k1, psso] 3 times, p3, C7F; rep from * to last 7 sts, p7.

28th row: As 22nd row.

29th row: P7, k7, *p4, [k2tog, yf] twice, KB1, k3, KB1, [yf, sl 1, k1, psso] twice, p4, k7; rep from * to last 7 sts, p7.

30th row: As 20th row.

31st row: P7, k7, *p5, k2tog, yf, KB1, k5, KB1, yf, sl 1, k1, psso, p5, k7; rep from * to last 7 sts, p7.

32nd row: As 20th row.

Rep these 32 rows.

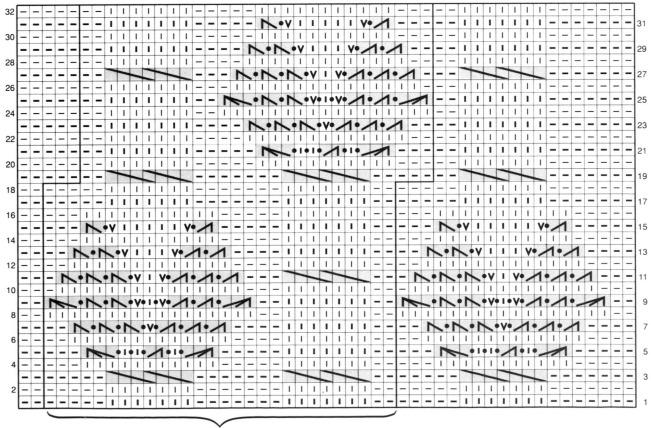

Rep these 28 sts

V = KB1, **⟋⟍** = k2tog, **⟍⟋** = sl 1, k1, psso, **•** = yf, **⟋** = k3tog, **⟍** = k3tog tbl.